CULTURAL READINGS OF IMPERIALISM
EDWARD SAID AND THE GRAVITY OF HISTORY

EDITED BY

KEITH ANSELL-PEARSON, BENITA PARRY

AND JUDITH SQUIRES

LAWRENCE & WISHART
LONDON

Lawrence & Wishart
99a Wallis Road, London E9 5LN

First published 1997
by Lawrence & Wishart

ISBN 0 85315 8401

British Library Cataloguing
in Publication data
A catalogue record for this book
is available from the British Library

Typesetting Art Services, Norwich
Printed and bound in Great Britain
by Redwood Books, Trowbridge.

CONTENTS

Keith Ansell-Pearson is Director of Graduate Research at the University of Warwick. He is the author of several books on Nietzsche and Deleuze, including *Deleuze and Philosophy* (1997).

Robert Bernasconi is the Moss Chair of Excellence in Philosophy at the University of Memphis. He is the author of *The Question of Language in Heidegger's History of Being* and *Heidegger in Question*. His current research is primarily in Hegel, continental philosophy and the history of racism.

Bryan Cheyette teaches English and Jewish literature at Queen Mary and Westfield College, University of London. He is co-editor of *Modernity, Culture and 'the Jew' (Polity Press, 1998).*

Laura Chrisman is lecturer in English at the University of Sussex. She is currently preparing a book on British imperial ideology of South Africa.

Moira Ferguson holds the James E. Ryan Chair in English and Women's Literature at the University of Nebraska - Lincoln. *The First Hundred Years: Nine Black Women Writers* is forthcoming from Routledge in 1997.

Kadiatu Kanneh is a lecturer in English at the University of Birmingham. She specialises in African, African-American and Black British literatures. *African Identities* is forthcoming from Routledge.

Neil Lazarus is Professor of English in the Department of Modern Culture and Media at Brown University, Rhode Island.

Masao Miyoshi teaches literature at the University of California, San Diego. *Globalization and Culture*, co-edited with Fredric Jameson, is forthcoming from Duke University Press.

Bhikhu Parekh is Professor of Political Theory in the Department of Politics at the University of Hull.

Benita Parry is the author of *Delusions and Discoveries: Studies on India in the British Imagination* (1972) and *Conrad and Imperialism* (1983).

Bruce Robbins is based in the Department of English, Rutgers University, New Jersey.

Ella Habiba Shohat is Professor of Cinema Studies and Women's Studies at the City University of New York. She is the author of the award winning *Unthinking Eurocentrism: Multiculturalism and the Media*, and editor of *Talking Visions: Multicultural feminism in a Transnational age*, forthcoming from New Museum and MIT Press.

Judith Squires is co-editor of *Cultural Remix: Theories of Politics and the Popular* and was, until 1997, editor of *new formations*. She lectures in the Politics Department at the University of Bristol.

Gauri Viswanathan is Associate Professor of English and Comparative literature at Columbia University, New York. She is the author of *Masks of Conquest: Literary Study and British Rule in India* (1989) and *Outside the fold: Conversion, Modernity and Belief* (Princeton UP, forthcoming).

David Wood is based at Vanderbilt University, Tennessee.

Robert Young is a Fellow of Wadham College, and Reader in English Language, Oxford University. He is the author of *Torn Halves: Political Conflict in Literary and Cultural Theory* (Manchester University Press 1996).

ACKNOWLEDGEMENTS

Most of the esssays included in this volume stem from an International Conference on *The Politics of Identity: Edward Said's Work and the Gravity of History* organised by the Centre for Research in Philosophy and Literature in Warwick University during March 1994. We are indebted to Warwick University for providing the finances and resources which made this Conference possible; and we thank Edward Said for attending the Conference, participating so fully in the debate within and outside the hall, and ensuring that the event was a joyous occasion.

The papers of Kadiatu Kanneh and Benita Parry were given at a Conference on *Culture and Imperialism* held at the University of Bristol in January 1994. The large attendance and animated exchanges at both gatherings attest to the singular impact which Said's work on imperialism and culture has made on interdisciplinary studies, and it is our hope that this collection not only reflects something of Said's generative role in this burgeoning discussion, but also emulates his commitment to the practice of 'secular criticism'.

INTRODUCTION

THE GRAVITY OF HISTORY

Said has been critical of 'cults like post-modernism, discourse analysis, New Historicism, deconstruction, neo-pragmatism', since they afford their adherents 'an astonishing sense of weightlessness with regard to the gravity of history.'[1] Both the magnetic force and the paramount importance of history are manifest in the essays in this collection however. Grappling with difficult questions concerning the complex relationship between culture and imperialism they undertake diverse explorations of the ideological, economic, political, racial, religious and sexual narratives of empire.

If there is a single strand running through the volume, it is the recall of Said's attention to the historically variable, complex and distinct processes at play in imperial and colonial articulations. However, although all the articles are concerned to reexamine the inflections of the imperial project in the West's cognitive traditions and received representational systems, this book is not an organic collection registering a reassuring unanimity of opinion. Hence our introduction seeks to draw attention to the incommensurability between some of the arguments of the contributors, and to allow the editors to join in the debate. Indeed, because the questions asked of the same and cognate problems have prompted disparate answers, the experience of reading these essays requires constant adjudication, and could be productively unsettling. Such analytic disjunctions are evidence of a volatile debate on matters relating to cultural difference and universals, national or ethnic identity and hybridity, imperial self-representation and the invention of other worlds, postcolonial theory and the dissident intellectual vocation. They also reflect the differing inferences that have been derived from Said's work; his discussion of national attachments, cultural positionings, political affiliations and critical consciousness have invited variable readings.[2] This becomes apparent, for example, when there is a consensus in understanding 'secular criticism' as intellectual work that is sceptical of received knowledge and opposed to orthodoxies, but disagreement in specifying the object of such deliberated disengagement: for Bruce Robbins, secular criticism implies an adversarial relationship to state, party and religious hegemonies; however, Gauri Viswanathan, in a bold move that may itself provoke dissent, seeks to extend this same oppositional quality to religious nonconformity, on the grounds that its heterodoxy necessarily disputes both ecclestistical authority and the consolidating ambitions of the secular state.

The possibility of such divergent appropriations is testimony to the sheer range of Said's theoretically eclectic practice, as well as to the nuances in his engagement with urgent contemporary issues of scholarly responsibility. Such multivalencies are perhaps intrinsic to the stance of a writer who situates himself on the borders of knowable communities, intellectual systems and theoretical modes. But they should not be read as signs of an olympian detachment from worldly circumstances; indeed Said's unfolding narrative - written by a consummate intellectual and connoisseur of many cultural forms - demonstrably makes known a solidarity with populations despised and rejected by the west's dominating social order, and afflicted by its continuing imperial project at home and abroad. This studied self-location is Said's major inspiration to the critical enterprise in which this volume aspires to participate: 'The intellectual's representations ... are always tied to and ought to remain an organic part of an ongoing experience in society: of the poor, the disadvantaged, the voiceless, the unrepresented, the powerless.'[3]

UNIVERSALISM AND NATIONALISM IN A DIVIDED WORLD

When Said commends 'universalism', it is in order to move 'beyond the easy certainties provided by our background, language, nationality', in pursuit of establishing and upholding 'a single standard' concerning 'freedom and justice'. This embrace of 'universal principles' is distinguished from 'the ideas of a universal norm of international behaviour [which] meant in effect the right of European power and European representations of other people to hold sway' (*Representations of the Intellectual*, ppxii, 9, 68-69). In a collection of essays such as ours, where many contributors examine the variable or situated usages of universalism, as westerncentric exclusion or international solidarity, what emerges is a shared concern with the deformations in critical thinking caused by the absence of 'universals', or by the failure to compose a manifold and inclusive perspective on different oppressions. Ella Shohat urges the necessity of a relational approach to dominations and resistances, and argues for a rupturing of the spatial and temporal boundaries of history as they are currently perceived. Insisting that specificity must not override the connectedness of histories, geographies and cultural identities, she juxtaposes 'Columbus, Palestine and Arab-Jews', in order to forge the historical and discursive linkages between the 'conquista practices' of fifteenth century Spain, at home and in the New World, the recent dispossession of the Palestinians, and the contemporary marginalisation of Sephardic Jews by Israel's official culture.

This meets Said's demand for a universal vocabulary, which can give 'greater human scope to what a particular race or nation suffered' (*Representations of the Intellectual*, p33), and which enables the affiliation of distinctive experiences of subjugation.[4] When this requirement is reiterated by Bryan Cheyette, it becomes the occasion for his faulting much postcolonial theory, including the work of Said, for marginalising or excluding 'the all too apparent history of antisemitism within imperial culture'; Cheyette argues that the gap between theories of anti-black racism, orientalism and antisemitism registers a failure to interrelate particular histories of victimisation (p106). The principal object of Cheyette's censure is the Fanon of *Black Skin, White Masks* who, Cheyette maintains, inscribes a tension between 'a particularist anti-colonial nationalism, and more universalist or transnational theories of racial oppression' (p115). Fanon acknowledges the complicity of European humanism with atrocities against Jews, hence bringing together the histories of colonialism and genocide, and associating the Jewish community with abused blacks; but, according to Cheyette, he also essentialises their whiteness, so that he effectively identifies the Jews with white oppressors. Furthermore, Cheyette argues, Fanon's theories of racial pathology, which distinguish between the Jews, as overdetermined from within, and Blacks, as overdetermined from outside, make absolute distinctions between anti-black racism and anti-semitism, thus blocking the possibility of universalising different oppressions. In the light of a body of writing that is, as Cheyette acknowledges, in constant flux and always polyvalent, this interpretation should be read alongside Neil Lazarus's essay. Lazarus's Fanon is reconstructed from a later work, *The Wretched of the Earth*, and emerges as the author of an unequivocally universalistic narrative of oppression, where decolonisation is envisaged as heralding the formation of a post-imperialist world and animating the growth of an 'international consciousness'.

A split of another order, which also impinges on interpretations of universalism, is opened up by the essays of Bruce Robbins and Neil Lazarus, who both invoke Said, but in defence of incompatible positions on nationalism. Robbins, who makes plain his own repudiation of all nationalist ideologies, regardless of their circumstances and agendas, cites Said's comment on the 'politics of secular interpretation' as proposing 'a way ... of avoiding the pitfalls of nationalism'. This is in order to substantiate his claim that Said uses 'secular' as 'an opposing term not to religion, but to nationalism'.[5] Because Robbins is concerned to reconcile an apparent contradiction in Said's position, he observes that Said 'has managed to defend the interests of the Palestinian national movement while maintaining an extremely sceptical view of nationalism as such' (p74), adding that the 'precarious but necessary authority' which Said gives to secular internationalism, is founded on 'an ambiguous border-crossing' (p84).

Since this gloss overlooks Said's distinction between patriotic/regressive and emergent/resistant nationalism, and would seem to detach Said's *internationalism* from any strategic or libidinal affiliation to *national* entities, Robbins's exposition should be considered together with Lazarus's understanding of Said as 'an open advocate of the project of national liberation' (p44). Lazarus reproves the 'constitutive metropolitan elitism' (p32) of critics who dismiss nationalism as a nostalgic and reactionary ideological enterprise, and disparage all its articulations everywhere as chauvinistic and socially divisive. Instead he is concerned to situate the category, in Anne McClintock's phrase, as 'an open site of political and ideological contestation' (p29). Hence he argues for recognising that nationalism in the Third World remains fundamental, since it is only on the inherited terrain of the nation 'that an articulation between secular intellectualism and popular consciousness can be forged' (p45).

This returns us to the question of construing a 'universalism' appropriate to a still conflictual world. For Robbins, a discourse of human rights has the capacity to provide the North American public with 'a vocabulary for widespread and heartfelt internationalist emotion', and serves as an effective counter to the resurgence of post-cold war nationalism in the United States. Such enunciations of universalism are, Robbins charges, ignored by proponents of an 'academic internationalism' such as Lazarus, who, because they are predisposed to a 'somewhat miraculous ideal', fail to devise a vocabulary 'that would offer postcolonial critics some articulation between nationalism and class' (p73).

Despite this accusation, it would appear that it is the purpose of both Lazarus and Masao Miyoshi to devise just such an idiom of 'nationalist internationalism', and one that *does* coherently articulate (inter)nationalism with class. Pointing to the accelerating immiseration and exploitation of third world populations, Lazarus argues that, for them, the question of the nation state has never before seemed so pressing or so central, because 'for capitalism to thrive, nationalism must wither away' (p34). In a closely related register, Miyoshi points to the nation state as 'the only political structure now that *could* protect people from the ungovernable disorder/unmediated violence' of transnational '"flexible" capital' (p55). Indeed, the essays of Miyoshi and Lazarus can be seen as enunciating an 'internationalism' that transcends the constraints of Robbins's version, where the distanced compassion for far-away people subjected to human rights violations does not seem to include the persecutions inflicted on populations by rulers who are clients of the United States; nor extend to the sufferings visited by the United States on its designated enemies. On the other hand, the 'universalism' enunciated by Miyoshi and Lazarus addresses the immediate necessity of opposing, intellectually and politically, the operations of a global capitalist system in the heartlands as well as the hinterlands of late imperialism.

UNIVERSALISM AS EUROCENTRISM

Whereas contributors are divided on the issue of whether nationalism is (in)compatible with 'universalism', all attempt to construe an innovative and oppositional universalism that counters the restricted and monistic notion endemic to European thought. The genesis of such exclusions is the subject of the papers by Robert Bernasconi and Bhikhu Parekh. Why, Bernasconi asks, has the question of the 'origin' of philosophy been so neglected among the community of philosophers? Is it because they cannot acknowledge their own unbearable origins in a place outside the West? Has there been a cover-up, and if so, was it motivated by racism? Bernasconi answers 'yes' to the first question, but, curiously, 'no' to the second, thereby circumventing any exploration of the connection between the Westernisation of philosphical discourse and the simultaneous processes outside the academy which led to the installation of the power of the West. The narrowing of the concept of philosophy, and 'the paradox of philosophy's parochialism', is thus accounted for by Bernasconi primarily in an *internal* history of paradigm shifts in philosophical thinking, and only secondarily in a 'chauvinism' operating in the social and political world, whose prevalence and dynamism within a specific historical moment remains unexamined.

While Bernasconi does draw attention to Western philosophical ethnocentrism and parochialism, he denies that philosophy is racist in intention or design - nor could it be, since, for him, it is the great abstract discourse of the perpetual other voice, the point at which thought transgresses the origin and becomes the simulated activity of the wanderer, the bastard, the vagrant, the madman. Bernasconi concludes by appealing to the academy to display a greater sensitivity to the exclusionary effects of the West's construction of a privileged discourse of philosophy. This position, although critical of institutional scholarship, preserves philosophy in its elevated and reified form, since the calling into question of philosophy is performed from within the discourse itself. This compounds the power of western philosophy, while neglecting the power of hitherto marginalised and relegated cognitive traditions and cultural formations to challenge and undermine its insular territory.

One concern of Bhikhu Parekh's essay is to show how European thought and European ways of life were universalised in the age of empire. It was assumed, even by those who accepted Indians and Blacks as belonging to the same species, that Europe was the human norm; and the consequence was that difference was reduced to the same, other versions being either early drafts of what was consummated by Europe, or failures to become what Europe was. Thus, although Locke posited the idea of man as being based on the capacity for rational discourse, possessed by all members of the species, his justification of English colonialism derived from equating a rational way of life with industry and the system of private property, conditions which were not satisfied by the populations of the Americas, thereby rendering their land liable for classification as vacant. When colonialism entered a new phase, a philosophical defence was required for appropriating the territories of the heavily populated continents of Asia and Africa. The vindication advanced by John Stuart Mill made a distinction between civilisation and backwardness: while human beings in the former societies were in 'the maturity of their faculties' and had 'attained the capacity of being guided to their own improvement by conviction or persuasion', non-European societies were in a state of infancy, or had been stationary for hundreds of years, and lacked the capability for self-regeneration.

Parekh's examination of three major traditions of European thought focuses on the importance of their definitions of 'the human', and their assumptions of a common human nature. These allowed Christianity, Liberalism and Marxism, all of which claimed an adherence to universalism, but were limited in their ability to accommodate diversity, to defend the imposition of their own cultural values, hence underwriting various colonial practices. There is, however, a twofold problem with treating Marxism alongside other systems which were ideologically and institutionally implicated in installing and maintaining empire. Because the compass of Parekh's discussion does not extend beyond Marx on India, subsequent analysis is overlooked: thus, for example, the significance of Rosa Luxemburg's study of imperialism as intrinsic to capitalism's trajectory is disregarded, and with it the recognition that any discussion on the making of capitalism's global system is unthinkable outside Marxist paradigms.[6] Furthermore, there is no acknowledgment of Marxism as a major resource for anti-colonialist theory, although its influence on the programmes of movements for national liberation, as well as its inflections in the writings of, for example, Aimé Césaire, Frantz Fanon, George Padmore, Amilcar Cabral, C.L.R. James and Walter Rodney, amply confirm Parekh's designation of Marxism as 'one of the most radical and emancipatory projects in Western thought' (p188) - which begs the question as to which other secular emancipatory project in Western or any thought is more radical in its purview and aspiration.

THE DIFFERENCE OF IDENTITY

The tensions within the larger debate on identity are apparent in the contest over the representation of Jewish identity conducted by Bryan Cheyette and Ella Shohat. They concur, although on different grounds, in rejecting the designation of the Jew as 'white', and in observing the perennial depiction of Jews in antisemitic discourse as an alien Eastern people; and both also refuse the received version of the Jewish experience written by Zionism. But their perspectives on the communities' cultural locations are at variance, while the histories they address are disparate. In questioning the Jew's presumed insertion in a supposed 'Western Judeo-Christian culture', Cheyette argues for including anti-semitism within 'Orientalist discourse', and inserting the history of anti-semitism into imperialist historiography. Challenging the fixed boundaries between black and white, East and West, Cheyette, who draws attention to perceptions of the Jew's uncontainable otherness in western literary representations (his specific instance is *Daniel Deronda*), is concerned to mark the Jew's equivocal position as 'white *and* black', as in *and* outside the dominant western tradition.

At an oblique angle to this ambivalently designated European location, Shohat chronicles the occluded story of the Sephardic communities in the Arabic and Islamic worlds, a narrative of Jewry beyond the West concealed in a Eurocentric Zionist historiography. This focus on 'Sephardic Arab-Jewish identity', Shohat maintains, counters the positioning of Arab and Jew as antonyms, recuperates the histories of 'flourishing syncretic Jewish communities all over the Islamic Middle East and North Africa' (p94), disposes of the 'master-narrative of universal Jewish victimisation' (p95), and disputes the notion of a single people participating in a common nationality, culture and experience of persecution. Significantly, while both Cheyette and Shohat finesse the making and articulations of distinctive Jewish identities, making known their equivocations and demonstrating their multifarious incarnations, neither is concerned to dispose of 'identity' either as concept or existential event.

Viswanathan's interest is in construing identity formation as a mediation between the homogenising tendencies required to fulfil citizenship functions, and the sectarianism of religious belief. The narratives produced 'in the crucial space of negotiation between national and religious identity', are perceived as displaying 'the contradictions embedded in the processual construction of national identity' (p154). They thus yielding 'the most visible light on the strains and stresses in community self-identification' (p154). For Viswanathan religious belief is not to be considered as a reference to doctrinal authority, but rather 'to the aspirations, understandings, expectations, needs and goals that constitute the self-definitions of people, the very content of which is denied or suppressed in the construction of social identity' (p159). To this end she examines the writings of John Henry Newman as an attempt to locate a middle ground between nation and religion, between consensual interpretation and private judgement, attributing the collapse of its syncretic possibilities to the contradictions between his radical, class-based social critique, and the orthodoxy of his religious position. However, she argues, the universalism underlying his positing of Catholicism as 'a transreligious, transnational force', that seeks to go beyond both citizenship and separatism, works regressively by failing to 'disentangle belief from structures of authority' (p155).

It is now accepted that communal subjectivities, which have been deployed both to oppress and to contest oppression, are crossed by various and competing identifications; and in observing how the 'anxious surveillance of the new industrial working class', which included the Irish immigration, brought forth observations of their increasing 'nigresence' or darkening, Robert Young shows how the permanence of racial type was extended to class differences, race in metropolitan class classification using the same language of zoology as was deployed in colonial situations. This, he suggests, 'provides clear historical corroboration of the traditional Marxist argument that race is simply an ideological screen for class' (p147). Because ethnic minorities within contemporary Britain are often characterised as such only 'because their position of special economic deprivation differentiates them from others ... as a group that suffers an unsual degree of economic exploitation', Young concludes: 'It is, as they say, no coincidence that we have reverted to the racist terminology of hybridity as the appropriate description of this characteristic of contemporary English culture.' (p148)

Young places diverse conceptualisations of the significance of racial identity within the context of an economic perspective, criticising the current tendency to adopt the 'racial terminology of hybridity' abstracted from pertaining social conditions. In a similar vein, Viswanathan faults 'modern criticism's predeliction for analysing religious discourse as disinterested and deliberately disengaged from material conflicts', and detached from articulating the political aspirations of the disenfranchised (p161). Her purpose is to show that religious sectarianism was used as 'an instrument for the attainment of working-class ends and the mode through which dissent is expressed' (p158); and the ease with which the demands of the English poor for the franchise shifted, from 'No Property!' to 'No Popery!', exemplifies for Viswanathan both the multiplicity of forms that expressions of class discontent could assume, and the intersection of class and cultural difference.

Other contributors appear to be less attentive to the complexities in the forms and conditions of identity construction. David Wood, for example, confiates identity with essentialism when he discerns an internal connection between violence and identity and contends that ethnic essentialism drives out doubt and complexity and legitimates violence. When the rejectionist premises of Wood are contrasted with those who are attuned to the variable social enunciations of subjectivity and selfhood, we have the makings of an implicit debate which converges on the problematic issue of identity construction and communal identifications.

'Identity', in the sense of something fixed, stable and enduring, has been under threat philosophically for the last two hundred years, at least since Hume, but it has also been under threat historically, as capital has begun to deterritorialise the social processes of production. Hence it could be argued that 'identity' is not only a metaphysical chimera, but also, and more importantly, a socio-historical redundancy. However, in suggesting that the quest for identity - a quest common to national struggles for liberation - is necessarily bound up with its other, 'violence', does not Wood misconstrue precisely that which he seeks to de-reify? For is a politics of identity ever a quest for 'identity'? Indeed, the importance of the 'capacity to make sense of our relation to the world', which Wood includes amongst the 'transcendental' requirements for sustaining identity, suggests that identity as a sign, a symptom of something deeper and more profound, serves rather as the means around which people collectivise in order to contest their subordinate position, and to wrest some autonomous power.[7] Moreover, since identity cannot be philosophically secured or stabilised in the face of historical modernity and accelerated cultural change, the question arises as to whether it should be treated as a philosophical notion at all. Any 'violence' it assumes has then to be analysed, not in terms of any intrinsic philosophical property it possesses, but always in the context of specific socio-historical dynamics. If modernisation is the only permanent feature of our late-modern social existence, then Marx's celebrated phrase about capitalist modernity - all that is solid melts into air, all that is holy is profaned - perhaps applies most potently to identity.

HYBRIDITY AND DIFFERENCE

Responses to the notion of hybridity vary among the contributors. Some embrace the notion but others are more sceptical. However all share the now incontrovertible notion that selfhood is constructed and not received, a product not an origin, negotiable and not fixed (the terms are those of Wood); other contributors also acknowledge the *affective* as well as the pragmatic dimensions of community identifications. As Shohat observes, for a people like the Palestinians who have been dispossessed of their lands, denied national-political rights and subjected to forcible dispersal, the longing for a lost homeland is not easily subsumed under 'essentialism'. Drawing attention to the ways in which nation states, in the wake of colonial partitions, have imposed a coherent sense of national identity precisely because of their 'fragile sense of cultural, even geographical belonging', Shohat acknowledges the conditions in which inventing a collective identity becomes inevitable (p89). Thus she defines the contemporary task as 'the remapping of national and ethnic racial identities against the deep scars of colonising partitions' (p104) - a suggestion that concurs with Bhikhu Parekh's observation that ethnic minorities view their cultures as an integral part of their identities (p178). Nor is Lazarus inclined to denigrate the invention of communal identities, contending instead that 'the concepts of "diversity", "mobility"... are of practical significance only to foreign elites and indigenous comprador classes' (p33); while Masao Miyoshi regards the insistence by the ex-colonial elites on the privilege of hybridity and multiple subjectships, together with their embrace of ambivalence and equivocation, as the signs of the intellectual ruled by the urgencies of capitalism's new global economy (p62).

Another and quite different sceptical note on the uses of hybridity is introduced by Robert Young, who unhinges race theory from an exclusively colonial context, and resituates it within a wider project of analysing European ethnicity. Young takes issue with the presumption that ethnic diversity is new to English culture by providing a detailed historical reading of

English 'hybridity', extending from twelfth century myths of racial origin, to the anthopological writing of the nineteenth century, and the rewriting of English history according to then current racial paradigms. Noting that nowadays 'the term hybridity has become widely used to characterise the ethnic diversity of contemporary British culture', Young points out that the histories of racial fusion have a long and complex past, and that in the 19th century when notions of 'species difference' were rife, mixed race or hybridity, perceived as a 'chaotic form of ethnic commotion' (p137), came to be associated with social and political anarchy.

There is an interesting tension between Parekh's critical exposition of the role of liberalism in denying the possibility of a politics of difference, and Young's focus on those responses to J.S.Mills's liberalism which condemn the rejection of 'the racial element' in his political thinking. Thus whereas Parekh represents liberalism as a force which in recommending assimilation hinders the recognition of difference, Young shows that its critics manifest a disturbing allegiance to racial stereotypes. Reading these essays together, we can discern the complexity of the debate surrounding the liberal commitment to tolerance of difference, and its accompanying strategy of realising such tolerance through the *transcendence* of difference within the public sphere, and 'a politics of difference'. Liberalism includes calls for fusion, hybridity, assimilation of racial identity, *and* demands for the categorisation of ethnic difference - and these demands have been based in both a negative desire to discriminate, oppress and exploit on the basis of otherness, *and* a positive desire to respect and understand cultural diversity.

TEXTS OF EMPIRE: RACE, POLITICAL ECONOMY AND GENDER IN IMPERIAL RHETORIC

Resonances of Said's pathbreaking work on how literary representations of empire participated in producing knowledge and perceptions of the historical world inflect the essays in this book which discuss the cognitive and aesthetic functions of colonialist and imperialist writing. Rejecting the search for a single universal analysis of colonialism's operation, Laura

Chrisman criticises the tendency towards synecdochic readings, which elide the distinct processes at play in imperial discourses. She calls for 'a methodology which can account for, and incorporate, differing imperial and colonial agendas' (p304), while exploring the ways in which 'the mechanics of imperial or colonial economic production' can inform and generate 'cultural anxieties and literary themes' (p295).

For Chrisman, Said's methodology acknowledges the 'overdetermined, historically variable complexities of metropolitan imperial cultures' and thus 'opens both a material and a theoretical space' for reading the texts of that culture in ways that differentiate them from white colonial discourse - a move which disposes of the assumption that 'the true psyche of the imperial West can only be mapped, and identified, in its colonial operations' (p293). This is especially important when the writing is part of a fantasy genre, 'the imperial romance', where nostalgic images of a pre-capitalist colonial world are construed as a corrective to processes of modernisation and capitalist accumulation in Britain, registering a diverse and contradictory formation that is more aligned with 'imperial-metropolitan than colonial ideology' (p304). As an example, Rider Haggard in King Solomons Mines 'uses African material to satisfy a primarily British readership's imaginary desires, and uses romance as a genre particularly well-suited to the symbolic resolution of material contradictions' (p304).

Moira Ferguson's subject is the travel account of an English woman, about two periods of residence in Sierra Leone during the late eighteenth century. This she reads as a fabrication, and by decoding its figurative language and restoring its silences, Ferguson profers the text as heteroglossic in its forms, replete with ironies, ruptures, and fluctuating responses. Ferguson attributes this polyphony to the complex location of an English woman in Africa, but her reading is in no doubt that in exercising both female and colonialist authority, Falconbridge's gendered narrative does not constitute an 'anti-conquest rhetoric'; rather, in advancing the brief for the ideology of European territorial expansion, it remains complicit with the colonial myth about Africa. In Ferguson's gloss, Falconbridge's 'ambivalent text' weaves between pro- and anti-slavery positions, mediating the black voices of the disappointed freed slaves settled in the territory, registering a compassion which is not-quite-sisterhood for the English prostitutes impressed as wives for the liberated slaves, and exposing the duplicity and injustice of the anti-slavery but pro-colonialist British administration.

Because Falconbridge's writing insists on asserting female authority, Ferguson argues, it registers 'a gendered colonial discourse for female travellers that claims both class and race privilege' (p258), producing a narrative that is a 'filament of overseas predation' (p262). Despite Ferguson's always sceptical reading of Falconbridge, she also makes radical claims for its panoply of meanings as extending and complicating the imperial trajectory (p259). Her concluding lines - 'All she did was give the colonial project a new twist, a novel context for reconstituting the cultural geography of Sierrra Leone and hence Englishness' - should give pause to those who would claim that a gendered perspective on the imperial project necessarily registers an identification of oppressions, or inevitably inscribes a critique of Europe's expansionist ideology.[8]

Some varieties of Africanist discourse are examined by Kadiatu Kanneh, who observes that postcolonial writers, when inventing their own 'Africas', must negotiate the inevitable complicities with received configurations, rhetorics and 'knowledge': the colonialist notion of Africa's cultural difference was derived from a racial ideology/typology, and translated as disjunction and inequality, the postcolonial appropriations of Africa perceive the confrontation of colonialism with indigenous social orders as a mutual encroachment, and engage with the ambiguities of multiple African identities, and grapple with the ethics of dialogues between difference.

In ironically reproducing the familiar colonialist rhetoric of both negation and celebration *vis-a-vis* Africa, Kanneh argues, Naipaul's *A Bend in the River* is simultaneously implicated and detached from the received version, so that, despite the text's consciously 'knowing' position, the novel is beset with the anxiety of seeing, interpreting and representing otherness. On the other hand, the dramatisation of cultural difference in Cheikh Hamidou Kane's *Ambiguous Adventure* is seen by Kanneh to entrench the idea of Africa's difference, even while considering the ambivalence of the notion; and although colonialism is proferred as 'a fatal clash between two value systems ... and a deeply disruptive collision between two fundamentally opposed metaphysics', the novel demonstrates the impossibility of a return to origins and the inevitability of interlocution.

Although Kanneh maintains that such dialogue *is* staged by Alice Walker in *Possessing the Secret of Joy*, she observes that Walker's proclivity for the notion of the collective nature of women's experience leads her to collapse the specific cultural practice of female circumcision into a metaphor for woman's global oppression. In addition, in projecting a collective human consciousness derived from Jungian theory, the novel promises a terrain free of difference; but it is a terrain in which the United States features as the microcosm of universal empathy. Thus although the fiction does acknowledge the disparaging narratives written by colonialist histories, its version of Africa as a damaged and dying culture is - despite the author's claim to the whole continent by virtue of her ancestry - produced from within North American and European conceptual frames, which severely limits the possibility of interlocution.

Some of the problems intimated by the readings of Ferguson and Kanneh are addressed by Chrisman, who faults those feminist postcolonial studies which allocate 'generative authority' to woman as a category, irrespective of class and racial difference, and inscribe a mystical version of woman's reproductive capabilities, thus remaining indifferent to the workings and conceptualisations of ideology and political economy within colonialist/imperialist culture. Chrisman therefore argues for reintroducing the notions of totality and mediation into feminist criticism: the notion of totality would allow an engagement 'with the structures in which literary subjects are given ideological value'; the notion of mediation would facilitate an engagement 'with the ways in which those values are produced'. Such moves relegitimate 'the critical study of fiction and literariness', by differentiating literature's aesthetic functions from those of the social sciences, and attending to the ambivalences of imaginative writing. A method which studies 'the collective properties of imaginative literature as a distinct modality within imperial writing', rather than as functionally interchangeable with other writing, will, Chrisman maintains, enable the elaboration of Said's example.

While Chrisman argues for distinguishing between white colonial discourses and those of metropolitan imperial culture, Parry makes a case for examining the shifts within the rhetoric of empire. When imperialism is considered as western capitalism's accelerated and concerted penetration of the non-capitalist world, it becomes apparent that it was a qualitatively different project from earlier colonialisms. This understanding permits us to examine how imperialism generated altered metropolitan modes of apprehending time and space, which impinged on perceptions of the domestic geography, inaugurating an exorbitant lexicon to construe an imperial mission and destiny, and stimulating new tropological ruses to explain, validate and enhance the west's global reterritorialising project.

Parry concedes that an interest in reiterated themes and motifs does facilitate reading the multiple signs of empire - whether conspicuous or ghostly - written across the body of metropolitan literature. But she questions the tendency in contemporary studies to concentrate on the reprise of topoi in its vast library, and to locate apprehensions of empire as recurrent archetypal forms in a repressed sub-text. Such strategies serve to divert attention from the particularities of *imperialist* representation. Instead she argues for attending to the innovation of rhetorical themes and figures, citing the work of Said and Fredric Jameson as exemplary practices which examine how the imperialist moment effected radical stylistic changes in the substance and form of the novel.[9]

Whereas many fictions normalised empire, and others registered uncertain apologies, Parry argues that Conrad's *Nostromo* is singular in its demystification of imperialism as historical event, ethical idea and social aspiration. This interrogation is dramatised not only in the novel's representational and tropological structure, as well as in a rhetoric which parodies imperialism's legitimating devices, but also in a narrative which, by ostentatiously deranging the linear form which Conrad inherited, subverts the authorised chronicle of the west's historical destiny, trajectory and achievement. But while suggesting that the novel is a dystopian narrative of the west's imperialist ascendency, Parry also observes that its critique, which can relinquish neither the contemplation of 'redeeming ideas' nor a dread of revolutionary energies, is constrained by an uneasy affiliation to those Western norms and values which imperialism is held to perform and violate.

THE DISSIDENT INTELLECTUAL VOCATION

The different conceptions of the role of the 'postcolonial critic' enunciated by Robbins, Lazarus and Miyoshi, together with their distinctive relationships to 'postcolonial criticism', emanate from divergent perceptions of both the contemporary global condition, and the assignments appropriate to intellectual work. Whereas for Lazarus and Miyoshi the asymmetries of the world system are a necessary function of Transnational Corporate Capitalism, Robbins finds the invocation of 'world capitalism' to be 'overtidy' or 'theological' in suggesting ubiquity and omnipotence, where in fact the flows of capital from the centre contend with flows of ideologies and images to the centre.[10] If this risks the charge of elitism, as does the metropolitan and class location of much postcolonial criticism, then, Robbins argues, we cannot sacrifice narratives of progress in the name of an ideal purity.

However, the dissenting commentaries have been directed at modes of postcolonial criticism which are exclusively concerned with the discursive, indifferent to both the political economy of oppression and the agency of oppositional movements, welcoming the advent of a supposedly transnational cultural hybridity, have been criticised for overlooking the fact that the reason for this state of affairs, which is capitalism's global reach, brings with it commodity fetishism and an international division of labour: 'As we talk about postcoloniality and postindustrialism in the metropolitan academia, we ignore those billions outside our on-going discourse for whom life has nothing "post" about it' (p54). This demur suggests that, rather than prematurely celebrating the arrival of the postcolonial era, the dissenting critic still needs to hold in view, as did Fanon, the image of a possible post-imperialist future.

For Miyoshi, scholarly discourse, even that which is engrossed in the issues of postcoloniality, multiculturalism, and difference, has been contaminated, because it is conducted within the space of Transnational Corporate Capitalism, where 'the oppositional vocabulary has been domesticated ... The abandonment of and indifference to the wretched of the earth fractures the credibility of their intellectual enterprise' (p62). Given this account of the unpropitious circumstances in which literary and theoretical discourse is now conducted, Miyoshi advocates that scholars must revive the notion of opposition and resistance in their practice. Miyoshi's way forward for the critical enterprise, which is cognisant of a conflictual world and passionately concerned with 'the forgotton and the unrepresented', is delivered in a register remote from Wood's meditation on whether philosophy can contribute to peace. These different lexicons are yet another sign of the fissures within a collection that began life as a common project, but emerged marked by the disjunctions between those critics who recognise that the dynamics of material processes necessarily inflect the critical enterprise, and thus demand of intellectuals a public commitment to explanations that will participate in effecting social transformation, and those critics who privelege the autonomous power of disciplinary work to change the world.

Despite such divergencies, the collection is held together by the recognition of empire's determinate place within modern western culture and thought; this acknowledgement does not imply that overseas empire was the only agency of constructing metropolitan knowledge and social meaning, but it does prompt a re-examination of disciplinary areas and texts once held to be immune from the ideological contamination of the imperial project. And it invites the appraisal of our own times as still implicated in the worlds imperialism made.

Keith Ansell-Pearson, Benita Parry, Judith Squires.

Notes

1. *Culture and Imperialism*, Chatto and Windus, London 1993, pp366-7.

2. See, for example, Tim Brennan, 'Places of Mind, Occupied Lands : Edward Said and Philology'; Abdul R. JanMohamed, 'Worldiness-without-World, Homelessness-as-Home: Toward a Definition of the Specular Border Intellectual'; and Jennifer Wicke and Michael Sprinker, 'Interview with Edward Said' in *Edward Said : A Critical Reader*, Michael Sprinker (ed), Blackwell, Oxford 1992.

3. Edward Said, *Representations of the Intellectual*, Vintage, London 1994, p84.

4. *Cf* Paul Gilroy, *The Black Atlantic*, Verso, London 1993, who urges the need to connect obviously different histories of persecution, citing in particular the parallels between the Black and Jewish experiences of enforced diaspora.

5. For a survey of prominent intellectual currents in American and European social theory which posit an antithesis between universalism and nationalism-as-pollution/unreason, see Jeffrey C. Alexander, 'Modern, Anti, Post and Neo', *New Left Review*, 210, March/April 1995, pp63-101.

6. See the diverse writings of Paul Sweezy, Samir Amin, Immanuel Wallerstein, Bill Warren, V G Kiernan, Michael Barratt Brown, Roger Owen, Bob Sutcliffe; as well as the materialist geographers David Harvey, Edward Soja, Neil Smith. For an overview, see Anthony Brewer, *Marxist Theories of Imperialism: A Critical Survey*, Routledge and Kegan Paul, London 1980, 2nd edition 1990.

7. This question has been rehearsed in different registers and on numerous occasions, most recently in Honi Fern Haber, *Beyond Postmodern Politics: Lyotard, Rorty, Foucault*, Routledge, London 1994. See also, for example, 'Minimal Selves', in *The Real Me: Post-modernism and the Question of Identity*, ICA Document 6, London 1987; Paul Smith, *Discerning the Subject*, University of Minnesota Press, Minneapolis 1988; Diana Fuss, *Essentially Speaking: Feminism, Nature and Difference*, Routledge, London 1989; *Identity: Community, Culture, Difference*, Jonathan Rutherford (ed), Lawrence and Wishart, London 1990.

8. For discussion of such problems, see, for example, Napur Chaudhuri and Margaret Strobel (eds), *Western Women and Imperialism: Complicity and Resistance*, Indiana University Press, Bloomington and Indianapolis 1992; Catherine Hall, *White, Male and Middle Class: Explorations in Feminism and History*, Polity Press, Cambridge 1992; Mary Louise Pratt, *Imperial Eyes: Travel Writing and Transculturation*, Routledge, London 1992; Vron Ware, *Beyond the Pale: White Women, Racism and History*, Verso, London 1992.

9. See *The Political Unconscious*, Methuen, London 1981 and *Modernism and Imperialism*, Field Day, Derry 1988.

10. Robbins here cites Arjun Appadurai, 'Disjuncture and Difference in the Global Cultural Economy', in *The Phantom Public Sphere*, Bruce Robbins (ed), University of Minnesota Press, Minneapolis 1993, pp269-295.

TRANSNATIONALISM AND THE ALLEGED DEATH OF THE NATION-STATE

Neil Lazarus

Over the course of the past decade, and, for very obvious geopolitical reasons especially since 1989, there has been something of an obsessive return to the subject of nationalism in Western-based cultural, historical, and social scientific scholarship. The unfolding of events in eastern Europe and the former Soviet Union, in India, in southern, central, and north eastern Africa, in the Maghreb, the Mashriq, and elsewhere, was nowhere anticipated. Despite this, the outpouring of Western based scholarship has tended to remain within the parameters of the established post-1945 ideologeme of nationalism: 'since the Second World War, in a conveniently European lapse of memory', as Tim Brennan has recently pointed out, 'studies of nationalism have not only increased; they have for the most part condemned the thing they studied.'[1] The sheet destructiveness of contemporary developments in Rwanda, Armenia and Azerbaijan, and in what less than five years ago was still Yugoslavia, has been taken to reveal a fundamental truth about all nationalisms everywhere: not merely that they are chauvinistic, but also that they only ever result in the violent intensification of already existing social divisions.

There is, of course, something deeply disingenuous about this kind of scholarship, emanating as it does from think tanks, policy centres and institutions of higher learning in the core capitalist *nations* of Britain, France, Germany, and the United States. The contemporary studies that deplore the 'resurgence' or 'persistence' of nationalism in Algeria or Serbia or Tajikistan are very often premised upon a convenient naturalisation of the trajectories of nationalism in the metropolitan West. 'Our' nationalisms, classed as finished projects, are taken somehow to have had benign effects: modernising, unifying, democratising.

'Their' still unfolding nationalisms, on the other hand, are categorised under the shop-worn rubrics of atavism, anarchy, irrationality, and power-mongering. Thus, arguably, the contemporary term 'ethnic nationalism', which seems to me to have little if any analytical substance, but which clearly plays an important role today in the construction and institutionalisation of ideological assumptions. Louis Snyder's remarkable 1954 taxonomy of nationalisms - 'integrative', 'disruptive', and 'aggressive' - might have lost its cold-war rationale, but it does not appear to have lost its credibility among political scientists.[2]

METROPOLITAN THEORIES OF NATIONALISM

For *dissenting* Western based scholars today, opposed to the smugly 'First Worldist' quality of many of the recent commentaries, the question of how to think *differently* about nationalism is proving to be a vexed one. In another era, the manifest volatility of nationalism might have caused progressive intellectuals to view it with cautious optimism as the open site of political and ideological contestation. Nationalist ideologies, as Anne McClintock has written, are always 'contested systems of representation enacted through social institutions, and legitimizing, or limiting people's access to the rights and resources of the nation-state'.[3] Stranded upon the perceived ruins of Marxism, however, and with their ears ringing with the cacophony of bourgeois triumphalism, many of today's progressive Western based intellectuals are tending to construe nationalism less as volatile than as inherently sinister. To these scholars, McClintock suggests, 'nationalisms are dangerous, not ... in the sense that they represent relations to political power and to the technologies of violence' but 'in the sense that they should be opposed'.[4] Thus Eric Hobsbawm, having characterised nationalism in the post-1945 period as 'a substitute for lost dreams' concludes his 1990 study, *Nations and Nationalism Since 1780*, by looking forward to a time when nationalism itself will have withered away.[5] He takes comfort from the fact that nationalism is being fiercely debated today among historians; this, he says, 'suggests that, as so often, the phenomenon is past its peak. The owl of Minerva which brings wisdom ... flies out at dusk. It is a good sign that it is now circling round nations and nationalism'.[6]

Hobsbawm's epistemo-political critique of nationalism differs from that of mainstream commentators in being directed as centrally to Western nationalisms as those of the East or the South. In other words, it involves a disavowal of nationalism as such. It is also representative of the position of many other contemporary theorists - radical and conservative alike - in being married to the broadly sociological argument that recent transformations in the structure of capitalism as a world system have rendered the nation state obsolete. The implication here is that as goes the nation state, so, in the long run, will go nationalism as an ideology. Hence the tendency to read the recent emergence of virulent and reactionary nationalist movements in, say, Germany or Russia or France or Serbia, as compensatory symptoms of the collapse of the distinctively modern formation of the sovereign nation or nation state. It is on this basis, for example, that Slavoj Zizek moves to distinguish between what he calls 'modern' and postmodern' forms of racism:

> The old racism was direct and raw - 'they' (Jews, blacks, Arabs, Eastern Europeans ...) are lazy, violent, plotting, eroding our national substance, etc., whereas the new racism is 'reflected', as it were squared racism, which is why it can well assume the form of its opposite, of the fight against racism. Etienne Balibar hit the mark by baptizing it 'metaracism'. How does a 'postmodern' racist react to the outbursts in Rostock? He of course begins by expressing his horror and repulsion at the neo-Nazi violence, yet he is quick to add that these events, deplorable as they are, must be seen in their context: they are actually a perverted, distorted expression and effect of a true problem, namely that in contemporary Babylon the experience of belonging to a well-defined ethnic community which gives meaning to the individual's life is losing ground; in short, the true culprits are cosmopolitic universalists who, in the name of 'multiculturalism', mix races and thereby set in motion natural self-defence mechanisms. Apartheid is thus

legitimized as the ultimate form of anti-racism, as an endeavour to prevent racial tension and conflicts.[7]

Hobsbawm is more prosaic, but he too seems convinced that, inasmuch as its material conditions of existence are manifestly dissolving, nationalism today can only be a nostalgic and reactionary ideological enterprise in strict terms, indeed, a luxury that no democratic consciousness can afford. It is not at all that he underestimates the continuing prominence of nationalist ideologies in sparking and directing global events. Rather, his argument is that:

In spite of its evident prominence, nationalism is historically less important [than it once was]. It is no longer, as it were, a global political programme, as it may be said to have been in the nineteenth and earlier twentieth centuries. It is at most a complicating factor, or a catalyst for other developments. It is not implausible to present the history of the Eurocentric nineteenth-century world as that of 'nation-building', as Walter Bagehot did. We still present the history of the major European states of Europe after 1870 in this manner, as in the title of Eugene Weber's Peasants into Frenchmen. *Is anyone likely to write the world history of the late twentieth and early twenty-first centuries in such terms? It is most unlikely.[8]*

There are, it seems to me, several problems with the conceptual schema here being exemplified by both Zizek and Hobsbawm, for all the obvious differences between their intellectual projects. One of these might be addressed briefly under the rubric of 'presentism'. For instance, I find it perplexing, that Zizek should use the categorical language of epochal periodisation - modern/postmodern - to characterise the emergence of 'new' forms of racism. It is not only that claims as to the 'radical novelty' of contemporary forms of consciousness and modes of social practice strike me as being eminently contestable - often, in fact, as empirically false.[9] It is also that, even if we were to grant the premise of such unprecedentedness, I do not see on what evidence it ought to be marked as registering a transformation of epochal

- that is, world-historical - proportions. In a somewhat different context, Peter Dews has observed that he finds Lyotard's 'inflation of the term "postmodernity" into a term of epochal diagnosis' profoundly unjustified.[10] It seems to me that this propensity to overstate the singularity of the present, its radical difference from the past, is by no means limited to Lyotard alone. On the contrary, as I have tried to show elsewhere in an essay on the limits of postmodernist social theory, it is today a pervasive and remarkable feature of the work of many of the most influential theorists of culture and society.[11]

It is clear that the contemporary restructuring of global capitalist social relations, ensuing on the one hand - in the West - from the crisis of profitability beginning in the early 1970s and the subsequent partial destruction of the welfarist class-compromise, and, on the other hand - in the East - from the collapse of historical communism, has had significant ideological effects, not least with respect to nationalism. What is altogether less clear, I feel, is the degree to which these effects can plausibly be read not only as constituting a trend but as pointing to an irreversible historical truth, one distinguishing today in any definitive sense from yesterday: the obsolescence of the nation state; the dissolution of nationalism; the reconfiguration of class relations; etc. 'Our world is being remade. Mass production, the mass consumer, the big city, big-brother state, the sprawling housing estate, and the nation state are in decline: flexibility, diversity, differentiation, mobility, communication, decentralisation and internationalisation are in the ascendant'.[12] The deathless words of Martin Jacques, from the 'New Times' manifesto of 1988, and easy to punch holes in, no doubt. But between Jacques and Hobsbawm and Zizek, there seem more commonalities than differences. All three are guilty of 'over-reading' the available evidence to support their initial assumptions as to the radical discontinuity between contemporary social existence and that of the recent past.

There is another sense in which the three theorists may be said to share assumptions. I refer of course to the constitutive metropolitan elitism of their presuppositions. This elitism is easiest to recognise in the cavalierly deployed 'our' of Jacques' opening sentence - 'our world is being remade'. This 'our' includes neither those people in the core capitalist states - a clear majority - whose livelihood and security have been jeopardised by the new strategies of resurgent post-Keynesian capitalism, nor those 'massed up workers', as A. Sivanandan has described them, 'on whose greater immiseration and exploitation the brave new western world of post-Fordism is being erected'.[13] For in Thailand, Egypt, Mexico and Kenya, the tide of poor people - landless peasants or 'rural proletarians' - flooding from the countryside to the big cities in search of jobs continues to rise exponentially. In Brazil, Nigeria, Korea, and El Salvador, the question of the nation state has never before seemed so pressing or so central. In Indonesia, Jamaica, Sri Lanka, and Malaysia, the concepts of 'diversity', 'mobility' and 'communication' are of practical significance only to foreign elite and indigenous comprador classes: to the overwhelming masses of local people, they merely spell out exploitation in new letters. As Debbie Nathan has recently argued, with reference to the current tightening of border controls between the US and Mexico, the instantiation of the New World Order works not to dissolve nationalism and to promote internationalism, but, on the contrary, to augment class division and to binarise class experience within the context of the existing nation-statist dispensation: 'the fact [is] that while greenbacks can go anywhere in the world, wetbacks can't. Under agreements like NAFTA, a goodly supply of Third World workers must be available at Third World prices. With factories in Mexico paying $5 a day and those in the United States $5 an hour, who in his or her right mind would bother staying on the south side? But with a well-sealed border, relocation opportunities are pretty much out'.[14] Dissolution of the nation state for capital; hardening and rigidification of it for labour.

Zizek's elitism - or, more narrowly, his 'First Worldism' - makes itself manifest in his extraordinarily naive and historically unselfconscious observation that 'the Chernobyl catastrophe made ridiculously obsolete such notions as "national sovereignty", exposing the power's ultimate impotence'.[15] Certainly, Chernobyl presented to the world a terrifying portent - yet another terrifying portent - of its own possible 'accidental' demise. And certainly, mere nation states were powerless to withstand or combat the resultant irradiation of vast areas of the world's surface. But did it really take *Chernobyl* to show that the sovereignty of nation states is severely limited?

Hasn't the cold fact of this severe limitation constituted the central, structuring action-horizon of most of the nations of the world today formally recognised as such? Perhaps it did come as a shock to some Americans or Europeans to have to contemplate the limits of national sovereignty. To a majority of the world's population, however, such contemplation has been the ineluctable stuff of everyday life for years, if not decades and even centuries. What is at issue here is nothing as mysterious or elusive as 'the power's ultimate impotence'. Rather, it is the very concretely and historically engineered impotence of imperialised social formations - even if they themselves are organised along statist lines - confronting imperialist power. What Zizek takes radiation to have shown just yesterday, has in fact been capitalism's manifest reality from the moment of its consolidation. And far from it being a question of the *obsolescence* of national sovereignty - 'ridiculous' or otherwise - the asymmetries of the world system are such that most nation states have yet to *win* sovereignty for themselves in any meaningful sense, let alone to outgrow it or have it grow obsolete. (Of course, some national formations have yet to secure statehood. For them, these are not, even in the purely technical sense, postcolonial times.)

Even Hobsbawm might be faulted on this score when, allowing the plausibility of Bagehot's representation of the nineteenth century under the rubric of nation-building, he argues that nationalism is no longer the 'global political programme' it once was. Naturally, Hobsbawm is well aware of the Eurocentrism of Bagehot's conceptualisation, and, correspondingly, of the insufficiency of its periodisation. With respect to the colonial world, 'nation building' has been very much a twentieth-century phenomenon also. But Hobsbawm wants to suggest that if formerly the culture of imperialism dictated that the whole world be carved up in accordance with the principle of compulsory nation-statism, today a countervailing set of directives is tending to come to the fore. In the 'nineteenth' century, capitalism and nationalism were mutually entailing; in the 'twenty first' century, nationalism must wither away so that capitalism may continue to thrive.

The problem with Hobsbawm's scenario is that it tends to view nationalism as a unitary phenomenon, and one that, whatever else one might want to say about it, has generally been successful in realising itself, often with ghastly consequences, over the course of the past two hundred years. Failing to distinguish adequately *between* nationalisms and *between* nation-building projects, Hobsbawm is inclined to project as normative and globally representative the models characteristic of the imperialist, metropolitan social formations. Nationalism on Hobsbawm's reading is an hegemonising enterprise that has, historically, been able to secure its own conditions of existence. That is to say, the modern nation has been able to construct itself ideologically as an 'imagined community', unique, different from other such communities, and materially capable, through its statist apparatuses, both of reproducing itself internally and of maintaining its sovereignty - territorial, political, economic, cultural - in the fact of external pressures and constraints. With respect to most of the imperialised world, however, such a nationalism is still a dream, a consummation devoutly to be wished.

NATIONALITARIANISM

Allow me here to draw two distinctions: first, between *imperialist* and *anti-imperialist* nationalist problematics; and second, within the context of anti-imperialist struggle, between *elite* or *bourgeois* nationalism and *nationalitarianism* (or *insurgent* nationalism). As Tim Brennan has pointed out, imperialist nationalisms have typically taken the form of 'project[s] of unity on the basis of conquest and economic expediency'.[16] These are appropriative nationalisms, in which conquest is succeeded by subsumption, of land or resources or the conquered population itself. Hence not only modern British, American, and Israeli nationalism, but also nineteenth century Zulu and, in the present conjuncture, Serbian nationalism. Anti-imperialist nationalisms, by contrast, are either predicated upon the 'project of consolidation following an act of *separation* from [an imperialist power]' or else are oriented toward that goal. Theirs is 'the task of reclaiming community from within boundaries defined by the very power whose presence denied community'.[17]

In his important study, *Nationalist Thought and the Colonial World*, Partha Chatterjee has undertaken to demonstrate the degree to which, even in its bourgeois manifestations, nationalism in the context of anticolonialism has needed to distinguish itself sharply from the metropolitan, imperialist nationalisms upon which, nevertheless, it is centrally predicated. Conceding that at the level of ideology, (bourgeois) anticolonial nationalism was inescapably derivative of European nationalist ideologies, Chatterjee nevertheless argues that, merely by virtue of its specificity as anticolonial nationalism, it was obliged to go beyond them:

> *Pitting itself against the reality of colonial rule ... [anticolonial] nationalism succeeds in producing a different discourse. The difference is marked, on the terrain of political-ideological discourse, by a political contest, a struggle for power, which nationalist thought must think about and set down in words. Its problematic forces it relentlessly to demarcate itself from the discourse of colonialism. Thus nationalist thinking is necessarily a struggle with an entire body of systematic knowledge ... Its politics impels it to open up that framework of knowledge which presumes to dominate it, to displace that framework, to subvert its authority, to challenge its morality.*

Yet in its very constitution as a discourse of power, nationalist thought cannot remain only a negation; it is also a positive discourse which seeks to replace the structure of colonial power with a new order, that of national power. Can nationalist thought produce a discourse of order while daring to negate the very foundations of a system of knowledge that has conquered the world? How far can it succeed in maintaining its difference from a discourse that seeks to dominate it?

A different discourse, yet one that is dominated by another: that is my hypothesis about nationalist thought.[18]

What is true of bourgeois nationalism in this regard is doubly true of nationalism as an insurgent configuration. Perhaps the central weakness of the reading of nationalism proffered by the leading contemporary theorists of colonial discourse is that it is incapable of accounting for the huge investment of 'the masses' of the colonised historically in various kinds of nationalist struggle - the 'involvement', as Ranajit Guha has put it, in the context of India, 'of the Indian people in vast numbers, sometimes in hundreds of thousands or even millions, in nationalist activities and ideals'.[19] Many of today's theorists of colonial discourse tend to follow the trajectory of liberal historical and anthropological scholarship in casting all forms of national consciousness as impositions upon more or less disunited 'ethnically' (or 'local knowledge') identified communities. In Guha's words, however,

> *What ... historical writing of this kind cannot do is to explain ... nationalism for us. For it fails to acknowledge, far less interpret, the contribution made by the people on their own, that is, independently of the elite to the making and development of ... nationalism. In this particular respect the poverty of this historiography is demonstrated beyond any doubt by its failure to understand and assess the mass articulation of this nationalism except ... in the currently ... fashionable terms of vertical mobilization by the manipulation of factions.*[20]

Referring to the Indian case, Guha argues that even in those instances in which 'the masses' were mobilised very self-consciously and wilfully by bourgeois nationalist elites, they 'managed to break away from their control and put the characteristic imprint of popular politics on campaigns initiated by the upper classes'.[21]

This is in some respects to specify the ideological bearings of nationalism in the context of anticolonial struggle. But Guha provides a definitive refutation of Hobsbawm's argument, it seems to me, in his demonstration that, in India at least, the nationalist project *failed* in both its bourgeois and its insurgent dimensions.[22] Thus, Guha writes of 'the failure of the Indian bourgeoisie to speak for the nation'.[23] This failure emerges for him as an inability on the part of the Indian elite during the colonial era to forge an articulated national ensemble out of the relatively autonomous domains of elite and popular politics. The bourgeoisie were unable to win the consent of the people, whose interests they failed to recognise, let alone represent: 'There were vast areas in the life and consciousness of the people which were never integrated into the ... hegemony [of the Indian bourgeoisie].[24] Moreover, the political dominance of the dominant classes could not be challenged effectively by any counterhegemonic alliance of workers and peasants:

> *The initiatives which originated from the domain of subaltern politics were not, on their part, powerful enough to develop the nationalist movement into a full-fledged struggle for national liberation. The working class was still not sufficiently mature in the objective conditions of its social being and in its consciousness as a class-for-itself, nor was it firmly allied yet with the peasantry. As a result it could do nothing to take over and complete the mission which the bourgeoisie had failed to realise. The outcome of it all was that the numerous peasant uprisings of the period, some of them massive in scope and rich in anticolonialist consciousness, waited in vain for a leadership to raise them above localism and generalize them into a nationwide anti-imperialist campaign'.[25]*

On Guha's interpretation, the social 'mission' that the Indian bourgeoisie failed to realise - the 'mission' that the Indian working class for its part was too weak to appropriate and bring to fruition in 'anything like a national liberation movement' - is to be characterised as an 'historic failure of the nation to come to its own'.

FANON AND BHABHA

The distinction drawn by Guha, between the practical ideology of the 'nationalist movement' and the ideology that might have characterised a working-class led 'nationwide anti-imperialist campaign', echoes Frantz Fanon's categorical distinction between bourgeois nationalism and another would-be hegemonic form of national consciousness - a liberationist, anti-imperialist, nationalist internationalism, represented in the Algerian arena by the radical anticolonial resistance movement, the Front de Liberation Nationale (FLN), to whose cause Fanon devoted himself actively between 1956 and 1961, the year of his death. Of this latter, 'nationalitarian' form of consciousness (the term is Anouar Abdel-Malek's), Fanon wrote that it 'is not nationalism' in the narrow sense; on the contrary, it 'is the only thing that will give us an international dimension ... it is national liberation which leads the nation to play its part on the stage of history. It is at the heart of national consciousness that international consciousness lives and grows'.[26]

But this is not, of course, how Fanon is increasingly tending to be read, at least not within the fields of 'colonial discourse analysis' or 'postcolonial studies'.[27] On the contrary, it is today common, as Benedict Anderson has written, 'for progressive, cosmopolitan intellectuals ... to insist on the near-pathological character of nationalism, its roots in fear and hatred of the other, and its affinities with racism'.[28] Within (post-) colonial studies, this contemporary move among Western-based scholars to disavow nationalism *tout court* receives a distinctive stamp, taking the form - as Benita Parry put it in an important and challenging essay published in 1987 - of a tendency to 'disparag[e] ... nationalist discourses of resistance'.[29] Not so long ago, to speak of Vietnam or Cuba or Algeria or Guinea-Bissau - to evoke the names of such figures as Che, Fidel, Ho, Amilcar Cabral, no matter how fetishistically - was to conjure up the spectre of national liberation, that is, of a decisive decolonisation capable, in Fanon's memorable phrase, of 'chang[ing] the order of the world'.[30] Today things are very different. It is not so much that the setbacks and defeats that have had to be endured throughout Africa and Asia and the Caribbean have been bitter and severe, though this is certainly true. Rather, contemporary theorists tend to argue that the national liberation movements never were what they were. Either, therefore, one will find Cabral and Fanon and Guevara being criticised for their supposed authoritarianism, naive utopianism, and ignorance of and contempt for the working and peasant classes in whose name they fought and campaigned; or else one will find these revolutionary activists being made

over, depoliticised and pressed into service as sophisticated
theorists of the impossibility of the social or of colonial narcissism.
For example, Christopher Miller, in his recent book *Theories of
Africans*, constructs a portrait, fully of a piece with bourgeois
nightmares of Robespierre, Lenin, or Mao, of Fanon as terrorist
and murderer, implacable, ruthless, and grimly doctrinaire.[31] On
the other hand, Homi Bhabha inverts the historical trajectory
of Fanon's thought in order to propose a vision of him as
preeminently a theorist of 'the colonial condition' of the
interpellative effectivity of colonial discourse.

On Bhabha's reading, Fanon's 'search for a dialectic of
deliverance' emerges as 'desperate' and 'doomed'. Bhabha
concedes the existence of a revolutionary-redemptive ethic in
Fanon, of course, grounded in an existentialist and dialectical
Marxist humanism, but he insists that the real value of Fanon's
work lies elsewhere, in a psychoanalytic interrogation of the
problematics of colonial desire. For Bhabha the strengths of *Black
Skin, White Masks* are that it 'shift[s] … the focus of cultural
racism from the politics of nationalism to the politics of
narcissism'; and that it ... 'rarely historicizes the colonial
experience. There is no master narrative or realist perspective
that provide a background of social and historical facts against
which emerge the problems of the individual or collective
psyche'.[32] On the basis of this construction, Bhabha casts Fanon's
recurring utilization of existential, dialectical, and Marxist-
humanist categories in the light of a sequence of unfortunate
lapses, or as a determinate failure of vision:

> *In his more analytic mode, Fanon can impede the
> exploration of the … ambivalent, uncertain questions of
> colonial desire. The state of emergency from which he writes
> demands more insurgent answers, more immediate
> identifications. At times Fanon attempts too close a
> correspondence between the* mise-en-scene *of unconscious
> fantasy and the phantoms of racist fear and hate that stalk
> the colonial scene; he turns too hastily from the
> ambivalences of identification to the antagonistic identities
> of political alienation and cultural discrimination; he is too
> quick to name the Other, to personalize its presence in the*

*language of colonial racism. These attempts, in Fanon's
words, to restore the dream to its proper political time and
cultural space can, at times, blunt the edge of Fanon's
brilliant illustrations of the complexity of psychic
projections in the pathological colonial relation ... Fanon
sometimes forgets that paranoia never preserves its position
of power, for the compulsive identification with a
persecutory 'They' is always an evacuation and emptying of
the 'I'.*[33]

Inasmuch as Bhabha wishes to construct a portrait of Fanon as
a poststructuralist *avant la lettre*, his writing is full of such
passages. The procedural logic of these passages is curious. Their
thrust is to represent Fanon's ideas as according fundamentally
with Bhabha's own epistemological and methodological
principles. To the extent that Fanon's explicit formulations seem
to render such a construction implausible, however, they need
to be reproved for preventing Fanon from saying what he would
have said, had he been able - that is, had he had the right words,
or the time to reflect, or the courage to follow through his best
insights. For example, the real contribution of Fanon's thought
is said by Bhabha to derive from his attention to the
'*antidialectical*' movement of the subaltern instance';[34] But since
it cannot be denied that his characteristic mode of
conceptualisation is profoundly dialectical, Fanon 'must
sometimes be reminded that the disavowal of the Other always
exacerbates the "edge" of identification, reveals that dangerous
place where identity and aggressivity are twinned'.[35] Similarly,
Fanon is said by Bhabha to 'warn ... against the intellectual
appropriation of the culture of the people (whatever they may
be) within a representationalist discourse that may be fixed and
reified in the annals of History'.[36] but since it has to be admitted
that Fanon's discourse is typically emphatically nationalitarian,
and therefore both historicist and representationalist, Bhabha
bids us understand that his (Fanon's) preeminent claim to our
attention is not as a theorist of decolonisation or revolution, but
of the 'subversive slippage of identity and authority'.[37] And again,
Fanon's thought is said by Bhabha to tend toward theoretical
antihumanism; but since it has to be admitted that his language

is more or less unwaveringly humanistic, Bhabha is obliged to
proffer the rationalisation that, for various reasons:

> *Fanon is fearful of his most radical insights: that the space*
> *of the body and its identification is a representational*
> *reality; that the politics of race will not be entirely contained*
> *within the humanist myth of Man or economic necessity or*
> *historical progress, for its psychic effects question such*
> *forms of determinism; that social sovereignty and human*
> *subjectivity are only realizable in the order of Otherness.*[38]

According to Bhabha, in short, Fanon's 'deep hunger for
humanism, despite [his] insight into the dark side of Man, must
be an overcompensation for the closed consciousness or "dual
narcissism" to which he attributes the depersonalisation of
colonial man'.[39]

Although I believe, therefore, that little warrant for Bhabha's
reading of colonial discourse is provided by Fanon's work - it is
clear among other things that Bhabha's Fanon would have been
unrecognizable to Fanon himself - I would not want to be
misunderstood as denying the suggestiveness of Bhabha's
intellectual production over the course of the past several years.
On the contrary, Bhabha has contributed very positively and
substantively to the contemporary theorisation of '(post)
coloniality' as an ideological configuration. But it is necessary to
specify the precise object of Bhabha's theorisation with great
circumspection. It might be supposed, on the grounds of his
discussion of ambivalence and hybridisation - 'Almost the same
but not white', he puns in 'Of Mimicry and Man': 'the difference
between being English and being Anglicized' - that Bhabha's
real object was colonised elitism. Bhabha's theorisation of colonial
discourse is, indeed, manifestly pertinent to a reading of colonised
elitism.[40] But I would like to suggest that the cardinal figure of
Bhabha's work is the marginal subject of (post) colonialism -
'marginal' not (necessarily) in the sense of being powerless or
'genuinely disenfranchised' (Gayatri Spivak's phrase), but in the
sense of existing at the margins, that is,'subject to' but not 'the
subject of' dominant discourse.

The particular burden of Bhabha's work is to demonstrate

that in the contemporary world-system, social identities are not only always compound and overdetermined, they are also unstable at their origins, and incapable of being stabilised. On this reading, the problematics of exile, migration and diaspora emerge as paradigmatic. Bhabha's characteristic concept-figures are the *mohajirs*, 'emigrants' from the countries of their birth and 'newcomers' in other countries (as Salman Rushdie puts it in *Shame*), multiply-rooted subjects dwelling fully neither within the 'First World' nor within the 'Third', but ranged across them, so to speak, athwart the international division of labour.[41] The space of such subjectivity is labelled 'postcolonial' by Bhabha:

> *The postcolonial space is now 'supplementary' to the metropolitan centre; it stands in a subaltern, adjunct relation that doesn't aggrandise the* presence *of the west but redraws its frontiers in the menacing, agonistic boundary of cultural difference that never quite adds up, always less than one nation and double.*[42]

As this formulation makes clear, Bhabha tends to use the concept of 'postcoloniality', as he has defined it, *against* nationalism. He writes that:

> *the postcolonial perspective ... attempts to revise those nationalist or 'nativist' pedagogies that set up the relation of Third and First World in a binary structure of opposition. The postcolonial perspective resists attempts to provide a holistic social explanation, forcing a recognition of the more complex cultural and political boundaries that exist on the cusp of these often opposed political spheres.*[43]

In 'DissemiNation', Bhabha praises Eric Hobsbawm for writing 'the history of the modern western nation from the perspective of the nation's margin and the migrants' exile'.[44] His general contention is that the problematic of nationalism is *exploded*, rendered both anachronistic and incoherent, by the questions that stem from any consideration of the situation of the marginal subjects of contemporary 'postcoloniality'. The 'atonality' of the discourse of 'postcoloniality' is in addition positively *disruptive*

of 'the powerful oratory of the unisonant'.[45] 'Postcoloniality' -
the standpoint of the migrant - is in these terms itself extremely
powerful: Bhabha speaks, thus, of a 'strange, empowering
knowledge ... that is at once schizoid and subversive' and which
emerges as a function of the condition of exile, migrancy,
diaspora.[46]

JAMESON'S 'INFORMATION'

In his 1991 essay, 'A Question of Survival', Bhabha devotes a
good deal of his time to reflecting on the significance of Edward
Said's book, *After the Last Sky*. On the basis of Said's commentary,
Bhabha draws the following conclusions, not only about
Palestinian identity but about the 'impossibility' of nationalist
discourse in general:

> *The opaque silence of the atonal overwritten space of the
> Palestinian - Abandon the metanarrative! - petrifies the
> present, barring access to any ... reflective,
> representationalist distance of knowledge, or time of return.
> The questions of the Other, 'What do you Palestinians
> want?', cannot simply be answered in the images of identity
> or the narrative of historicism, because they are also asked
> in the language of Desire:* He is saying this to me but what
> does he want? *And that question cannot be replied to
> directly because it leads us past the place of meaning or
> truth and leads us to the enunciative level, to the moment
> that determines unique and limited existence of the
> utterance - the broken, fragmentary composition of the
> Palestinian: the atonal void ... The silence or void
> dangerously decomposes the narrative of the national
> culture (p97).*

Two points need to be made about this formulation. First, it is
important to draw attention to the tendentiousness of Bhabha's
reading of Said. As earlier with respect to Fanon, here too he
seems simply to appropriate Said, to assimilate him to his own
theoretical interests and preoccupations. In his essay, 'Yeats and
Decolonization', Said distinguishes between the 'insufficient'

moment of 'national anti-imperialism' and 'liberationist anti-imperialist resistance'.[47] Like Fanon and Guha, Said seems to me to emerge in his work - even in an introspective text like *After the Last Sky* - as well as in his political practice as an open advocate of the project of national liberation; this commits him to a nationalitarian politics - that is, to a discourse of representation predicated upon the assumption that it is indeed possible for a movement or alliance or party to 'speak for the nation'. This longstanding commitment on Said's part is not only ignored, but actually transmuted into its opposite, in Bhabha's commentary. The injunction to 'abandon the metanarrative', for instance, finds little sanction in Said's thought.

Second, and more important, it seems to me that Bhabha's claims both for the representativeness and for the 'disruptive' effectivity of the kind of subjectivity allegedly embodied in 'the Palestinian' are considerably overstated. It is not only that the Palestinian situation is socially and historically *sui generis*, and really cannot be taken as a generative model. It is also that, even if, in the contemporary world-system, the subjects whom Bhabha addresses under the labels of exile, migration and diaspora, are vastly more numerous than at any time previously, they cannot reasonably be said to be paradigmatic or constitutive of 'postcoloniality' as such. By the same token even if the category of the migrant or diasporic subject significantly complicates any easy espousal of nationalism in terms of belonging or territoriality, it is scarcely sufficient to undermine the credibility of those contemporary anti-imperialist discourses - in South Africa, in Palestine, in El Salvador for instance - that present themselves as nationalist.

Allow me to conclude, very abruptly, by referring to Fredric Jameson's controversial article on 'Third-world Literature in the Era of Multinational Capitalism'. Jameson opens this article rather strangely, by casting himself as an eavesdropper on 'recent conversations among third-world intellectuals'.[48] What Jameson 'overhears', of course, is that 'a certain nationalism is fundamental in the third world'; and this 'mak[es] it legitimate' in his view, 'to ask whether it [nationalism] is all that bad in the end' (p65). One would have wanted a decidedly more precise formulation, obviously; yet the 'information' that Jameson relays to us remains valuable, nevertheless. For it seems to me that 'a certain nationalism' *is* fundamental in the 'Third World'. It is fundamental, arguably, because it is today and for the foreseeable future still only on the inherited terrain of the *nation* that an articulation between secular intellectualism and popular consciousness can be forged; and *this* is important, in turn, because in the era of transnational capitalism it is only on the basis of such a universalistic articulation - that is, on the basis of nationalitarian struggle - that it is possible to imagine a postcapitalist world order.

Notes

1. Tim Brennan, 'The National Longing for Form', in *Nation and Narration*, Homi K. Bhabha (ed), Routledge, London 1990, p57.

2. See Louis L. Snyder, *The Meaning of Nationalism*, Rutgers University Press, New Brunswick 1954.

3. Anne McClintock, '"No Longer in a Future Heaven": Women and Nationalism in South Africa', *Transition* 51, 1991, pp104-5.

4. *Ibid*, p104.

5. Eric J. Hobsbawm, *Nations and Nationalism Since 1780. Programme, Myth, Reality*, Cambridge University Press, Cambridge 1990, p178.

6. *Ibid*, p183.

7. Slavoj Zizek, *Tarrying with the Negative. Kant, Hegel, and the Critique of Ideology*, Duke University Press, Durham 1993, p226.

8. Hobsbawm, *op cit*, pp181-82.

9. Ernesto Laclau and Chantal Mouffe, 'Post-Marxism without Apologies', *New Left Review* 166, November-December 1987, p80.

10. Peter Dews, Editor's Introduction, Jürgen Habermas, *Autonomy and Solidarity. Interviews*, Verso, London 1986, p27.

11. See Neil Lazarus, 'Doubting the New World Order: Marxism and Postmodernist Social Theory', *differences. A Journal of Feminist Cultural Studies* 3, no. 3, Fall 1991, pp94-138.

12. Martin Jacques, Editor's Introduction to a special issue on 'New Times', *Marxism Today*, October 1988, p1.

13. A. Sivanandan, 'All that Melts Into Air Is Solid: The Hokum of New Times', *Race & Class* 31, no. 3, 1990, p6.

14. Debbie Nathan, *The Nation*.

15. Zizek, *op cit*, p237.

16. Brennan, *op cit*, p58.

17. *Ibid*.

18. Partha Chatterjee, *Nationalist Thought and the Colonial World: A Derivative Discourse?*, Oxford University Press, Delhi 1986, pp40,42.

19. Ranajit Ghua, 'On Some Aspects of the Historiography of Colonial India', *Subaltern Studies I. Writings on South Asian History and Society*, Ranajit Guha (ed), Oxford University Press, Delhi 1986, p3.

20. *Ibid*.

21. *Ibid*, p6.

22. In this respect, see also the relevant sections of Basil Davidson's *The Black Man's Burden. Africa and the Curse of the Nation State*, Times Books, New York 1992.

23. Guha, *op cit*, p5.

24. *Ibid*, pp5-6.

25. *Ibid*, p6.

26. Frantz Fanon, *The Wretched of the Earth*, trans. Constance Farringdon, Grove Press, New York 1968, pp247-48.

27. For a discussion of the 'appropriation' of Fanon in the work of contemporary scholars in these fields, see Cedric Robinson, 'The Appropriation of Frantz Fanon', *Race & Class* 35, no. 1, 1993, pp79-91.

28. Benedict Anderson, *Imagined Communities. Reflections on the Origin and Spread of Nationalism*, Verso, London 1991, p141.

29. Benita Parry, 'Problems in Current Theories of Colonial Discourse' *Oxford Literary Review 9*, nos. 1-2, 1987, p35.

30. Fanon, *op cit*, p36.

31. Christopher Miller, *Theories of Africans: Francophone Literature and Anthropology in Africa*, University of Chicago Press, Chicago 1990.

32. Homi Bhabha, 'Remembering Fanon: Self, Psyche, and the Colonial Condition', in *Remaking History*, Barbara Kruger and Phil Mariani (eds), Bay Press, Seattle 1989, pp146, 136.

33. *Ibid*, p142.

34. Homi Bhabha, 'Interrogating Identity: The Postcolonial Prerogative', in *Anatomy of Racism*, David Theo Goldberg (ed), University of Minnesota Press, Minneapolis 1990, p198.

35. Bhabha, 'Remembering', *op cit*, p144.

36. Homi K. Bhabha, 'DissemiNation: Time, Narrative, and the Margins of the Modern Nation;, in *Nation and Narration*, *op cit.*

37. Bhabha, "Remembering": 146. "Nowhere" Bhabha adds, "is this slippage more visible than in [Fanon's] work itself, where a range of texts and traditions - from the classical repertoire to the quotidien, conversational culture of racism - vie to utter that last word that remains unspoken. Nowhere is this slippage more significantly experienced than in the impossibility of inferring from the texts of Fanon a pacific image of 'society' or the 'state' as a homogeneous philosophical or representational unity. The 'social' is always an unresolved ensemble of antagonistic interlocutions between positions of power and poverty, knowledge and oppression, history and fantasy, surveillance and subversion. It is for this reason - above all else - that we should turn to Fanon (146-47).

38. *Ibid*, pp142-43.

39. *Ibid*, p143.

40. Homi Bhabha, 'Of Mimicry and Man: The Ambivalence of Colonial Discourse', *October* 28, 1984, p130.

41. Salman Rushdie, *Shame*, Alfred A. Knopf, New York 1983, pp89-90.

42. Bhabha, 'DissemiNation', p318.

43. Homi Bhabha, 'Freedom's Basis in the Indeterminate', *October* 61, 1992, pp47-48.

44. Bhabha, 'DissemiNation', p291.

45. Homi Bhabha, 'A Question of Survival: Nations and Psychic States, in *Psychoanalysis and Cultural Theory: Thresholds*, James Donald (ed), St. Martin's Press, New York 1991, p90.

46. Bhabha, 'DissemiNation', p319.

47. Edward W. Said, 'Yeats and Decolonization', in Terry Eagleton, Frederic Jameson, Edward W. Said, *Nationalism, Colonialism, and Literature*, University of Minnesota Press, Minneapolis 1990, p76. It is interesting that Said revises this formulation of the distinction between these two moments of nationalist anti-imperialism in the version of 'Yeats and Decolonization' that appears in his book, *Culture and Imperialism*, Alfred A. Knopf, New York 1993. (See pp224-25).

48. Frederic Jameson, 'Third-World Literature in the Era of Multinational Capitalism'. *Social Text* 15, 1986, p65.

SITES OF RESISTANCE IN THE GLOBAL ECONOMY

Masao Miyoshi

Nike contractors used to make their shoes in South Korea but moved to Indonesia as wages rose. In Indonesia they pay young girls $1.35 for sewing shoes all day. Overtime is often mandatory. There is no union protection. A pair of Nikes sell in the United States for $45-80, but costs only $5.60 to produce. Michael Jordan's reported $20 million fee for promoting the brand was more than Nike's entire payroll of these young workers in its six factories in 1992.[1] Rumour is now spreading that Nike may move its operation again, this time to Vietnam. Labour in this communist country is reliable and, more important, its costs are once again lower.

The 'global' economy is a given of our life now. Transnational corporations cross borders to maximise productivity. This worldwide project to restructure industry for the maximum profit reorders society and culture as we have known it for centuries. First, I will briefly mention a few key points concerning transnational corporatism, then speculate on possible sites for contesting the global forces, and finally examine the role of the university as it is placed within the global corporate system.

THE 'GLOBAL' ECONOMY

Since the rise of capitalism, there have been general reorganisations of work and life. The earlier industrial revolutions, however, did not globally proliferate but remained regional at the crucial beginning stage. Uneven distribution of technology and industry as well as of labour and resources, and consequently of wealth and prosperity, resulted in the patterns of exploitation within the West itself, of course; but the imbalance was far more devastating between the two sides of the West and the non-West divide. We are all familiar with this story.

Said

Industrial transnationalisation was a function of the postwar high-tech revolution in automation, synthetic chemistry, electronics, and of course, computerised information, communication, transportation, and manufacture. In the half century since, global linkage has become unprecedentedly efficient. Temporal and spatial compression is an indisputable reality now.[2] Capital can move freely in time and space as long as the target area guarantees: (1) a stable political structure (often meaning dictatorship); (2) viable labour conditions (that is, cheaply trained or trainable labour plus the absence of unionism, feminism, and human rights); (3) reasonable infrastructure; (4) lower tax rates (favoured treatment by the host governments); and (5) indifference to the environment. In this age of technologically altered spatiality, it is now mobile private corporations, and not the geographically rooted nation states, that drive the world economy.[3]

The relationship between the state and the trading companies in modern Western countries has never been clearly delineated. Nevertheless, the sense of the nation state as more or less unitary had some validity earlier. Trading companies before the 1960s were still defined within the national borders and controlled by the government, which at least at times responded to the demands of its people, in the liberal capitalist nations. The development of transnational corporations (TNCs) in the 1960s and thereafter changed the picture dramatically. The TNCs were far more autonomous, and as they grew more powerful, and escaped from governmental control, they jettisoned the nation (that is, the aggregate of citizens and public space) leaving it to its own devices.

On the other hand, 'Free Trade' is never really free. Ever since Adam Smith, the idea of free trade has been the central doctrine of liberal capitalism. And yet the actual history of the US trade was openly protectionist until very recent days. The United States turned into a trading nation in the mid-1970s, for the first time, when TNC operation became a significant economic factor - in the sense that the US-originated and joint-venture corporations overseas began to ship their manufactured goods back to the United States. It was at this time that general trade tariffs were lowered in the US. Even then, however, US protectionism was not abandoned. It was simply shifted, to non-tariff barriers, such as 'voluntary' export restrictions. And through such narrowly aimed protectionist means, market distortions have continued to this day. What's interesting here is that the US workers' Average Weekly Earning began to decline steadily from the 1970s, as TNCs increasingly relocated capital, labour, and plant.[4]

The challenges from European and Japanese economies intensified during the 1970s. The US production system was stagnant because of the vast waste in Vietnam and other cold war commitments, as well as the political and industrial arrogance that had mitigated against industrial innovation since 1945. In response, Presidents Reagan and Bush initiated radical economic and fiscal reforms, to substantially transfer wealth from the poor to the rich. In the name of productivity and efficiency, much of public service was redefined as waste. Thus federal budgets for public works, education, and welfare were constantly challenged unless related to national 'security'. Privatisation of public programmes and institutions was the order of the day, and profit and self-interest were the only acceptable 'rational' motives.[5] In tune with such privileging of individual incentive, TNCs were unapologetic for their restructuring programmes. The corporate pay-scales were broadened to allow spectacular salaries to the top CEOs, while maintaining the barest minimum wage level for the multitude of workers. Industrial relocation and undersizing were approved of with near unanimity everywhere in the industrial and newly industrialised economies.[6] In the US many employers are abandoning traditional employee benefits - health insurance and retirement security - and national programmes such as the universal health care proposal and Social Security System are not assured of wide support. The end of the cold war has accelerated this trend rather than delivered the promised 'peace dividends'.

The economic situation has remained essentially unchanged under the Clinton administration. The larger corporations become larger, just as the rich become richer. This concentration of wealth is enabled by the transnationalisation of capital, labour, and market. The disappearance of jobs in industrialised nations is more serious than is shown in the unemployment statistics. Three out of four workers who lost their jobs in 1992 did not go back to the same type of jobs, according to one US study.[7] Those who regain jobs are often underemployed (overqualified) or subemployed (part time; no benefits). And temporary workers (also called 'contingency' workers) are now increasingly the mainstay of corporate employment.[8] And industrial companies are shedding workers by the thousand, even in the weapons industry. And undersizing is hardly an American event. The world's 500 ranking corporations lay off 400,000 workers annually - regardless of the increase in their profts.[9] The loss of jobs, the lowering of wages, the reduction in public services, and the rise of ultra elitism are common throughout the trans-nationalised world.

Sharp differences remain between the fully industrialized zones and the still developing nations. First, globalisation does not affect the North and South equally. For example, the effects of NAFTA on Northern American workers will be serious, but minuscule compared with the destructive impact on Mexican workers. And Mexico, with a per capita income of $3,200, is one of the better off nations of the world. Second, the political stability required by TNC operation often leads to the effective suppression of democratic demands. Thus in the Newly Industrialised Economies (NIEs) of the Northeast Asia - Korea, Taiwan, Hong Kong, and Singapore - the 'austerity' budget and the curtailment of human rights were ruthless for many years, and only recently have Taiwan and Korea relaxed their states of emergency.[10]

Thirdly, the Chiapas uprising serves as a good instance of the TNC destruction of the natural environment in developing nations. The Mexican lumber business has been indiscriminately cutting down tropical trees for years to clear the land for cattle ranchers and to export hardwood. The result is both the devastation of the Mayan Indian habitat and the deforestation of a vast area. Driven out of their forest, the Indians have been migrating northward to the US border, seeking employment at the maquilas in blighted living conditions. The ultimate effects of the ecological damage will not be known for generations. There are numerous examples of such deforestation, desertification, and displacement in Brazil, Congo, Malaysia, Indonesia, Thailand, West Africa, and elsewhere.[11] Disruptions of the planetary ecosystem are familiar to us all, but there is as of now no regulatory organisation with enforcement power even over the most egregious TNC performances.

Fourthly, the radical alteration of human habitats means the destruction of local and regional culture. The maximum profit principle does not hesitate to destroy the everyday life of local society if it does not willingly convert itself into an attractive commodity. Even officially 'traditional' artifacts - music, poetry, arts - are tested on their marketability, and all folk and ceremonial products and performances are similarly examined. 'Traditional' arts and forms are fragmented and decontextualised so as to be staged, museumized, collected, or merchandised. Even the local resistance and nativist resentment are open to the seduction of cosumerism, as can be seen in the history of graffiti art and rap music. New meanings are attached to all cultural products through aestheticization and/or pricing. Tourism and entertainment seem to be the triumphalist destination of all, and local, national, and regional differences are always on the verge of reduction to mere variants in the universal theme park, informed by the TNC world view.

In a fundamental way, the idea of national culture was a manufacture of the bourgeois West all along. As a part of the nation-state building programme, a 'culture' was selected, edited, and privileged to represent each nation somewhere around the end of the eighteenth century and throughout the nineteenth. But the age of transnational corporatism alters the idea once again. National culture is increasingly irrelevant; multiculturalism holds the day now as a tradeable commodity. All major films are produced for the world market, transcending local idiosyncrasies. People's everyday life, where alone 'difference' is vital and significant, is ignored. In the international bazaar of exportable goods, difference is in style only, as in clothing, cooking, or entertainment. With the decline of the nation state, the whole idea of culture is itself rapidly emptying. The disappearance of such official 'traditional' culture may be an occasion for celebration; the destruction of a people's way of life, however, is altogether different. It signifies the triumph of consumerism over local life, a place, a presence.

There are now 5.5 billion people on earth. Of these, less than one billion people, who live in the United States, Europe, Japan, and other transnational trade zones in the former Third World nations, are elites in this TNC age.[12] (I should reiterate here that residence in the trilateral regions does not guarantee a membership in transnational elitism: in every industrial nation a large proportion of workers are permanently unemployed, underemployed, and displaced.) The highly skilled TNC elites have, and will continue to have, disproportionate income and freedom, with which to master the new global spatiality. The rest - about 4 to 5 billion people - will live, increasingly, outside the capital flow, under brutal circumstances. Absorption into global consumerism is distressing enough; abandonment as useless is still worse. Without a nation state structure shielding them from the conditions of ravaged earth, utter chaos cannot be ruled out as their future prospect. Already in Sub-Sahara Africa - from Guinea and Zaire, Sudan and Somalia, to the Ivory Coast and Liberia - famine and slaughter are spreading with little governmental control. Strongmen and thugs are free to roam, and murder and pillage are unrestrained. We witnessed a full-scale genocide in Rwanda as the world stood by. Many areas in the former colonies in Africa, Eastern Europe, the Middle East, Central America, the Indian Subcontinent, and possibly inland China, in short a vast majority of the world, are threatened with unmediated disorder resulting from overpopulation, poverty, and civil violence. Forsaken by the industrialised elites as unprofitable, the majority of humanity faces a bleak future. As we talk about postcoloniality and postindustrialism in metropolitan academia, we ignore those billions outside our on-going discourse for whom life has nothing 'post' about it. Thus the inescapable question: in this age of ultra TNC elitism, is resistance at all possible?

RESISTANCE AND HOPE

Globalism by definition does not recognise the outside. Even those areas that are abandoned and ignored by TNCs are at least on their map. If all were inside the TNC space, there could be no 'outside' or 'otherness', thus no conflict. In that sense, it is understandable that the current trend of intellectuals, the ultra elite of the TNC zones, is to expunge words like 'opposition' and 'resistance' from their critical vocabulary. Fukuyama, Baudrillard, Lyotard, and Foucault prevail. As discourse, presumably, enables all presences, and nothing exists outside discourse, so there is nothing outside of the 'global' economy. In other words, discursive inclusivity and political-economic integration are both unbounded, leaving out nothing - or rather, leaving no 'outside' space for any 'other' idea/object to exist. Such discursive and political-economic extension, however, can be no more than a fantasy. We only need to examine the contours of discourse and of globalised trade. The fact of the matter is that the 'global' economy is global only in the sense that giant corporations have free access to every place in the world, if they so choose; but the profit motive restricts their expansion. Thus the vast majority of humanity is totally shut out from it. The 'global' economy is in fact nothing but a strategy for maximum exclusion. Exactly in the same way, the discourse is coextensive strictly with the discourser's interest. Despite Wittgenstein and Foucault, there is always an outside to language and discourse. And to the extent that the money and production flow is beneficial only to the privileged few and inaccessible to the rest, resistance is not only possible but is inevitable. Discourse must acknowledge the idea of resistance and opposition.

Where does it begin then? Where can hope be found? We should begin by reexamining the obvious. Firstly, as people have always tried, and we persist in trying, to take back the state. The nation state structure has never been adequate for people, and the baggage of nationalism and ethnocentrism that comes along with it is almost always dangerous.[13] Yet our distrust of the state is outweighed now by the need for administrative mediation between people and 'flexible' capital, between people and chaos. The state is the only political structure now that *could* protect people from ungovernable disorder/unmediated violence. The state as we know it has never worked, yet even that form of state is better present than absent, if only to accomplish some of the projects described below. Secondly, a fully empowered representative interstate organisation - what the United Nations ought to have been - must be invented. Global labour, environment, health, education, information as well as economy and peace must be negotiated by North and South together. Not the United Nations, which is largely an instrument of the industrial nations, especially the United States, but a world assembly reorganised to represent and reconcile conflicting interests - and united for human survival - must be constructed. Thirdly, the intensification of grassroots activities (Non-Governmental Organisations,) must accompany such attempts to take back and reinvent the state against TNCs. The state and TNCs must continually be made aware of the extra-state civil possibilities as well as the interstate organisation. Fourthly, transnational labour unions especially need to be organised. To combat the TNCs, nationally defined labour unions are totally deficient. While national labour unions are preoccupied with the policy of self-protection against overseas workers, TNCs will transfer their operations beyond the national borders. Only transnational labour unions can face up to the TNCs, and this movement must begin among the comparatively higher-paid workers of developed nations.

It must be admitted that these four suggestions - the reclaimed state, interstate organisation, grassroots programmes, transnationally organised labour - are nothing new, and they may well be thought of as proven failures: the fragmentation of the nation state is a part of what originally occasioned this paper; the global governmental form as we have it now is thoroughly appropriated by the TNCs and G7; most NGO activities in poorer countries cannot bypass the existing state structure, which is usually thoroughly corrupt and ineffectual; and labour unions are by definition self-interested. Any alliance with poorly paid workers abroad is nearly impossible to imagine, even though that is the only way to fight back the effectively allied TNCs. These are, however, the only political means for the survival and protection of people at this moment.[14]

There are other, even more theoretical, grounds for ultimate hope. First of all, even the TNC phase of capitalism will have to face the crisis of overaccumulation sooner or later. Because of its hyper-accelerated 'productivity,' the need for the absorption of surplus capital and labour will be ultimately greater than ever before. The world's poor must in the long run be supplied with cash to buy products, and for that, they must be provided with work. That means that the superefficient system of wealth acquisition must be readjusted for improved dispersal of wealth- - enough to keep people buying, and so alive - or vice versa. For the foreseeable future such an adjustment will probably be confined to Western Europe, the United States, Canada, Australia, New Zealand, South Africa, and Japan, where 80 per cent of world capital circulates. The East Asian NIEs will be added to the list before long; then, subsequently, TNC zones in other areas. If the trickle-down effect is not all myth, wealth might spread - albeit rather thinly and slowly.

Secondly, eventually the limits to environmental destruction will be recognised by all - including TNCs. The planet is truly more global than the 'global' economy, and the effects of its irreversible depletion and dilapidation will be shared by all, with no exception. Even the most obdurate industry will have to realise sooner or later the ultimate limits and non-transferability of eco-destructions, and such fear of absolute overconsumption is bound to enter even the most self-serving calculations of corporate planners. Environmental terminality is the twentieth and twenty-first centuries' answer to the nineteenth century's myth of growth and progress. And the poor of the South can turn the situation into bargaining chips.[15]

Thirdly, late capitalism has produced a situation that could allow workers to shift the direction of its economic operations. As has been often pointed out, the ownership of corporate capital is no longer predominantly in the hand of private individuals or families ('the capitalist class'), but in public institutions.[16] Over one half of the stock in developed countries is now owned by institutional investors, especially the pension funds in Britain and the United States. This fact has an explosive consequence if the owners' rights are correctly exercised. At present investment managers are very much like corporate managers, earning immense salaries, bonuses, and perks from generating corporate profits. Fiduciaries, however, can be charged with legal responsibilities for protecting not only specific investments but also the trust as a whole. For instance, a pension plan presumably should ensure the workers reasonable security after retirement, and TNC policies for the transfer of capital, labour, and market overseas may thus be found to be a contravention of the workers' welfare. Specific corporations invested with the institutional funds might make great profits, but that does not fulfill the fiducial responsibilities entirely: if such profits fail to benefit the individual workers' future, the whole investment policy needs to be challenged. In short, the investor-workers can exercise their proprietary rights and powers over the management of the TNCs in which they own shares of capital. For example, to the extent that outside support made any contributions, the divestment movement was a significant factor in the fall of the white rule in South Africa. Workers' direct participation in the management of pension investment is not a far-fetched project, but a perfectly reasonable course of action to control the direction of TNC operations.[17]

Fourthly, as long as extreme inequity in wealth and welfare persists, resentment and opposition are bound to rise. However skilled and sophisticated in suppressive technology, the corporate world cannot keep control indefinitely. For example, the Zapatista National Liberation Army rebellion still continues in New Mexico. Although people elsewhere seem politically paralyzed generally, there is no reason to believe that they will remain inactive for good. We may simply not know what is happening: there are always local movements beneath the conglomerate news and information. A nun at a Catholic church in Chiapas, described the ZNLA insurrection, 'This was like a plant that had never died but never grew either. Now the earth beneath them has moved, and the plant is growing.'[18]

At the darkest moment of despondence, we should try to remember that no matter how the history of the 1960s may be rewritten, it was the resisters and protesters, together with the Vietnamese, who ended the war in Vietnam. All the follies and errors of the time, and the nostalgic, patriotic, and bored renarrativisations, do not alter history one bit. Likewise, apartheid was felled solely by those who struggled and sacrificed for justice and independence, and their supporters. The future of South Africa might be bloody again, political suppression may only be replaced by economic domination. But it does not alter history: white rule was defeated by those who fought back.

THE USES OF THE UNIVERSITY

Those of us who are members of universities need to think of our own site of work. We know that today the university is actually a corporarion in style and substance.[19] Professors are allowed to make nearly any assertion, for or against the state, for or against TNCs, but the reason is not academic freedom. Corporatism is so effective that any criticism is at once repossessed by converting disagreement into preagreement, and opposition into diversity. Flexibility and multiplicity are, however, merely apparent. The university maintains its authority through its system of hierarchy, reinforced by means of carefully graduated privilege and power. Academic elitism is no less pernicious than TNC ultra elitism in as much as it satisfies the most vocal and inhibits the least, producing acquiescence in both.

A successful critic freely circulates his/her views, which will then make the scholar a success, a celebrity, and a commodity. The star system works; few can resist such bewitchery - especially because it is couched in terms of intellectual and scholarly excellence. Though paltry in absolute terms, comfort and luxury visibly accompany university pay, rank, and honours. Through civilities and pleasantries, it can promote the pleasure of collegiality. At times, sheer marginalisation can silence the articulate, too. Assured of these satisfactions and impotences, which, generate pervasive silence, corporatism is now aloof to the substance of our teaching and learning. It is far less nervous now about faculty and student speeches and activities than, say, twenty years ago. It knows that the university harbors hardly any subversives now. The university may in fact be among the most conservative institutions, with TNC interests firmly entrenched and protected.

At the same time, everyone in academia knows that corporatism is set to downsize the educational enterprise, just like any other industry. It can banish whomever it finds undesirable, together with the unproductive. It now understands that the university is not the best - i.e., most cost-effective - institution for worker training. TNCs can create their own training programmes. They can also import from abroad ready-made physicians, engineers, and skilled workers at minimum production costs. As to cultural creativity, energy and inventiveness are sought elsewhere, for more vital - that is commercially successful - producers and productions. They are available on the street. And as for literary and cultural criticism, corporatism cannot expend with anything more eagerly than that. Not because it can be subversive, but because it is redundant and useless - overproduced and oversupplied as well as unproductive.

Thus, the corporate reorganisation of academic institutions seems inevitable. The projects of undersizing and restructuring have already begun. We may in fact some day find ourselves being hauled outside of academia, among those disempowered whom we haven't taken note of for the last half century. It is, however, precisely here that our moment of resistance and opposition could arrive. We could then begin our serious task. However, like the programmes of reconstructing the TNC-dominated world, corporate academicism cannot be restructured overnight. In the interim, we need specific projects to alter the general scheme of learning and education, as well as to reinforce our not always sustained morale.

We have been long alerted to the exclusivism that is inherent in the Enlightenment notion of universality. The Enlightenment idea of 'universal' meant simply European/male/propertied/heterosexual, while those who are outside such 'norm' - i.e., most people on earth - were considered subnormal exceptions or accidental particulars. We also know that what constitutes and organises the departmental and disciplinary structure of today's university is the same Enlightenment elitism. This eighteenth - century universalism is part of the philosophy of progress and evolution that endorsed the nineteenth-century imperialism of the West. The university, as imagined by Fichte, Wilhelm von Humboldt, John Henry Newman, and Matthew Arnold, has been a response to the two-century-long call for the mobilisation of Western adventurists. Thus recent challenges from the margins - ethnics, feminists, colonials, homosexuals, and underclass - are an overdue acknowledgment of the distortions inherent in the European provincialism that passed for universalism. And this is a salutary step.

Across many universities recently, one recognises a deep

uncertainty regarding the nature of departmental disciplines. In every department the faculty and students are seriously in doubt about the grounds for the 'canon' and 'requirements'. Rare are professors who still work in the field and discipline in which they wrote their doctoral theses decades earlier. What was once agreed on as the centre and boundaries of a field is no longer widely agreed; disciplinary methodologies and regional specialisations, too, are hotly contested everywhere. Under pressure from feminism, identity politics, and multiculturalism, conventional disciplines are forced to loosen their boundaries and transnationalise their expertise. Long frowned upon by established scholars, 'interdisciplinary' studies are now emerging as saviours of curriculum and scholarship, from the structural failure of the university. The failure of the university however is far more fundamental than taxonomical. Interdisciplinarity needs to do more and go further than it has been so far willing to do, before drawing the boundaries of criticism and scholarship. Obviously, I am referring here to parallel and cognate developments between economy and scholarship.

We have remarked that those who are excluded from transnational corporatism are also left out of the texts of criticism. Scholarly discourse, even of those deeply engrossed with the issues of postcoloniality, multiculturalism, and difference (in ethnicity, gender, and class), is conducted within the TNC space, inside the insiders' globe. And our urgent university reorganisation project requires breaking out of this confinement and straying outside. First of all, transnational ultra elite discourse - very much like TNC capitalism - resumes and repeats the traditional Eurocentric exclusionism that was crucially indicted by Third-World intellectuals, in the period around the Second World War, and the diasporan intellectuals later in the 1970s. The difference between the current postcolonial TNC intellectuals and the old metropolitan Eurocentrists is becoming more and more miniscule. After all the years of the Orientalism debate, since Edward Said's book started it, the oppositionist vocabulary has been domesticated: the old 'self' and the old 'other' are now comfortable with each other, and together they ignore the new 'other'. Binarism is out, blurriness is in. Today's 'anti-Orientalists' are deeply imbued with Orientalist arrogance and exclusivism. Worse, the ex-colonials want to remain both inside and outside; thus they insist on the privilege of 'hybridity' as their birthright.[20] And they join the postmodernists for whom the 'multiple subjectships' are the official agent of the new socialist strategy.[21] Ambivalence and equivocation - contradiction and evasion, really - rule the TNC intellectuals.

Secondly, literary and theoretical discourse is drastically losing its audience. No one except for determined academic cadres and aspirants participates in it. The books and journals that publish them have a cliquish circulation. One recalls that their point of departure and raison d'être once - in the 1960s and 1970s - lay in a passionate concern with the forgotten and unrepresented, which was a matter of vital importance to a far wider range of readers. The abandonment of, and indifference to, the wretched of the earth fractures the credibility of their intellectual enterprise. Gibberish - not so much in terminology as in substance - attracts graduate students and mature scholars alike, precisely because it is incomprehensible to many and thus exclusive. Articles in scholarly journals read amazingly identically, citation by citation, term by term, paragraph by paragraph. Their attention is almost always riveted on each other's publications, seldom ever venturing out to the outside world. Ideas rapidly circulate the world over, skimming the scholarly consciousness which is ever ready for the next move - just like TNC investments. Conformism in gibberish is the doctrine that best befits the TNC academia because it enhances the exclusivism and obscurantism inherent in the TNC doctrine.

In order to regain moral and intellectual legitimacy, scholars in TNC societies need to resuscitate the idea of opposition and resistance. They, we, need to identify the victims and the victimisers once again, and define our relations to them.

As long as we are inside the university, we will not be able to participate directly in the material improvement of the dispossessed four to five billion people of the world. We can, however, still write about them so that their conditions can be better known. We cannot represent them, nor can we be surrogates. But we can report what we know, and seek to counter the information emanating from three other dubious sources: media, corporations, and state. We can disturb and upset our intellectual routines by teaching what we are not expected to. There is a positive merit in simply disrupting the smooth operation of bureaucratic discourse in as much as the academic institutionalisation was implicated in the project of colonialism and transnationalism. We can break out of the vicious circle of mutual reference and mutual endorsement among scholars. We can in a small way revitalise our knowledge and learning by being scrupulously intellectual and remaining staunchly sceptical about scholarly journals, books, and conferences as well as university regulations and department rules on intellectual matters - even when we discuss postmodernism, multiculturalism, postcolonialism, feminism, or identity politics. To do anything in order to disturb exclusivism of any kind, to forcibly expand and include knowledge and learning, and thereby expose globalism for its exclusivism - that is the only way we can intellectually survive during these interim years under the 'global' economy.

Many of my friends have read this paper in various stages. I am thankful for the following for helpful comments and suggestions, although errors are, of course, entirely my own: Martha L. Archibald, Paul Bove, Noam Chomsky, H.D. Harootunian, Takeo Hoshi, Fredric Jameson, George Mariscal, Edward Said, Dan Schiller and Don Wayne.

Notes

1. Nike contends that it is distanced from this labour issue because its plants belong to contractors who are responsible for the management. For further elaboration, see Richard J. Barnet and John Cavenagh, *Global Dreams: Imperial Corporations and the New World Order*, Simon and Shuster, New York 1994, pp325-329; and Donald Katz, 'Pusan, Republic of Korea,' in *Just Do It: The Nike Spirit in the Corporate World,* Random House, New York 1994, pp 160-206.

2. See David Harvey, *The Condition of Postmodernity* , Basil Blackwell, Oxford 1989, Parts II and III, pp 121-323.

3. See my 'A Borderless World? From Colonialism to Transnationalism and the Decline of the Nation-State', *Critical Inquiry*, Vol. 19, No. 4, pp726-751.

4 After the peak of over $350 in 1973, it fell to around $310 in 1986. US Department of Commerce and Bureau of the Census, *Historical Statistics of the United States: Colonial Times to 1970* and the annual *Economic Reports to the President*. Cited also by Harvey, p131.

5. Privatisation is of course not an American phenomenon, but global. The most dramatic instance is in the former socialist states. See, for example, 'The Special Report' articles on Russia, Eastern Europe, and Latin America in *Business Week*, 21 October 1991.

6. As for the European corporations shifting jobs to low-wage countries, see Roger Cohen, 'Europeans Fear Unemployment Will Not Fade with Recession', *The New York Times*, June 13, 1993.

7. David Rosenbaum, 'Jobs', *The New York Times,* 3 October 1993.

8. Jaclyn Fierman, 'The Contingency Work Force', *Fortune*, 24 January 1994, pp 30-36.

9. Clairmonte and Cavanagh, *Le Monde diplomatique*, March 1994, p27.

10. It could be argued that dictatorship would have emerged in these nations regardless of economic globalism. The Phillipines and Indonesia are good examples that might support this idea. But the point is that transnationalisation does not alter the oprressive situation of these countries, but rather serves to create and or maintain it. Indonesian genocide in East Timor was carried out with U S, European, and Japanese Capital. Iraq's dictatorship may have been a target of TNC global policy, but the Saudi Arabian and Kuwaiti rulers are not. Mexico's PRI has long suppressed the poverty-stricken workers, and the passage of NAFTA has nothing to offer them.

11. According to a 1991 UN Environment Programme report, 25 per cent of the global land surface is threatened with desertification.

12. Riccardo Petrella, 'World City-States of the Future', *New Perspectives Quarterly*, 24, Fall 1991, pp 59-64. See also Robert B. Reich, *The Work of Nations: Preparing Ourselves for Twenty-First Century Capitalism*, Alfred A. Knopf, New York 1991; and my article 'A Borderless World?'

13. The nation state has been inadequate even in the West where it was invented. The nation state structure in the non-West is merely an imposition by the former masters and thus has even less legitimacy.

14. There are a few bright spots scattered in the world. The Grameen Bank of Bangladesh is a shining NGO example. An innovative loan assistance project largely organised among poor uneducated village women, it has grown to be a sizeable financial organisation without compromising its original intents. It is spreading to American urban ghettos and attracting interests of public officials of industrial nations such as Norway and the United States. Also, among the educated youths

in the industrialised nations, there are signs of rejecting mainline economic life, preferring bartering and craft to corporate life-style. Interesting enough, though it is too early and too local to place great hope on such developments. For Grameen Bank, see Andreas Fuglesang and Dale Chandler, *Participation as Process: What We Can Learn from Grameen Bank, Bangladesh*, Norwegian Ministry of Development Cooperation, 1986; and David S. Gibbons, *The Grameen Reader,* Universiti Sains Malaysia, 1992. The People's Plan for the Twenty-First Century (PP21), a project started around the Pacific-Asia Resource Center in Tokyo, is also an interesting development. The Center publishes *AMPO: Japan-Asia Quarterly Reviews.* See also Martin Hart-Landsberg, 'Post-NAFTA Politics: Learning from Asia', *Monthly Review,* June 1994, pp12-21.

15. Richard J. Barnet and John Cavanagh argue that the executives of leading TNCs are capable of global thinking 'far more developed than that exhibited by most officials of national governments'. However, they do not elaborate the point. *Global Dreams: Imperial Corporations and the New World Order* Simon and Schuster, New York 1994, p18. Bruce Rich's *Mortgaging the Earth* discusses signs of criticism of development policy within the World Bank, although it is not the dominant force.

16. For instance, Peter F. Drucker, *Post-Capitalist Society,* Harper Business, New York 1993, especially Chapters 2 and 3.

17. Corporate governance is in fact currently attracting considerable attention. The main interest has so far been in the increase of profits, and certainly not in employee welfare or environmental protection. However the potential for enlightened management by public shareholders do exist. See 'A Survey of Corporate Governance', *The Economist,* 29 January 1994. The topic is in circulation in Japan, too. *Asahi Shinbun,* for instance, published a four-part series on it in June 1994.

18. Tim Golden, '"Awakened" Peasant Farmers Overrunning Mexican Towns,' *The New York Times*, 9 February 1994. See also, Alma Guillermoprieto, 'Letter from Mexico', *The New Yorker*, 16 May 1994.

19. Clark Kerr, *The Uses of the University*, The University of California Press, Berkley 1964, is one of the earliest assessments of the role of the thoroughly socialised and corporatised university. It was a shocking admission in 1964 and became one of the causes of the Free Speech Movement at Berkley. A mere three decades later, everyone takes for granted Kerr's notion of 'multiuniversity'.

20. Homi Bhabha, *The Location of Culture*, Routledge, London 1994. Nestor Garcia Canclini also uses the idea of 'hibridas' 'Memory and Innovation in the Theory of Art,' *The South Atlantic Quarterly*, Vol 92, No 3 (Summer 1993), so does Bruno Latour, *We Have Never Been*

Modern, Harvard University Press, 1994. Although their contexts are different, they all derive the concept from a desire for blurring distinctions - with similar ideological and practical implications.

21. Ernest Laclau and Chantal Mouffe, *Hegemony and Social Strategy: Towards a Radical Democratic Politic*, Verso, London and New York 1985.

SECULARISM, ELITISM, PROGRESS AND OTHER TRANSGRESSIONS: ON EDWARD SAID'S 'VOYAGE IN'

Bruce Robbins

In February 1994 the *New York Times* published an article by Richard Rorty entitled 'The Unpatriotic Academy.' It begins as follows:

> *Most of us, despite the outrage we may feel about governmental cowardice or corruption, and despite our despair over what is being done to the weakest and poorest among us, still identify with our country. We take pride in being citizens of a self-invented, self-reforming, enduring constitutional democracy. We think of the United States as having glorious-if tarnished-national traditions.*
> *Many of the exceptions to this rule are found in colleges and universities, in the academic departments that have become sanctuaries for left-wing political views'.*

He is 'glad there are such sanctuaries', Rorty says. But he wishes 'we had a left more broadly based, less self-involved and less jargon-ridden than our present one'. And he also finds a bigger problem with this left:

> *it is unpatriotic. In the name of 'the politics of difference,' it refuses to rejoice in the country it inhabits. It repudiates the idea of a national identity, and the emotion of national pride. This repudiation is the difference between traditional American pluralism and the new movement called multiculturalism.*[1]

After a brief caricature of multiculturalism, which he sees as an attempt to keep all of America's different communities 'at odds with one another'. Rorty hastens to his conclusion:

> *If in the interests of ideological purity, or out of the need to stay as angry as possible, the academic left insists on a 'politics of difference', it will become increasingly isolated and ineffective. An unpatriotic left has never achieved anything. A left that refuses to take pride in its country will have no impact on that country's politics, and will eventually become an object of contempt.*

A collection like this is perhaps not the best place to respond with the appropriate gusto to Rorty's false prophecy of 'contempt' (which is not a prophecy at all, in that it clearly describes a contempt he already feels). But it is worth noting the unlikelihood that the proper places would ever lend themselves to the proper responses. I doubt whether the *New York Times*, for instance, would print a history lesson about what happened when, as Rorty's hero John Dewey advocated, the American left suddenly did turn patriotic and helped plunge the nation into the unprecedented and purposeless slaughter of the First World War. I doubt whether many American television stations would devote an hour of prime time to the notion (not unfamiliar in the universities) that the American version of multiculturalism has been working not against but in the service of American nationalism, as we saw for example in the Arab-targeted pride about US women in uniform that lent ideological support to US efforts during the Gulf War. Anyone who watched the debates over NAFTA during or after the 1992 presidential campaign may well wonder what discursive space is available, if any, for a position that does *not* identify itself firmly and unequivocally with the US national interest - that *does* identify itself, say, with the wage scales of Mexican workers.

In short, there is undoubtedly a split between the American public and the academic left, and both parties undoubtedly suffer from it, but the cause to which Rorty attributes this split doesn't go very far towards explaining it. It would seem more accurate to identify the problem not as the academic left's fastidious recoil from national pride (something of which I do not after all see overwhelming evidence), but rather as the marked absence of anything resembling internationalism from the media-dominated public sphere *outside* the academy. The divide could hardly therefore be remedied, as Rorty stops just short of proposing, by mass recitations of the Pledge of Allegiance throughout the nation's institutions of higher learning. But this does not mean that those whom Gayatri Spivak calls 'postcolonial critics' can afford complacently to ignore what Rorty's flag-waving means to them.

Rorty offers an inadvertent but nonetheless urgent corrective, for example, to those within the academic left (for example, Neil Lazarus) who have been arguing that a cosmopolitan anti-nationalism is now the canonical position of Washington and Wall Street, America's chosen means of universalising its hegemony and breaking down Third World resistance.[2] As Rorty's outburst suggests, the resurgence of post-cold war nationalism in the United States seems rather to be taking the pragmatic, non-universalistic direction of *Realpolitik*, a grimly amoral pushing of 'our' national interest against everyone else's in what is presumed to be a trans-national competition of equally valid, necessarily national interests. The rise of *Realpolitik* need not mean that universalism, stained as it is by associations with Eurocentrism and global capitalism, must be the object of a political transvaluation; nor does it mean that that one must pretend to recognise in the real world today the somewhat miraculous ideal that Lazarus describes as 'a liberationist, anti-imperialist nationalist internationalism' (p72). But it does mean that what Rorty calls a 'politics of difference' may seem increasingly to be describing the international status quo rather than protesting against it; and that it can avoid that self-neutralisation only by daring to explore the interests it might share with a politics of sameness.

One such venture would be a reconsideration of the discourse of human rights. If postcolonial critics in the US want to unite their efforts with the concerns of Americans (and non-Americans) outside the universities, there is no need to do so on Rorty's terms, the terms of flagrant and unrepentant ethnocentrism. Ordinary Americans identify with America's 'glorious' traditions, it is true, but that has never been all they identify with. (This is in part because, if the media have frequently played shamelessly to national pride, that has never been the only sort of identification they have fostered.) Thus the academic left's

Said

bridge-building might well begin with those imperfect but pervasive and passionate forms that internationalist thought has already in fact taken outside the academy. Whether one thinks about the US public's tortured fascination with Bosnia and Rwanda, or about China's prisons and Israel's Occupied Territories, it is clear that the discourse of human rights does offer a vocabulary for widespread and heartfelt internationalist emotion. Yet this is an internationalist discourse that *academic* internationalism in the humanities has had little dialogue with. There are of course strictly political reasons for this. After the heroic moment of Fanon, Césaire, and Cabral, after the solidarity movements linking First World progressives to struggles in South Africa, Latin America, and the Middle East, the discourse of human rights will naturally look like a diminished thing, thin and directionless when it is not simply a tool of the other side. But the weightier reason is, I think, a more local one. Of late cultural difference has been one or even *the* major rationale for knowledge-production in the humanities, and the universalising discourse of human rights seems to set itself straightforwardly against it. Yet, once again, if one were to decide (*pace* Rorty) that American nationalism remains the single most dangerous force loose in the world today, one might have to rethink the reflex defence of culture against universalism that has been so persistent a part of concern with colonial and postcolonial subjects. One would have to cultivate, rather than discount, any and all seeds of non- or anti-nationalist feeling that American political culture has allowed to exist.

One further conclusion that might be drawn from Rorty's critique of academic internationalism - the conclusion that I want to follow out in the remainder of this essay - concerns the folly of what appears to be a gathering consensus, within postcolonial studies itself, that the institutional rise of the field is somehow an anomaly and an embarrassment. To judge from recent essays and conference presentations, the best thing to do with postcoloniality's success story is to subject it to the most scathing critique possible. Gleeful and increasingly unrestrained attacks on the metropolitan location of postcolonial studies and the power, privileges, and priorities that stem from that location conveniently forget, however, the point that Rorty unintentionally makes: the legitimacy and the institutional toehold enjoyed by such studies in the metropolis remain extremely fragile. It is often claimed that critical attention to the (post)colonial deviously serves the interests of neo-imperialism. Unfortunately, nothing obliges neo-imperialism to agree that its interests are so served, and there are no guarantees that it will act accordingly. Indeed, Rorty's effusion is one sign among many that post-cold war nationalism in the United States does *not* wish to recognise its supposed interest in sustaining all those left-wing critics, many of them originally from Third World countries, who are teaching unpatriotic lessons to American youth. And if the tendency to delegitimate and defund continues, the ultra-left paranoid view of the rise of postcolonial criticism will appear retrospectively to have been as misguided (to paraphrase Régis Debray) as Communist attacks on progressive French universities on the eve of the Nazi invasion.[3]

The broad public appeal of sentiments like Rorty's - an appeal it would be dangerous to underestimate - relies in large part on an element that is only hinted at in the *New York Times* piece. In earlier and rhetorically similar complaints, Rorty has borrowed the theme of class - paradoxically, from the right - as a weapon against what he calls, with undisguised contempt, 'the English department left'. 'The English department left has lots of thoughts about race and gender, but almost no ideas about class.'[4] From Reagan through Dinesh D'Souza, the US right has specialised in defending the poor and suffering precisely and exclusively to the extent that the poor and suffering of the US can be successfully invoked to the discomfiture of women, African-Americans, and non-Americans (preferably of the Third World), all of whom are momentarily assumed to be exempt from poverty and suffering.[5] Dinesh D'Souza, whose Republican patrons have not been notable for their support of labour unions or working mothers or any other working-class causes, has made a debater's arsenal out of the blatant hypocrisy of class talk like this. Rorty himself cites David Bromwich, who declares unforgettably that 'race and gender are our great diversions', proving his commitment to the working class by blithely writing off the two modes in which the majority of its American members live their daily inequality.[6]

At the same time, Bromwich also turns the institutional radicals' oft-repeated charge of elitism back against them: they are, he says, an 'the anti-elitist humanities elite' (p115). Faced with concrete evidence of achievement by feminists (other cultural radicals, he suggests, have achieved nothing), he asks, 'But for whose benefit? - outside, of course, the ranks of the middle class to which the academics themselves belong' (p117). Now if you take the charge that feminists and other cultural radicals have neglected the interests of (in Rorty's words) 'the weakest and poorest among us', if you add to it the charge that they have thereby served and disguised their own class interests, and if you then top it off with Rorty's new polemic about their lack of patriotism, you get a composite denunciation of the academic left that replays the heady performances of Hitler and Stalin: an attack on 'rootless cosmopolitans' who don't really feel for 'the nation' or its people because they are a privileged, greedy, mobile elite. As a Jew, I find it hard to hold back the more or less rash, more or less approximate epithets that come to mind when I see populist appeals like this begin to take ominous shape. But rather than linking this invective to the resurgent language of nationalism in, say, Eastern and Central Europe, it seems more useful to investigate an even stranger parallel: the way it mirrors a great deal of polemic within the field of postcolonial studies itself.

There is a certain sarcasm about the socio-geographical position of postcolonial studies that seems irresistible even to observers who are otherwise quite opposed to each other, like Aijaz Ahmad and his many critics; it takes the form of a more or less personal belittling of the field's practitioners, identified as upwardly mobile both in terms of their place of origin (Third World) and their class of destination (bourgeois). According to Kwame Anthony Appiah, 'Postcoloniality is the condition of what we might ungenerously call a comprador intelligentsia: of a relatively small, Western-style, Western-trained, group of writers and thinkers who mediate the trade in cultural commodities of western capitalism at the periphery.'[7] According to Arif Dirlik, 'postcoloniality is the condition of the intelligentsia of global capitalism', and 'the popularity that the term *postcoloniality* has achieved in the last few years has less to do with its rigorousness as a concept or with the new vistas it has opened up for critical inquiry than it does with the increased visibility of academic intellectuals of Third World origin as pacesetters in cultural criticism.'[8] For 'Third World intellectuals who have arrived in First World academe,' Dirlik argues, 'postcolonial discourse is an expression not so much of agony over identity, as it often appears, but of newfound power' (p339).

Now it should be possible to admit the partial truth of this observation, it seems to me, without also agreeing with the crushing conclusions that Dirlik draws from it about the illegitimacy and misguidedness of postcolonial studies generally-conclusions which obviously offer comfort to such outsiders as Rorty and Bromwich. Yes, the existence of postcolonial discourse *does* express 'newfound power', as well as agonies of identity. And so? Would this not be the case for any successful intellectual movement, any movement that wins provisional popular and/or institutional support for its terms and agendas, whatever the criteria of progressiveness it is judged by? Or have we actually come to believe that any success in winning support is in itself a fatal sign of cooptation, or evidence that the movement was never progressive to begin with? If not, then the failure to answer the many critiques like this, indeed the seemingly masochistic tendency to repeat and delight in them, would seem to indicate an incoherence at the point where class and (inter)nationalism intersect that is rather mysterious. And this incoherence is also dangerous. For the lack of a vocabulary that would offer postcolonial critics some articulation between nationalism and class other than Rorty's also means the inability to represent themselves and what they do in public. What postcolonial studies needs, it seems to me, is not a political purge or purification (although, like everyone else, I have my own points of disagreement with various routine assumptions), but a different and impious view of its own authority (such as it is), some narrative of how it arrived at that authority, and some explanation of what that authority has to do with the trans-national circle or sphere to which it holds itself newly accountable.

This is more than I am presently prepared to do myself. But it is with this task in mind that I would like to make some remarks about the recent work of Edward Said, and in particular about the distinctive version of internationalism that clusters around his favoured phrases 'secular criticism' and the 'secular intellectual.'[9] Said is of course one of the few academic figures in the US who have managed to give public voice both to serious criticism of American foreign policy and, with more difficulty, to solidarities that are not centred on or limited to the unquestioned priority of the American national interest. Most remarkably, he has managed to defend the interests of the Palestinian national movement while maintaining an extremely sceptical view of nationalism as such. Indeed, perhaps the most crucial meaning of 'secular', in his usage, is as an opposing term not to religion but to nationalism. In the interview with Jennifer Wicke and Michael Sprinker published in Sprinker's *Edward Said: A Critical Reader*, Said sets the 'ideal of secular interpretation and secular work' against 'submerged feelings of identity, of tribal solidarity', of community that is 'geographically and homogeneously defined'.[10] 'The dense fabric of secular life,' Said says, is what 'can't be herded under the rubric of national identity or can't be made entirely to respond to this phony idea of a paranoid frontier separating "us" from "them"- which is a repetition of the old sort of orientalist model.' 'The politics of secular interpretation proposes a way ... of avoiding the pitfalls of nationalism' (p233).

Now the word secular has usually served as a figure for the authority of a putatively universal reason, or (narratively speaking) as the ideal endpoint of progress in the intellectual domain. In appropriating the word as a sort of insignia, then, Said clearly runs the risk of (in Tim Brennan's words) 'assuming the nineteenth century mantle of progress and enlightenment.'[11] Naturally enough, this usage has not gone uncontested among critics of Eurocentrism. R. Radhakrishnan, for example, objects to how '"the secular" as a western norm is made to operate naturally and therefore namelessly.'[12] 'What we have to realize,' Peter van der Veer writes in *Orientalism and the Postcolonial Predicament*, 'is that the very distinction between religious and secular is a product of the Enlightenment that was used in orientalism to draw a sharp opposition between irrational, religious behavior of the Oriental and rational secularism, which enabled the westerner to rule the Oriental.'[13] Meanwhile, the Subaltern Studies group have stressed the further connection between secularism and indigenous elites. Extending the argument from western orientalists to the secularism of Indian nationalist elites, Ranajit Guha argues for instance that the latter's 'abstract and sterile discourse ... can do little to illuminate the combination of sectarianism and militancy which is so important a feature of our rural history.'[14] Or, as Dipesh Chakrabarty puts it, secular nationalism in India has meant 'an act of appropriation by elite (and elitist) Indians, on behalf of their project of building an Indian state, of diverse historical struggles of the subaltern classes' (pp52-53).[15] The case against elites and the case against secularism seem to be the same case.

Having seen a certain *ressentiment* directed at his professional renown and his privileged position in an elite metropolitan university, Said shows some bravery in standing together with so authoritative a term as secularism. And, at the same time, his descriptions of the intellectual also try to evade this authority. As he says in the Wicke/Sprinker interview, his version of secularism is an attempt to avoid nationalism's us-and-them without on the contrary espousing what he calls '"universal values"' (p235).[16] If he speaks positively of 'globalism' and 'worldliness' (p242), he says a distinct no to 'cosmopolitanism and intellectual tourism' (p242), to any internationalism that would express a 'superior detachment ... a general all-encompassing love for all of humanity' (p235). In other words, the word secular seems to aim at a version of internationalism that would do without the direct authoritative backing either of a putatively universal class, as in the Marxist version, or of disinterested rationality. Is it, then, a sort of postmodern secularism that attempts to do without *any* authority?[17]

Here another implication of secular is pertinent: the suggestion that the so-called clerisy must learn to work without the quasi-theological guarantees and quasi-theological self-conceptions that have served it in the past. At the end of his final Reith lecture in the summer of 1993, now published in *Raritan*, Said declared that

> *the true intellectual is a secular being. However much*
> *intellectuals pretend that their representations are of higher*
> *things or ultimate values, morality begins with their*
> *activity in this secular world of ours - where it takes place,*
> *whose interests it serves.*[18]

Rather than some sort of exemplary otherworldliness, being a
secular intellectual seems here to mean resigning oneself to an
inevitable profane untidiness, an impurity, a political
incorrectness. Yet it also seems to draw energy and authority
from that refusal of virtue. And this is perhaps because, implicitly,
it entails biting the not entirely bitter bullet of institutional
privilege. According to the Oxford English Dictionary, secularism
is 'the doctrine that morality should be based solely in regard to
the well-being of mankind in the present life to the exclusion of
all considerations drawn from belief in God or in a future state.'
If intellectuals should be 'worldly' or even 'profane', at least
partially subdued to the untidiness of an unjust and hierarchical
world, then perhaps they must do some strategic acquiescing in
institutional or professional hierarchies.

The last lines of the final Reith lecture, go as follows: 'as an
intellectual you are the one who can choose between actively
representing the truth to the best of your ability, or passively
allowing a patron or an authority to direct you. For the secular
intellectual, *those* gods always fail' (p14). Add to this the refusal
of all orthodoxy and dogma, of any 'kind of absolute certainty'
or any 'total, seamless view of reality' (p13), and you get a secular
intellectual who submits to *no* authority, even that of his or her
own beliefs or findings.[19] Given this somewhat deconstructive
thrust of the term secular - not just anti-nationalist, but against
any grounding of intellectual mission and activity - one would
imagine that Said would be quite harsh with Julien Benda's *La
Trahison des clercs*, a text that grounds its attractive anti-
nationalism upon a shamelessly sacred view of the intellectual.
Surprisingly, he is not.[20] On the key issue of the clercs' betrayal,
he comes down on Benda's side. Which is to say that he implicitly
endorses, here and throughout the Reith lectures, the sense of
high vocation without which there could *be* no betrayal. This
stubborn fidelity to an ideal of vocation is clearly one reason

why his work is so moving to so many people. But it is all the more reason to ask on what grounds, on what secular authority this sense of mission might be based. The question is absolutely crucial, for it seems to promise, as against Rorty, a *different difference* between intellectuals and non-intellectuals, an articulation between the two that does not demand that the first simply dissolve into the second, and at the same time an authority that is specifically and uncompromisingly internationalist.

The secular ideal of the intellectual who 'speaks truth to power', which Said celebrates in Benda and elsewhere, pays no explicit attention to the decisive question - the same question in another form - of *why power would listen*, what might *make* it listen, what makes *anyone* listen. That is, it has nothing explicit to say about the source of *counter-authority* that intellectuals must be assumed to counterpose to 'power'. This absence of critical or countervailing authority is all the more evident given that the term secular functions elsewhere in Said so as to frustrate the usual answers to the authority question: the dogmatic authority of disinterested truth and the authority of an ethnically purified local or national community, as we have already seen, and also - here we gesture back in the direction of Rorty's militant anti-professionalism - the borrowed sanctity of the *professional* community. In the introduction to *The World, the Text, and the Critic*, entitled 'Secular Criticism'. Said mobilises the term secular in an attack on what he calls, again from the theological lexicon, the 'cult of professional expertise' (p2), with its sense of 'vocation' and its 'quasi-religious quietism' (p25).[21]

What sorts of authority might there be, then? One hint comes from Said's most sympathetic words about Julien Benda, which suggest a sort of *economy* of authority. Intellectuals, Said says, 'have to be in a state of almost permanent opposition to the status quo'. And this is why 'Benda's intellectuals are perforce a small, highly visible group'. Here intellectual authority would seem to come from the presumed rarity or scarcity of those willing to confront non-intellectual authority. It would come, that is, from a 'rarefaction' of intellectuals - I borrow the term from Said's influential appreciation of Foucault - that formally resembles the dread concept of elitism, but that offers the restrictiveness of the group an ethico-political legitimacy (the unusual courage needed for opposition to the status quo) rather than a meritocratic one. Or perhaps it would be fairer to say that rather than the profession deciding who is a competent scholar, it is power that decides who is a real intellectual, whose dissent is painful or threatening enough to be worthy of public expressions of dislike. The authority of the intellectual is a faithful inversion of the authority of power itself, and is thus dependent upon it. Here the amoral connotations of secularism are not far beneath the surface. Practically speaking, an *ethical* scarcity defined by opposition will be indistinguishable from a *social* scarcity that is a potential source of profit and prestige. An undesired visibility, resulting from the political hostility of the powers that be, can and perhaps must be exchanged for celebrity, the prized, often apolitical currency of honours and economic rewards.

This line of thought seems interestingly continuous with another answer to the question of where intellectuals get such authority as they possess - Anna Boschetti's analysis of the success of Sartre. For Boschetti, Sartre's trick was to manage a transfer to one domain of cultural capital accumulated in another domain; thus Sartre brings the prestige of the Ecole Normale Superieure and the discipline of philosophy to literature, and he then brings that newly accumulated sum to his political activities, the government's dramatic reactions to which feed back into his literary and philosophical esteem.[22] For all its problems, the concept of cultural capital makes a valuable stab at quantifying and mapping such transfers, translating an otherwise vague 'guardianship of the archives' into a diversified and dynamic economy of cultural resources. And this import/export model brings out some distinctive features of - indeed, enables us to recognise as such - the authorising story of the intellectual that Said calls, in *Culture and Imperialism*, 'the voyage in'- the movement of Third World writers, intellectuals, and texts into the metropolis and their successful integration there.

From one point of view, this movement could obviously be described as a form of upward mobility, and to these as to other such narratives, critics have reacted with various degrees of alarm. Can Third World fictions and careers that aim at and are embraced by the metropolis ultimately signify anything other than an opportunistic affirmation of the metropolis? Gayatri Chakravorty Spivak for example makes a pointed parallel between the current First World enthusiasm for Third World writers and the earlier divide-and-conquer strategy of colonialism, which simultaneously served the interests of the colonial power and of a native-born 'aspiring elite'. Do we see here again, she asks, 'the old scenario of empowering a privileged group or a group susceptible to upward mobility as the authentic inhabitants of the margin'?[23]

Faced with the collective *Bildungsroman* of Third World writers who have come to live and work in the metropolis, thereby repeating (with a transnational difference) the country-to-the-city journey so characteristic of the nineteenth-century European novel, Said in contrast is rather cheerful. You can see the cheerfulness, for example, in his innovative treatment of the novel of disillusionment. In an indirect reply to Franco Moretti's darkly Lukacsian view of the genre, Said appreciatively displays Third World reversals of *Heart of Darkness*, like Tayeb Salih's *Season of Migration to the North*. Moretti sees the genre dying when European men, losing faith in their own projects, have tired of it. Said's insistence on its continuing vitality in the hands of Third World men and women would appear on the contrary to express the intelligent optimism of a stratum or category that is still rising, energetic, confident of its powers.

The grounds of this qualified optimism - what another great Palestininan stylist has called 'pessoptimism' - are clearly not that the story of an upwardly mobile elite can literally be everyone's story. It's hard to imagine that American readers would react so favorably to Jamaica Kincaid or Bharati Mukherjee, say, if they thought the entire Third World was being advised to emulate their upwardly mobile au pair heroines and head for the nearest international airport. Said's point, rather, is that the center can be and has been changed. There has been what he calls 'adversarial internationalization in an age of continued imperial structures' (p244). Opposition has arisen in the modern metropolis - an opposition there was little sense of in *Orientalism*. In the universities, the 'impingement' of Third World intellectuals on metropolitan space has resulted in 'the transformation of the very terrain of the disciplines'. This implies, I would like to add, that the story of Third World intellectual migration has conferred a certain authority upon oppositional intellectuals in and from the First World, including many for whom the work of representing colonial and postcolonial experience must unequivocally *be* work, that is, cannot even be misperceived as a matter of simple identity. And all this has been possible - this is the key point - because of the risky and unstable fusion of personal mobility and impersonal representativeness: 'anti-imperialist intellectual and scholarly work done by writers from the peripheries who have immigrated to or are visiting the metropolis is usually an extension into the metropolis of large-scale mass movements.'[24]

Let me offer a brief and schematic national contrast. In what I might call the French model of intellectual authority, as in Anna Boschetti and Pierre Bourdieu, the sole source of cultural capital is existing institutions. Bourdieu's model of the 'oblate', for example, describes the rewards given to a poor child, without social capital, whose upward mobility has depended entirely on the educational institution that elevated him and to which he responds with unconditional loyalty. Conservative reaction against disciplinary change often comes, Bourdieu writes in *Homo Academicus*, from 'those I call "oblates", and who, consigned from childhood to the school institution (they are often children of the lower or middle classes or sons of teachers) are totally dedicated to it' (pxxiv):[25]

> *The oblates are always inclined to think that without the church there is no salvation - especially when they become the high priests of an institution of cultural reproduction which, in consecrating them, consecrates their active and above all passive ignorance of any other cultural world. Victims of their elite status, these deserving, but miraculously lucky, survivors present a curious mixture of arrogance and inadequacy which immediately strikes the foreign observer ... They offer to the academic institution which they have chosen because it chose them, and vice versa, a support which, being so totally conditioned, has something total, absolute, and unconditional about it (p100-101).*

In this model, no authority is ascribed to the place from which the mobile 'oblate' sets out; all authority is imagined to flow from the institutional destination. There is no possibility that the protagonist's initial poverty might serve in any way the (legitimating) purposes of the institution, nor - more important - that the protagonist's rise from that origin might help change that destination in any way, or change the composition of the cultural capital subsequently transmitted to others.

Said's 'voyage in' narrative redistributes the emphasis radically. While it does not underestimate the continuing authority of metropolitan institutions, neither does it treat the composition of cultural capital as fixed once and for all, or assume that to accept it is necessarily to offer the donor unconditional loyalty in return. National origin matters; transfers from the periphery to the centre do not leave the centre as it was. The trans-national story of upward mobility is not just a claiming of authority, but a redefinition of authority, and a redefinition that can have many beneficiaries, for it means a recomposition as well as a redistribution of cultural capital. In short, progress is possible.

Ironically, critiques of postcolonial studies which declare their fidelity to Marxist orthodoxy also turn out to be those which, unlike Marx, seem to preclude the untidily dialectical existence of progress. Arif Dirlik, for example, agrees that success stories like this one must offer some answer to the crucial question of where the newfound authority comes from: 'merely pointing to the ascendant role that intellectuals of Third World origin have played in propagating *postcolonial* as a critical orientation within First World academia begs the question as to why they and their intellectual concerns and orientations have been accorded the respectability that they have.' In Dirlik's view, the metropolitan success of Third World intellectuals that has given the term postcolonial its currency has been 'dependent on the conceptual needs of the social, political, and cultural problems thrown up by [a] new world situation', that is, by changes in world capitalism (p330). 'In their very globalism, the cultural requirements of transnational corporations can no longer afford the cultural parochialism of an earlier day'; they have 'a need to internationalize academic institutions (which often takes the form not of promoting scholarship in a conventional sense but of 'importing' and 'exporting' students and faculty').[26]

The messiness of the word secular seems a necessary antidote to this invocation of world capitalism, an invocation which might be described either as over-tidy or as theological. For Dirlik, global capitalism is assumed to be not only 'organized' (a matter of dispute among Marxist economists) but ubiquitous and omnipotent; whatever happens expresses its will, a will that is undialectically unified and, in terms of its effects on Third World peoples, invariably malignant. There is no room here for a cunning of reason that, to cite Marx's famous discussion of the British in India, could bring forth a certain political progress even from the worst horrors of colonialism. It is hard to see how, within this worldview, any progress is conceivable that would not, upon its emergence, immediately demand to be reinterpreted as the result of capitalism's disguised but malevolent intentions.

The common assumption for all of us who begin, in the study of colonial and postcolonial culture, with the intolerable facts of global suffering and injustice, ought surely to be, on the contrary, that progress is an absolute necessity. Of course, as Anne McClintock points out, the word itself is entangled with a history of racism and Eurocentric self-congratulation, and so too is 'postcolonial'.[27] Of course, any historical instance of progress will obligatorily be compromised in any number of ways, as the rise of postcolonial studies is compromised by its metropolitan and class location. But this does not mean it is so contaminated as to be unsayable; we are not so rich in instances that we can afford to throw any out in the name of an ideal purity. For progress must be believed to be possible before it can be fought for, and narratives of progress, including narratives of upward mobility, do just this work. Thus such narratives cannot be disposed of by the simple thought that for most of the world's people, there has been no upward mobility. The incongruities between narratives of upward mobility and the static or declining state of the world cannot be corrected by some voluntary gesture of self-discipline whereby narrative would henceforth allow no image of fulfilled desire not statistically guaranteed by actual improvement on the part of X thousands or millions of people. For narratives, including meta-narratives, are obliged to make use of desire, and there is no politics without them. As Alan Sinfield has noted, the rise of British 'left culturism', including the careers of Raymond Williams, E.P. Thompson, and Richard Hoggart, was after all by no means an easy or inevitable fact of post-war cultural life; and their legitimation was secured in part by narratives of 'upward mobility through education', which was 'a story that society, or parts of it, wanted to tell itself, not a record of experience.'[28] Anyone who sees postcolonial studies as a ruse of world capitalism should be prepared to say that the cultural scene would have been better off without these figures, or that the current scene would be better off without the equally contingent presence of figures like Said, Gayatri Spivak, and Stuart Hall.

In describing what he calls 'the global cultural economy', Arjun Appadurai has distinguished between 'finanscapes', or flows of capital, and 'ideoscapes', or flows of ideologies and images. His point is that there is a 'disjuncture' between these flows; no one of them (he provisionally distinguishes five levels) is a mere effect of any other.[29] No account of global capitalism can afford to forget this disjuncture, which makes a space for redistributions of cultural capital that are neither simply metaphorical nor simply epiphenomena of the real thing. I am trying to suggest, a bit obliquely, that the new internationalism or multiculturalism of the academic left can be seen as one effect of a recomposition of cultural capital - an effect that Said's 'voyage in' narrative risks the charge of elitism in order to authorise and legitimate. The power of *anti*-elitism, whether in Rorty's denunciation of rootless cosmopolitans or elsewhere, does not of course depend on *refusing* narratives of upward mobility, but only on *controlling* them. Said's 'voyage in' can I think be seen as a courageous and well-timed effort to take back these narratives, to use them in a different sharing out of intellectual authority. It is more than incidental that, in so doing, it also offers an implicit answer to the enigma of where the postcolonial critic's secular authority comes from. The authority of internationalism, according to this narrative, comes from the national itself, or even from nationalism - though not everyone's nationalism, and not a nationalism that can itself be unchanged by taking part in the operation.[30]

In the vocabulary of Abdul JanMohamed, we could perhaps say that the precarious but necessary authority that Said gives to secular internationalism is founded on an ambiguous border-crossing: neither simply an exile (which privileges the place of origin), nor simply an immigration (which privileges the destination), but both an exile and an immigration at once.[31] Thinking back to Rorty, it is tempting to stress the Americanness of the optimistic narrative that Said thus counterposes to the French 'oblation', and even to stress the legitimate pride one might feel in belonging, in this somewhat modified version of John F. Kennedy's words, to 'a nation of immigrants'. With all due respect to Rorty, however, and all due gratitude that the US offers more support than he realizes for the multicultural project of changing the centre, I think I would prefer to express an affiliation internationally, with the many otherwise situated groups and individuals, in the US and elsewhere, who take this secular project as their own.

An earlier and shorter version of this paper appeared in Social Text 40, 1994.

Notes

1. Richard Rorty, 'The Unpatriotic Academy', *The New York Times*, 13 February 1994.

2. See for example Neil Lazarus, 'Disavowing Decolonization: Fanon, Nationalism, and the Problematic of Representation in Current Theories of Colonial Discourse', *Research in African Literatures*, 24, Winter 1993, pp69-98.

3. Régis Debray, *Teachers, Writers, Celebrities: The Intellectuals of Modern France*, trans. David Macey, intro. Francis Mulhern, Verso, London 1981, pp58-59.

4. Richard Rorty, Reply to Andrew Ross, *Dissent*, Spring 1992. See also Rorty, 'Intellectuals in Politics', *Dissent*, Fall 1991.

5. It would seem that if one were genuinely committed to altering the situation of the working (which is to say frequently unemployed) class in this country, then one would naturally support a strong gender-and-race agenda. For women, African-Americans, and Chicanos are largely who the working class is *in fact*, if not who it is for the rhetorical purposes of the neoconservatives. See my review of Bromwich's *Politics By Other*

Means in *Modern Language Quarterly*, 54:4, December 1993, pp567-572.

6. David Bromwich, *Politics By Other Means: Higher Education and Group Thinking*, Yale UP, New Haven 1992, p118.

7. Kwame Anthony Appiah, *In My Father's House: Africa in the Philosophy of Culture*, Oxford UP, New York 1992, p149.

8. Arif Dirlik, 'The Postcolonial Aura: Third World Criticism in the Age of Global Capitalism', *Critical Inquiry*, 20:2, Winter 1994, pp356, 329. Dirlik's argument is amplified in *After the Revolution: Waking to Global Capitalism*, Wesleyam University Press, Hanover, NH, 1994.

9. It would also be interesting to consider at least two of Said's idiosyncratic uses of 'secular', which have to do especially with scholarship: 1) the association of the secular with a distinctively slow historical rhythm, the temporality of scholarship; and 2) its association with a sort of Weberian existential heroism of scholarship, one that does without the usual versions of transcendent reassurance.

10. Michael Sprinker (ed), *Edward W. Said: A Critical Reader*, Blackwells, London 1992, pp232-33.

11. Tim Brennan, 'Places of Mind, Occupied Lands: Edward Said and Philology', in Michael Sprinker (ed), *op cit*, p92.

12. R. Radhakrishnan, 'Postcoloniality and the Boundaries of Identity', *Callalloo*, 16:4, 1993, p754.

13. Peter van der Veer, 'The Foreign Hand: Orientalist Discourse in Sociology and Communalism', *Orientalism and the Postcolonial Predicament: Perspectives on South Asia*, Carol A. Breckenridge and Peter van der Veer (eds), University of Pennsylvania Press, Philadelphia 1993, p39.

14. Ranajit Guha, 'The Prose of Counter-Insurgency', *Selected Subaltern Studies*, Ranajit Guha and Gayatri Chakravorty Spivak (eds.), Oxford UP, Delhi 1988, p83.

15. Dipesh Chakrabarty, 'The Death of History? Historical Consciousness and the Culture of Late Capitalism', *Public Culture*, 4:2, Spring 1992: 'nationalist history, in spite of its anti-imperialist stance and substance, shared a deeply embedded meta-narrative with imperialist accounts of British India. This was the meta-narrative of the modern state' (p52).

16. See however Chatterjee's essay in the Sprinker volume, 'Their Own Words? An Essay for Edward Said', which defends, within nationalism, the 'many possibilities of authentic, creative, and plural development of social identities which were violently disrupted by the political history of the post-colonial state seeking to replicate the modular forms of the

modern nation-state' (p216).

17. Note the uses of 'authority' in *Beginnings*, vis-a-vis molestation: a coinage which is emphatically *not* anti-authoritarian. Edward W. Said, *Beginnings: Intention and Method*, Basic Books, New York 1975.

18. Edward W. Said, 'Gods that Always Fail', *Raritan*, 13:4, Spring 1994, p13.

19. One's own beliefs and findings, in Said's view, quickly and inevitably harden into authorities.

20. See Edward Said, *Representations of the Intellectual*, Pantheon, New York 1994, pp5-6.

21. Edward W. Said, *The World, the Text, and the Critic*, Harvard UP, Cambridge 1983, pp2, 25.

22. Anna Boschetti, *The Intellectual Enterprise: Sartre and 'Les Temps modernes'*, trans. Richard C. McCleary, Northwestern UP, Evanston, IL, 1988.

23. Gayatri Chakravorty Spivak, 'Poststructuralism, Marginality, Postcoloniality, and Value', *Literary Theory Today*, Peter Collier and Helga Geyer-Ryan (eds), Cornell UP, Ithaca, 1990, pp222, 224.

24. Edward W. Said, *Culture and Imperialism*, Knopf, New York 1993, p244.

25. Pierre Bourdieu, *Homo Academicus* trans. Peter Collier, Stanford UP, Stanford, 1988. Note the irony that the secular scholar can only hold to his institution with a religious irrationality.

26. Dirlik, *op cit*, pp330, 354-55.

27. Anne McClintock, 'The Angel of Progress: Pitfalls of the Term "Postcolonialism"', *Social Text*, 31/32, 1992, pp84-98.

28. Alan Sinfield, Literature, Politics, and Culture in Postwar Britain, University of California Press, Berkeley 1989, p234.

29. Arjun Appadurai, 'Disjuncture and Difference in the Global Cultural Economy', in Bruce Robbins (ed), The Phantom Public Sphere, University of Minnesota Press, Minneapolis 1993, pp269-295.

30. Here I am combining two points articulated by Neil Lazarus in 'Disavowing Decolonization'. First, Lazarus suggests, in defence of Fredric Jameson, that a certain nationalism is indeed fundamental in the 'Third World', for 'it is only on the terrain of the nation that an articulation between cosmopolitan intellectualism and popular consciousness can be forged' (p91). Second, Lazarus notes Said's

emphasis on 'the accomplishments not only of anticolonial *nationalism* but also of radical *intellectualism* as irreducible', that is, a contribution that 'could not have been provided by any other form of labor-power, by any other social practice, in any other arena' (p92). I add to this only a polemical insistence on how much Said's synthesis means in and to the metropolis. See also Lazarus's discussion of Said in 'Postcolonialism and the Dilemma of Nationalism: Aijaz Ahmad's Critique of Third-Worldism', *Diaspora*, 2:3, Winter 1993, pp373-400.

31. Abdul JanMohamed, 'Worldliness-without-World, Homelessness-as-Home', in Sprinker, *Edward W. Said*, pp96-120.

COLUMBUS, PALESTINE AND ARAB-JEWS: TOWARD A RELATIONAL APPROACH TO COMMUNITY IDENTITY

Ella Shohat

Recent postcolonial theory has at times shied away from grounding its writings in historical context and cultural specificity. While innumerable poststructuralist essays elaborate abstract versions of 'difference' and 'alterity', few offer a communally participatory and politicised knowledge of non-European cultures. At the same time, however, the professionalised study of compartmentalised historical periods and geographical regions (as in Middle East and Latin American Studies) has often resulted in an overly specific focus that overlooks the interconnectedness of histories, geographies, and cultural identities. In *Unthinking Eurocentrism*, Robert Stam and I argue for a relational approach to multicultural studies that does not segregate historical periods and geographical regions into neatly fenced off areas of expertise, and which does not speak of communities in isolation, but 'in relation'.[1] Rather than pit a rotating chain of resisting communities against a western dominant (a strategy that privileges the 'West' if only as constant antagonist), we argue for stressing the horizontal and vertical links threading communities and histories together in a conflictual network. Analysing the overlapping multiplicities of identities and affiliations that link diverse resistant discourses helps us transcend some of the politically debilitating effects of disciplinary and community boundaries.

The kind of connections we have in mind operate on a number of levels. First, it is important to make connections in temporal terms. While postcolonial studies privilege the imperial era of the nineteenth and twentieth centuries, one might argue for grounding the discussion in a longer history of multiply located colonialisms and resistances, tracing the issues at least as far back as 1492. We propose connections, second, in spatial/

geographical terms, placing debates about identity and
representation in a broader context which embraces the
Americas, Asia and Africa. We also argue for connections in
disciplinary and conceptual terms, forging links between debates
usually compartmentalised (at least in the US): on the one hand,
postcolonial theory associated with issues of colonial discourse,
imperial imaginary and national narrations, and, on the other,
the diverse 'Ethnic Studies', focusing on issues of 'minorities',
race and multiculturalism. The point is to place the often
ghettoized discourses about geographies - 'here' versus 'there' -
and about time - 'now' versus 'then' - in illuminating dialogue.
A relational approach, one that operates at once within, between,
and beyond the nation-state framework, calls attention to the
conflictual hybrid interplay of communities within and across
borders.

'Columbus, Palestine, and Arab-Jews' already juxtaposes
disparate entities to point to the ways in which nation states,
epecially in the wake of colonial partitions, have imposed a
coherent sense of national identity precisely because of their
fragile sense of cultural, even geographical, belonging. The
formation of postcolonial nation states often involved a double
process of, on the one hand, joining diverse ethicities and regions
that had been separate under colonialism, and, on the other,
partitioning regions in a way that forced regional redefinitions
(Iraq/Kuwait), or a cross-shuffling of populations (Pakistan/India,
Israel/Palestine, in relation to Palestinians and Arab Jews). Given
the 'minority' / 'majority' battles 'from within' and the war waged
by border-crossers (refugees, exiles, immigrants) 'from without',
Eurocentric historiography has had a crucial role in handing
out passports to its legitimate races, ethnicities, nations. And in
the words of Mahmoud Darwish's well-known poem, 'Passport'
(*Joowaz sufr*): 'ar min al ism, min al intima? fi tarba rabit'ha
bilyadyn?' ('Stripped of my name, my identity? On a soil I
nourished with my own hands?'). The same colonial logic that
dismantled Palestine had already dismantled the 'Turtle Island'
of the Americas. Thus, the first illegal alien, Columbus, remains
a celebrated discoverer, while indigenous Mexicans 'infiltrate' a
barbed border everyday to a homeland once theirs.

Here, by way of demonstration of the 'relational' method, I

Said

will focus on Sephardic Arab-Jewish (known in the Israeli context as Mizrahi) identity as it intersects with other communities and discourses in diverse contexts over time. I will take as a point of departure the 1992 quincentennial commemorations of the expulsions of Sephardic Jews from Spain, to argue that any revisionist effort to re-articulate Arab-Jewish identity in a contemporary context that has posited Arab and Jew as antonyms can only be disentangled through a series of positionings vis-a-vis diverse communities and identites (Arab-Muslim, Arab-Christian, Palestinian, Euro-Israeli, Euro-American-Jewish, Indigenous-American, African-American, Chicano/a), which would challenge the devastating consequences that the Zionist-orientalist binarism of East versus West, Arab versus Jew has had for Arab Jews (or Jewish-Arabs). Linking, de-linking, and relinking, at once spatial and temporal, thus becomes part of adversary scholarship working against taboo formulations, policed identities, and censored affiliations.

'Your Highnesses completed the war against the Moors', Columbus wrote in a letter addressed to the Spanish throne, 'after having chased all the Jews ... and sent me to the said regions of India in order to convert the people there to our Holy Faith.'[2] In 1492 the defeat of the Muslims and the expulsion of Sephardi Jews from Spain converged with the conquest of what came to be called the New World. But while the celebrations of Columbus's voyages have provoked lively opposition, the Eurocentric framing of the 'other 1492' has not been questioned. Apart from some enthusiastic scholastic energy dedicated to dubious pride as to the possibility that Columbus could once and for all be claimed as a (secret) Jew, Expulsion events navigated within the calm seas of Old World paradigms. Furthermore, the two separate quincentenary commemorations, both taking place in the Americas, Europe and the Middle East, have seldom acknowledged the historical and discursive linkages between these two constellations of events. To examine the relationship between contemporary discourses about the two '1492's might therefore illuminate the role scholarly and popular narratives of history play in nation-building myths and geopolitical alliances.

The Spanish-Christian war against Muslims and Jews was politically, economically and ideologically linked to the caravels' arrival in Española. Triumphant over the Muslims, Spain invested in the project of Columbus, whose voyages were partly financed by wealth taken from the defeated Muslims and confiscated from Jews through the Inquisition.[3] The reconquista's policies of settling Christians in the newly (re)conquered areas of Spain, as well as the gradual institutionalisation of expulsions, conversions, and killings of Muslims and Jews in Christian territories, prepared the grounds for similar conquista practices across the Atlantic. Under the marital-political union of Ferdinand (Aragon) and Isabella (Castille), victorious Christian-Spain, soon to become an Empire, strengthened its sense of nationhood, subjugating indigenous Americans and Africans. Discourses about Muslims and Jews during Spain's continental expansion crossed the Atlantic, arming the conquistadors with a ready-made 'us versus them' ideology aimed at the regions of India, but in fact applied first toward the indigenous of the accidentally 'discovered' continent. The colonial misrecognition inherent in the name 'Indian' underlines the linked imaginaries of the East and West Indies. India awaited its colonised turn with the arrival of Vasco de Gama (1498) and the Portuguese conquest of Goa (1510). If in the fifteenth century the only European hope for conquering the East - given the Muslim domination of the continental route - was via sailing to the West, the nineteenth century consolidation of European imperialism in the East was facilitated by Europe's previous self-aggrandizing at the expense of the Americas and Africa.

Although Moorish Spain testifies to syncretic multi-culturalism avant-la-lettre, the reconquista ideology of *Limpieza de Sangre*, as an early exercise in European 'self-purification', sought to expel, or forcibly convert, Muslims and Jews. The Crusades, which inaugurated 'Europe' by reconquering the Mediterranean area, catalysed Europeans' awareness of their own geocultural identity and established the principle that wars conducted in the interests of the Holy Church were axiomatically just. The campaigns against Muslims and Jews as well as against other 'agents of Satan', heretics and witches, made available a mammoth apparatus of racism and sexism for recycling in the 'new' continents. Anti-semitism and anti-infidelism provided a conceptual and disciplinary framework which, after being turned against Europe's immediate or internal others was then projected outward against Europe's distant or external others.[4] Prince Henry ('the Navigator'), the pioneer of Portuguese exploration, had himself been a Crusader against the Moors at the battle of Ceuta. Amerigo Vespucci, writing about his voyages, similarly, drew on the stock of Jewish and Muslim stereotypes to characterise the savage, the infidel, the indigenous man as a dangerous sexual omnivore and indigenous woman as a luringly yielding nature.[5] In this sense, the metonymic links between Jews and Muslims - their literal neighbouring and their shared histories - are turned into metaphorical and analogical links in relation to the peoples of the Americas.[6] The point is not that there is a complete equivalence between Europe's oppressive relations toward Jews and Muslims and toward indigenous peoples; the point is that European Christian demonology pre-figured colonialist racism.

If the genocide of indigenous Americans and Africans is no more than a bit of historical marginalia, the linked persecutions in Iberia of Sephardi Jews and Muslims, of Conversos and Muriscos, are also submerged. The quincentennial elision of the Arab-Muslim part of the narrative was especially striking. During the centuries-long *reconquista*, not all Muslims and Jews withdrew with the Arab forces. Those Muslims who remained after the change of rule were known as *mudejars*, deriving from the Arabic *mudajjin*, 'permitted to remain', with a suggestion of 'tamed', 'domesticated'. The Spanish Inquisition, institutionalised in 1478, did not pass over the Muslims. Apart from the 1492 expulsion of 3 million Muslims and 300,000 Sephardi Jews, in 1499 mass burning of Islamic books and forced coversions took place, and in 1502 the Muslims of Granada were given the choice of baptism or exile. In 1525-26, Muslims of other provinces were given the same choice. In 1566 there was a revival of anti-Muslim legislation, and between 1609 and 1614 came edicts of expulsions. In other words, the same inquisitional measures taken against the Jewish Conversos who were found to be secretly practicing Judaism were taken against the Moriscos found to be practicing Islam, measures culminating in edicts of expulsion addressed specifically to Muslims. As a result, many fled to North Africa, where, like Sephardi Jews, they maintained certain aspects of their Hispanicised Arab culture.

This well documented history found little echo in the events promoted by the International Committee - Sepharad '92 whose major funds came from the US, Spain, and Israel.[7] Spain, which still has to come to terms with its present-day racist immigration policies towards - among others - Arab North Africans, embraced its 'Golden Age' after centuries of denial, while reserving a regrettable mea culpa only for the official spokespersons of 'the Jews'. As for all other representatives, including conservative upper-middle class Zionist Sephardim, the elision of comparative discussions of the Muslim and Jewish (Sephardi) situations in Christian Spain was largely rooted, I would argue, in present-day Middle Eastern politics. The 1992 commemorations entailed a serious present-day battle over the representations of 'Jewish identity' in terms of an East/West axis, a battle dating back to the nineteenth century beginings of Zionist nationalism.

Zionist historiography, when it does refer to Islamic-Jewish history, consists of a morbidly selective 'tracing the dots' from pogrom to pogrom. (The word 'pogrom' itself derives from and is reflective of the Eastern-European Jewish experience.)[8] Subordinated to a Eurocentric historiography, most quincentenary events lamented yet another tragic episode in a homogeneous, static history of relentless persecution. Not surprisingly, the screening at an Expulsion conference of *El Santo Oficio*, a film about the Inquisition in the New World, and the persecution of Sephardi conversos, elicited such remarks as: 'You think it's different today?', 'That's also what the Nazis did to us. That's what the Arabs would do if they could'. (A curious claim since the Arab Muslims had a millenium-long opportunity to install an inquisition against Middle Eastern Jews - or against Christian minorities - but never did.) Such common remarks underline the commemorations' role as a stage for demonstrating (Euro)Israeli nationalism as the only possible logical answer to horrific events in the history of Jews. The inquisition of Sephardi Jews is seen merely as a foreshadowing of the Jewish Holocaust.

In this paradigm, the traumas left by Nazi genocidal practices are simplistically projected onto the experiences of Jews in Muslim countries, and onto the Israeli-Palestinian conflict.[9]

My point here is not to idealise the situation of the Jews of Islam, but rather to suggest that Zionist discourse has subsumed Islamic-Jewish history into a Christian-Jewish history, while also undermining comparative studies of Middle Eastern Jews in the context of diverse religious and ethnic minorities in the Middle East/North Africa. On the occasion of the quincentenary, the Zionist perspective privileged Sephardi-Jewish relations with European-Christianity over those with Arab-Islam, projecting Eurocentric maps of Christians and Jews as West and Muslims as East, and ignoring the fact that at the time of the expulsion syncretic Jewish communities were flourishing all over the Islamic Middle East and North Africa. Quincentennial events not only rendered the inter-relations between Jewish conversos and indigenous conversos invisible, but also undermined the Sephardic-Jewish and Muslim cultural symbiosis. The only Muslim country that has received some quincentennial attention is Turkey, partly due to Sultan Beyazid II's ordering his governers in 1492 to receive the expelled Jews cordially. But no less important is Turkey's contemporary regional alliances, its national fissured identity between East and West. Unlike Arab-Muslim countries, where expelled Sephardim also settled (Morocco, Tunisia, Egypt), Turkey has not participated in the Israeli-Arab conflict, nor in the non-allied embargo that has for decades regionally isolated Israel until the recent orchestration of Arab diplomatic recognition. Yet, even in the case of Turkey, the quincentennial emphasis was less on Muslim-Jewish relations than on the voyages of refuge, and, anachronistically, on the Turkish (national) as opposed to Muslim (religious) shelter.

In this rewriting of history, present-day Muslim-Arabs are merely one more 'non-Jewish' obstacle to the Jewish-Israeli national trajectory. The idea of the unique, common victimization of all Jews at all times provides a crucial underpinning of official Israeli disocurse. The notion of uniqueness precludes analogies and metonymies, thus producing a selective reading of 'Jewish history', one that hijacks the Jews of Islam from their Judeo-

Islamic geography, and subordinates it to that of the European-Ashkenazi *shtetl*. This double process entails the performance of commonalities among Jews in the public sphere so as to suggest a homogeneous national past, while silencing any more globalised and historicised narrative that would see Jews not simply through their religious commonalities but also in relation to their contextual cultures, institutions, and practices. Given this approach, and given the Israeli-Arab conflict, no wonder that the Jews of Islam, and more specifically Arab Jews, have posed a challenge to any simplistic definition of Jewish, and particularly of the emergent Jewish Euro-Israeli, identity.

The selective readings of Middle Eastern history, in other words, make two processes apparent: the rejection of an Arab and Muslim context for Jewish institutions, identity, and history; as well as their unproblematised subordination into a 'universal' Jewish experience. In the Zionist 'proof' of a single Jewish experience, there are no parallels or overlappings with other religious and ethnic communities, whether in terms of a Jewish hyphenated and syncretic culture or in terms of linked analogous oppressions. All Jews are defined as closer to each other than to the cultures of which they have been a part. Thus the religious Jewish aspect of diverse intricated and interwoven Jewish identities has been given primacy, a categorisation tantamount to dismembering the identity of a community. And indeed, the Euro-Israeli separation of the 'Jewish' part from the 'Middle Eastern' part, in the case of Middle Eastern Jews, has resulted in practically dismantling the Jewish communities of the Muslim world, as well as in pressures exerted on Mizrahim (orientals) to re-align their Jewish identity accordinq to Zionist Euro-Israeli paradigms. Since the beginnings of European Zionism, the Jews of Islam have faced, for the first time in their history, the imposed dilemma of choosing between Jewishness and Arabness, in a geopolitical context that perpetuated the equation between Arabness and Middle Easterness and Islam, on the one hand, and between Jewishness and Europeanness and Westerness on the other.

The master-narrative of universal Jewish victimization has been crucial for legitimising an anomalous nationalist project of 'ingathering of the Diaspora from the four corners of the globe';

but this can also be defined as forcing displacements of peoples from widely diverse geographies, languages, cultures and histories, a project in which, in other words, a state created a nation. This master narrative has also been crucial for the claim that the 'Jewish nation' faces a common historical enemy - the Muslim-Arab - implying a double edged amnesia with regards to both the Judeo-Islamic history and the colonial partition of Palestine. False analogies between the Arabs and Nazis, and in 1992 with Inquisitors, become not merely a staple of Zionist rhetoric, but also a symptom of a Jewish European nightmare projected onto the structurally distinct political dynamics of the Israeli/Palestinian conflict. In a historical context of Sephardi-Jews experiencing within the Muslim world a history utterly distinct from that which haunted the European memories of Ashkenazi Jews, and in a context of the massacres and dispossession of Palestinian people, the conflation of the Muslim-Arab with the archetypical (European) oppressors of Jew downplays the colonial-settler history of Euro-Israel itself.

But the neat division of Israel as West and Palestine as East, I would argue, ignores some of the fundamental contradictions within Zionist discourse itself. Central to Zionism is the notion of return to origins located in the Middle East. Thus it often points to its linguistic return to Semitic Hebrew, and to its sustaining of a religious idiom intimately linked with the topography of the Middle East, as a 'proof' of the Eastern origins of European Jews - a crucial aspect of the Zionist claim for the land. And although Jews have often been depicted in anti-Semitic discourse as an alien 'Eastern' people within the West, the paradox of Israel is that it presumed to end a diaspora, which was characterized by Jewish ritualistic nostalgia for the East, only to found a state whose ideological and geopolitical orientation has been almost exclusively toward the West. Herzl called for a Western-style capitalist-democratic miniature state, to be made possible by the grace of imperial patrons such as England or Germany, while Ben Gurion formulated his visionary utopia of Israel as that of a 'Switzerland of the Middle East'. Although European Jews have historically been the victims of anti-Semitic orientalism, Israel as a state has become the perpetrator of orientalist attitudes and actions whose consequences have been the dispossession of Palestinians. The ideological roots of Zionism can be traced to the conditions of nineteenth- and early twentieth-century Europe, not only as a reaction against anti-Semitism but also in response to the rapid expansion of capitalism and of European empire- building. Israel, in this sense, has clearly been allied to first world imperialist interests, has deployed Eurocentric-inflected discourse, and has exercised colonialist policies toward Palestinian land and people.

The question is further complicated by the socialist pretensions, and at times the socialist achievements, of Zionism. In nationalist Zionist discourse, the conflict between the socialist ideology of Zionism and the real praxis of Euro-Jewish colonization in Palestine was resolved through the reassuring thesis that the Arab masses, subjected to feudalism and exploited by their own countrymen, could only benefit from the emanation of Zionist praxis.[10] This hegemonic socialist-humanist discourse has also hidden the negative dialectics of wealth and poverty between First and Third World Jews behind a mystifying facade of egalitarianism. The Zionist mission of ending the Jewish exile from the 'promised land' was never the beneficient enterprise portrayed by official discourse, since from the first decade of this century Arab Jews were perceived as a source of cheap labour which could replace the dispossessed Palestinian *fellahin*.[11] The 'Jews in the form of Arabs' thus could prevent any Palestinian declaration that the land belongs to those who work it, and contribute to the Jewish national demographic needs.[12] The Eurocentric projection of Middle Eastern Jews as coming to the 'land of milk and honey' from desolate backwaters, from societies lacking all contact with scientific-technological civilization, once again set up an orientalist rescue trope. Zionist discourse has cultivated the impression that Sephardi culture prior to Zionism was static and passive, and like the fallow land of Palestine, as suggested by Edward Said, lying in wait for the impregnating infusion of European dynamism.[13] While presenting Palestine as an empty land to be transformed by Jewish labour, the Zionist 'Founding Fathers' presented Arab-Jews as passive vessels to be shaped by the revivifying spirit of Promethean Zionism.

The Euro-Zionist problematic relation to the question of East and West has generated a deployment of opposing paradigms that often results in hysterical responses to any questioning of its projected 'Western identity'. Zionism viewed Europe both as ideal ego and as the signifier of ghettoes, persecutions and Holocaust. Within this perspective, the 'Diaspora Jew' was an extra-territorial rootless wanderer, someone living 'outside of history'. Posited in genderized language as the masculine redeemer of the passive Diaspora Jew, the mythologized *sabra* simultaneously signified the destruction of the Diasporic Jewish entity. The prototypical newly emerging Jew in Palestine - physically strong, with blonde hair and blue eyes, healthy looking and cleansed of all 'Jewish inferiority complexes', and a cultivator of the land - was conceived as an anti-thesis to the Zionist virtually anti-Semitic image of the 'Diaspora Jew'. The *sabra* which was modelled on the Romantic ideal, largely influenced by the German *Jungend Kultur*, generated a culture in which any expression of weakness came to be disdained as 'galuti' - that which belongs to the diaspora. Zionism, in other words, viewed itself as an embodiment of European nationalist ideals to be realised outside of Europe, in the East, and in relation to the pariahs of Europe, the Jews. Thus, the sabra was celebrated as eternal youth devoid of parents, as though born from a spontaneous generation of nature, as, for example, in Moshe Shamir's key nationalist novel of the 1948 generation *Bemo Yadav* (In His Own Hands), which introduces the hero as follows: 'Elik was born from the sea'. In this paradoxical idiosyncratic version of the Freudian *familienroman*, Euro-Zionist parents raised their children to see themselves as historical foundlings worthy of more dignified, romantic, and powerful progenitors. Zionism posited itself as an extension of Europe in the Middle East, carrying its Enlightenment banner of the civilising mission.

If the West has been viewed ambivalently as the place of oppression to be liberated from, as well as a kind of object of desire to form a 'normal' part of it, the East has also signified a contemporary ambivalence. On the one hand, it is a place associated with 'backwardness', 'underdevelopment', a land swamped, in the words of 1950s propaganda films, with 'mosquitos, scorpions, and Arabs'. On the other, the East has symbolised solace, the return to geographical origins, and reunification with biblical history. The obsessive negation of the

'Diaspora' which began with the Haskalah (European-Jewish Enliqhtenment) and the return to the homeland of Zion, led, at times, to the exotic affirmation of Arab 'primitiveness', as a desirable image to be appropriated by the native-born sabra. The Arab was projected as the incarnation of the ancient, the pre-exiled Jews, the Semitic not yet corrupted by wanderings in exile, and therefore, to a certain extent, as the authentic Jew. This projection, however, co-existed with a simultaneous denial of Palestine. In Israeli archeology the deep stratum, in the literal and figurative sense, is associated with the Israeli Jews, while the surface level is associated with the Arabs, as a recent 'superficial' historical element without millenial 'roots'. Since the Arabs are seen as 'guests' in the land, their presence must be downplayed, much as the surface of the land has at times been 'remodelled' to hide or bury remnants of Arab life. The linguistic, lexical expression of this digging into the land is the toponymic archaeology of place names. Some Arabic names of villages, it was discovered, were close to or based on the biblical Hebrew names; in some cases therefore, Arabic names were replaced with old-new Hebrew ones.

Yet despite the importance of the idea of Return, it is no less important to see Zionist representations of Palestine in the context of other settlers' narratives. Palestine is linked to the Columbus narrative of the Americas in more ways than would at first appear. The Columbus narrative prepared the ground for an enthusiastic reception of Zionist discourse within Euro-America. The Israeli/Palestinian conflict as a whole, touches, I would argue, on some sensitive historical nerves within 'America' itself. As a product of schizophrenic master-narratives, colonial-settler state on the one hand and anti-colonial republic on the other, 'America' has been subliminally more attuned to the Zionist than to the Palestinian nationalist discourse. Zionist discourse contains a liberatory narrative vis-a-vis Europe which in many ways is pertinent to the Puritans. The New World of the Middle East like the New World of America was concerned with creating a New Man. The image of the sabra as a new (Jewish) man evokes the American Adam. The American hero has been celebrated as prelapsarian Adam, as a New Man emancipated from history (i.e. European history) before whom all the world and time lay available, much as the sabra was conceived as the anti-thesis of the 'old world' European Jew. The American Adam and the sabra masculinist archetypes implied not only their status as creators, blessed with the divine prerogative of naming the elements of the scene about them, but also their fundamental innocence. The notions of an American Adam and an Israeli sabra elided a number of crucial facts, notably that there were other civilizations in the Promised Land; that the settlers were not creating 'being from nothingness' and that the settlers, in both cases, had scarcely jettisoned all their Old World cultural baggage, their deeply ingrained Eurocentric attitudes and discourses. Here the gendered metaphor of the 'virgin land', present both in Zionist and American pioneer discourses, suggests that the land is implicitly available for defloration and fecundation. Assumed to lack owners, it therefore becomes the property of its 'discoverers' and cultivators who transform the wilderness into a garden, those who 'make the desert bloom'.

In the case of Zionist discourse, the concept of 'return to the mother land', as I have pointed out, suggests a double relation to the land, having to do with an ambivalent relation to the 'East' as the place of Judaic origins as well as the locus for implementing the 'West'. The sabra embodied the humanitarian and liberationist project of Zionism, carrying the same banner of the 'civilizing mission' that European powers proclaimed during their surge into 'found lands'. The classical images of sabra pioneers as settlers on the Middle Eastern frontiers, fighting Indian-like Arabs, along with the reverberations of the early American biblical discourse encapsulated in such notions as 'Adam', '(New) Canaan', and 'Promised Land', have all facilitated the feeling of Israel as an extention of 'us' - the US. Furthermore, both the US and Israel fought against British colonialism, while also practising colonial policies towards the indigenous peoples. Finally, I would argue for a triangular structural analogy by which the Palestinians represent the aboriginal 'Indians' of Euro-Israeli discourse, while the Sephardim, as imported cheap labour, constitute the 'Blacks' of Israel. (Taking their name from the American movement, the Israeli 'Black Panthers', for example, sabotaged the myth of the melting pot by showing that there was in Israel not one but two Jewish communities - one white, one black.) The manifest Palestinian refusal to play the assigned role of the presumably doomed 'Indians' of the transplanted (far) Western narrative has testified to an alternative narrative in whose narration Edward Said has been in the forefront. The story of Sephardim - as the Jewish victims of Zionism - also remains to be heard.

The same historical process that dispossessed Palestinians of their property, lands and national-political rights, was intimately linked to the process that affected the dispossession of Arab Jews from their property, lands and rootedness in Arab countries, as well as their uprootedness from that history and culture within Israel itself. But while Palestinians have fostered the collective militancy of nostalgia in exile, Sephardim, trapped in a no-exit situation, have been forbidden to nourish memories of at least partially belonging to the peoples across the river Jordan, across the mountains of Lebanon, and across the Sinai desert and Suez Canal. The pervasive notion of 'one people', reunited in their ancient homeland, actively disauthorizes any affectionate memory of life before the State of Israel. Quincenntenial events luxuriated in the landscapes, sounds, and smells of the lost Andalusian home, but silence muffled an even longer historical imaginary, in Cairo, Baghdad, Damascus - and hid an even more recent loss. For centuries, both Muslim and Jewish poets eulogized Andalusia. In contemporary Palestinian poetry Andalusia is not simply a closed chapter of Arab grandeur, for it allegorizes Palestine. But the parallelism between Andalusia and Palestine stops precisely at the point of reclaiming a Palestinian future.

The 1992 discussions of expulsion brought out the 'wandering Jew' motif as perennially displaced people. But the Jews of the Middle East and North Africa, for the most part, had stable 'non wandering' lives in the Islamic world. As splendidly captured in the work of Amitav Gosh's *In an Antique Land*, the Sephardim who have moved within the regions of Asia and Africa, from the Mediterranean to the Indian Ocean, did it more for commercial, religious, or scholarly purposes than for reasons of persecution. Ironically, the major displacement took place in recent years when Arab Jews were uprooted, dispossesed, and dislodged due to the collaboration between Israel and some of the Arab governments under the orchestration of Western colonial powers who termed their solution for the 'question of Palestine' as a 'population exchange'.[14] Sephardim who have managed to leave Israel, often in (an indirect) response to institutionalised racism there, have dislocated themselves yet again, this time to the US, Europe, and Latin America. In an historical twist, today it is to the Muslim-Arab countries of their origins to which most Middle Eastern Jews cannot travel, let alone fantasize a return - the ultimate taboo.

The commonalities between Middle Eastern Jews and Muslims are a thorny reminder of the Middle Eastern character of the majority of Jews in Israel today. Not surprisingly, quincentenary events in Europe, Middle East and the Americas have centred on the Spanishness of Sephardi culture (largely on Ladino or Judeo-Español language and music), while marginalising the fact that Jews in Iberia formed part of a larger Judeo-Islamic culture of North Africa, the Middle East, and the European Balkan area of the Ottoman Empire. The erasure of the Arab dimension of Sephardim-Mizrahim has been crucial to the Zionist perspective, since the Middle Easterness of Sephardi Jews questions the very definitions and boundaries of the Euro-Israeli national project.

The taboo around the Arabness of Sephardi history and culture is clearly manifested in Israeli academic and media attacks on Sephardi intellectuals who refuse to define themselves simply as Israelis, and who dare to assert their Arabness in the public sphere.[15] The Ashkenazi anxiety around Sephardi-Mizrahi identity underlines that Sephardi Jews have represented a problematic entity for Euro-Israeli hegemony. The Sephardi difference has destabilized Zionist claims for representing a single Jewish people, premised not only on a common religious background but also on common nationality. The strong cultural and historical links that Middle Eastern Jews have shared with the Arab-Muslim world, stronger in many respects than those they shared with the European Jews, threatened the conception of a homogeneous nation akin to those on which European nationalist movements were based. Arab-ness and oriental-ness have been consistently stigmatized as evils to be uprooted, creating a situation where Arab Jews were urged to see Judaism and Zionism as synonyms and Jewishness and Arabness as antonyms. Distinguishing the 'evil' East (the Muslim Arab) from the 'good' East (the Jewish Arab), Israel has taken upon itself to 'cleanse' Arab Jews of their Arab-ness and redeem them from their 'primal sin' of belonging to the Orient. This conceptualisation of East and West has important implications in this age of the 'peace treaty' since it avoids the inherent question of the majority of the population within Israel being from the Middle East - Palestinians citizens of Israel as well as Mizrahi-Sephardi Jews.

The leitmotif of Zionist texts was the cry to be a 'normal civilized nation'; but these *ostjuden*, perenially marginalised by Europe, realized their desire of becoming European, ironically, in the Middle East, this time on the back of their own 'Ostjuden', the Eastern Jews. The Israeli establishment, therefore, has made systematic efforts to suppress Sephardi-Mizrahi cultural identity. The Zionist establishment has systematically attempted to eradicate the Middle Easternness of those other Jews - for example, by marginalizing these histories in school curricula, and by rendering Mizrahi cultural production and grass-root political activities invisible in the media. However, Sephardi popular culture, despite its obvious shifts since the partition of Palestine, has clearly manifested its vibrant intertextual dialogue with Arab, Turkish, Iranian, and Indian popular cultures. (Oriental-Arabic music produced by Sephardim - at times in collaboration with Israeli-Palestinains - is consumed by Palestinians in Israel and across the borders in the Arab world often without being labeled as originating in Israel.) This creativity is partly nourished through an enthusiastic consumption of Jordanian, Lebanese and Egyptian television programmes and films, and Arabic video-music performances, which rupture theEuro-Israeli public sphere.

In Israel 'orientals' (mizrahim) signifies radical politics, evoking a common experience shared by all Asian and African Jews in Israel, despite our different origins. On the part of radical Sephardi movements, it also suggests a resistant discourse that calls for linkages to the East asopposed to the hegemonic discourse of 'we of the West'. Sephardi Jews, along with

Palestinians within Israel proper (Israeli-Palestinians), compose the majority of the citizens of a state which has rigidly imposed an anti-Middle Eastern agenda. In a first-of-its-kind meeting between Sephardi-Mizrahi Jews and PLO Palestinians held at the symbolic site of Toledo, Spain, in 1989, we insisted that a comprehensive peace would mean more than settling political borders, and would require the erasure of the East/West cultural borders between Israel and Palestine; and thus the remapping of national and ethnic racial identities against the deep scars of colonising partitions.

Parts of this essay appeared in preliminary form in Middle East Report, *No. 178, September-October 1992 and* Third Text, *No.21, Winter 1992-93. This essay is also included in* Beyond Orientalism *edited by Dilip Basu and Edmund Burk, to be published by the University of Michigan Press.*

Notes

1. I thank Robert Stam for allowing me to use here some 'shared territory' from our book *Unthinking Eurocentrism: Multiculturalism and the Media*, Routledge, London 1994.

2. Quoted in Jean Comby, '1492: Le Choc des Cultures et l'Evagelization du Monde', *Dossiers de l"episcopat Francais*, No. 14, October 1990.

3. See Charles Duff, *The Truth about Columbus*, Random House, New York: 1936.

4. Jan Pieterse makes the more general point that many of the themes of European imperialism traced antecedents to the European and Mediterranean sphere. Thus the theme of civilization against barbarism was a carry over from Greek and Roman antiquity, the theme of Christianity against pagans was the keynote of European expanison culminating in the Crusades, and the Christian theme of 'mission' was fused with 'civilization' in the *mission civilisatrice*. See Pietersee, *Empire and Emancipation*, Pluto, London 1990, p240.

5. For details see Jan Carew, *Fulcrums of Change: Origins of Racism in the Americas and Other Essays*, Africa World Press, Trenton 1988.

6. The indigenous peoples of the Americas similarly were offically protected from massacres by the throne only once they converted to Christianity.

7. See for example, W. Montgomery Watt and Pierre Cachia, *A History of Islamic Spain*, Edinburgh University Press, Edinburgh 1977; James T. Monroe, *Hispano-Arabic Poetry*, University of California Press, Berkley 1974.

8. This picture of an ageless and relentless oppression and humiliation, ignores the fact that, on the whole, Jews of Islam - a minority among several other religious and ethnic communities in the Middle East and North Africa - lived relatively comfortably within Arab-Muslim society.

9. For a more complex analysis see for example, Ilan Halevi, *A History of the Jews: Ancient and Modern*, Zed Books, London 1987; Maxime Rodinson, *Cult, Ghetto, and State: The Persistance of the Jewish Question*, Al Saqi Books, London 1983; Ella Shohat, *Israeli Cinema: East/West and the Politics of Representation*, University of Texas Press, Austin 1989. Ammiel Alacaly, *After Jews and Arabs: Remaking Levantine Culture*, University of Minnesota Press, Minneapolis 1993.

10. See Maxime Rodinson, *Israel: A Colonial-Settler State?*, translated by David Thorstad, Monad Press, New York 1973.

11. See Yoseff Meir, *Hatnua haTzionit veYehudei Teman* (*The Zionist Movement and the Jews of Yemmen*), Sifriat Afikim, Tel Aviv 1982; G.N. Giladi, *Discord in Zion: Conflict Between Ashkenazi and Sephardi Jews in Israel*, Scorpion Publishing, London 1990. Also Ella Shohat, 'Sephardim in Israel: Zionism from the Standpoint of Its Jewish Victims', *Social Text* 19/20, vol7, nos 1-2 (Fall 1988). Reprinted in Anne McClintock, Aamir Mufti and Ella Shohat (eds), *Dangerous Liaisons: Gender, Nation, and Post-Colonial Perspectives*, University of Minnesota Press, Menneapolis and London 1997.

12. The phrase was used already at the first decade of this century by the early engineers of 'Aliya' of Jews from the regions of the Ottoman Empire. See Yoseff Meir, *The Zionist Movement and the Jews of Yemmen*.

13. See Edward Said, *The Question of Palestine*, Times Books, New York 1979.

14. See for example, Abbas Shiblak, *The Lure of Zion*; Gideon Giladi, *Discord in Zion*.

15. For example, attacks on the Iraqi-Israeli author Shimon Ballas after the publication of his novel *And He is an Other*, Zmora Bitan, Tel Aviv 1991, as well as on myself after the Hebrew publication of my book *Israeli Cinema: East/West and the Politics of Representation* (published as Hakolnoa haIsraeli: Histpria veIdiologia), Breirot, Tel Aviv 1991.

WHITE SKIN, BLACK MASKS:
JEWS AND JEWISHNESS IN THE WRITINGS OF
GEORGE ELIOT AND FRANTZ FANON

Bryan Cheyette

It is often assumed that post-colonial theory cannot, by definition, replicate the oppressive discourses which are, in part, the object of its study. None is more aware than Edward Said of the hazards of reproducing what he calls, in his *Culture and Imperialism* (1993), a historical analysis based upon 'essentialism and exclusiveness' (p35) or the 'politics of separate identity' (p401).[1] In his latest work, *Representations of the Intellectual*, Said has argued that this 'new tribalism' or 'absence of universals' now threatens to deform secular critical thinking in general (p68). As a means of contesting a new doctrinal tribalism, I want to examine the ways in which the history of antisemitism has either been marginalised or excluded within post-colonial theory. My contention is that the immense (but slowly shrinking) gap between post-colonial and post-holocaust studies - or the gap between theories of anti-black racism, orientalism and antisemitism - at worst adds to this divisive new tribalism and, at best, does not sufficiently universalise and intertwine particular histories of victimisation.

These criticisms of post-colonial theory, I should stress from the beginning, are not a one-way street. By emphasising the continuities as well as the discontinuities between post-colonial and post-holocaust studies, I want to question the orthodoxies and absences on all sides. My longer work was written both to expose the racial discourse about Jews at the heart of English national culture and also to radically rethink the dominant and received historiography of antisemitism. The danger is that this historiography essentialises Jews as uniquely timeless, unchanging victims and therefore positions the history of antisemitism outside of the social, political and historical processes which gave rise to this history in the first place. One need hardly add that the language of victimhood has, since the Second World War, fed into many nationalisms - in, for example, the context of Israel/Palestine or former Yugoslavia - and this language is used, on all sides, to justify the most horrendous crimes. In his *Representations of the Intellectual*, Said cites the example of the South African Boers who were once victims of British Imperialism but went on to assert their historical experience through the doctrines of Apartheid (p33). Many have been aware, not least Frantz Fanon, of the dangers of collapsing post-colonial liberation into the seemingly unstoppable appeal of ethnic or national 'rootedness' which inevitably results in the dominance of a single national narrative. This misguided response to colonialism is also played out in relation to post-Holocaust national narratives with, as James Young has argued, Israel having a self-proclaimed redemptive relationship to the Holocaust.[2]

I am not saying, in a banal sense, that we must 'learn', whatever that means, from each other's history of oppression; although we might at least begin to read each other's histories. At this stage, what seems most compelling is the question of what is at stake within post-colonial theory if we do not rethink our conceptions of 'the West' in relation to the history of antisemitism. In other words, what anxiety, on all sides, is caused by bringing together post-colonial and post-Holocaust history? Why, for example, does Henry Louis Gates's aptly named and rightly influential anthology, *'Race', Writing and Difference* (1986), include little or no discussion of Western antisemitism among its essays, which Tzvetan Todorov, in particular, objected to? What is more, Gates in this volume, subsequently reprinted in his *Loose Canons: Notes on the Culture Wars*, speaks consistently of a homogenous and dominant white 'Western Judeo-Christian' culture. Said, in his *Culture and Imperialism*, follows Gates in this regard. Where within this supposed 'common culture' does 'the Jew' - other than as an aspect of dominant 'white' oppression - fit? To be fair, Gates has subsequently problematised his notion of an homogenous white 'Judeo-Christian' power in his ongoing work on black antisemitism and Jewish racism, which begins to recognise the ambivalent position of 'the Jew' within this seemingly 'common culture'. Gates' recent work, which contrasts starkly with his earlier writings, has been appropriately followed by Paul Gilroy and Cornell West, who both strive for an exemplary but gestural understanding of the mutuality between the black and Jewish diasporas.[3] Such interventions, however, are still at odds with much post-colonial theory.

More typically, Robert Young in his *White Mythologies: Writing History and the West*, speaks of the history of antisemitism as a form of internal Orientalism in the West, thereby simultaneously including and excluding it from the realm of his inquiry.[4] This equivocal gesture is done without linking the history of antisemitism to the main varient of internalised Western Orientalism which was German Orientalism, and which is, significantly, also missing from Said's *Orientalism*. To be sure Said, in this formative work, does rightly describe Orientalism as a 'strange secret sharer of Western antisemitism' (p27). But he also speaks of the 'Jew of pre-Nazi Europe' (p286) as being eventually 'bifurcated': 'one Semite went the way of Orientalism, the other, the Arab, was forced to go the way of the Oriental' (p307). As if to emphasis the manichaean divide between post-War Arab and Jewish 'Semites', Said's *Culture and Imperialism* does not mention the all too apparent history of antisemitism within Imperial culture. As his recent *The Politics of Dispossession: The Struggle for Palestinian Self-Determination 1969-1994* makes clear, however, there is an obvious political dimension to Said's simultaneous inclusion and exclusion of the history of antisemitism. What *The Politics of Dispossession* shows, above all, is the extent to which the representation of the Holocaust has been used as a tool of Palestinian oppression (pp167-69). But it is precisely because Jewish suffering has been so crudely essentialised, in the name of Israeli nationalism, that it needs to be engaged with in a non-nationalist, or what Said calls in *Culture and Imperialism* a 'hybrid', context.

What is at stake when we rename antisemitism 'Orientalism' (or vice versa) or when we write of the history of racism in 'the West' without including antisemitism or other forms of racism not necessarily reduced to the issue of skin colour or colonial domination? This lack of 'double consciousness', in the words of Paul Gilroy (echoing W. E. B. Du Bois), can surely only ever reinforce a new tribalism. I want to examine two radically differing texts - George Eliot's *Daniel Deronda* (1876) and Frantz Fanon's *Black Skin, White Masks* (1952) - to show in some detail the pitfalls of constructing either an exclusively 'black' victimhood or, its mirror image, an exclusively 'white' all-prevailing European culture. My argument is that 'the Jew', in these works, throws both of these manichaean categories into disarray. By bringing together these admittedly disparate texts, I hope to illustrate the dangers of *unambivalent* readings with particular regard to the presumed 'whiteness' of European Jewry. In other words, I want to challenge the mountain of certainties that continues to separate a post-Holocaust reconstitution of 'the West' from its post-colonial counterpart. Far from seeing the history of anti-black racism or Orientalism as mutually exclusive in relation to the history of antisemitism, I want to attempt to establish some of the ways in which these various histories may be interrelated.

Before looking at George Eliot's *Daniel Deronda* in more detail, I will begin with a rather lengthy quote from a letter by Eliot, written in February 1848, which contains her well-known reaction to Benjamin Disraeli's Imperialist Young England Trilogy. Eliot wished especially to dismiss Disraeli's theories of Jewish or Semitic racial superiority and purity. After stating that such theories have 'not a leg to stand on', she continues:

Extermination up to a certain point seems to be the law for the inferior races - for the rest, fusion both for physical and moral ends. It appears to me that the law by which privileged classes degenerate from continual intermarriage must act on a larger scale in deteriorating whole races. The nations have been always kept apart until they have sufficiently developed their idiosyncrasies and then some great revolutionary force has been called into action by which the genius of a particular nation becomes the common mind of humanity. Looking at the matter aesthetically, our ideal of beauty is never formed on the characteristics of a single race. I confess the types of the 'pure races', however handsome, always impress me disagreeably - there is an undefined feeling that I am

> *looking not at man but at a speciman of an order under Cuvier's class, Bimana. The negroes certainly puzzle me - all the other races seem plainly destined to extermination or fusion not excepting even the 'Hebrew-Caucasian'. But the negroes are too important physiologically and geographically for one to think of their extermination, while the repulsion between them and the other races seems too strong for fusion to take place to any great extent.*[5]

While this letter obviously predates *Daniel Deronda* by nearly three decades, many of its propositions remain at the heart of George Eliot's last novel. Her sense of racial determinism and the conflation of 'race' with society or class; her aesthetisation of 'race'; her belief that 'some great revolutionary force' will bring together essentially separate nations; the rigid classification of different races and nations based, here, on the physiology of Georges Cuvier; and, finally, the racial destiny of Jews and blacks represented in the starkest of terms as the choice between 'extermination or fusion'. All of these narratives reappear in more complex forms in *Daniel Deronda*, and there is a sense in which Eliot, in her later work, is arguing vehemently with many of these propositions while still accepting their fundamental assumptions.

A key example of Eliot's racial assumptions being replicated in *Daniel Deronda* can be seen in the strangely incongruous but revealing authorial aside about half way into the novel: 'And one man differs from another, as we all differ from the Bosjesman [Bushman]' (p370). The influence of Georges Cuvier on Eliot, at this point, is especially apparent as Cuvier, in *The Animal Kingdom* (1831), had notoriously described the 'Negro race' as 'evidently approximate to the monkey tribe' and as having 'always remained in the most complete state of barbarism'.[6] As Martin Bernal has demonstrated in his *Black Athena*, a good deal of the racial discourse surrounding a supposedly irredeemable black inferiority is implicitly concerned with the presumed 'whiteness' of European culture. The apprehension in Victorian Britain surrounding the 'colour' of the 'ancient Egyptians' or the 'race' of the Semites was, Bernal argues, a bid to expunge the 'afroasiatic roots' of European classical civilisation. Using the racialised language of Disraeli, George Eliot in *Daniel Deronda* wished to show that Jews, because of their perceived 'whiteness', could be Europeanised as 'purer Caucasians' (p562).[7] Virtually in the next breath, however, Eliot describes the lowly Mr Cohen as having an 'oily cheerfulness', which tended to 'look mongrel' (p562), and which caused the hostility of the local Londoners. The issue of whether Jews are 'pure' or 'impure', 'white' or 'black', European or Oriental, produces a range of radically competing narratives in *Daniel Deronda*.

Immediately after her imperious reference to the absolute alterity of the 'Bosjesman' of South Africa, Daniel Deronda is said to have 'something of the knight-errant in his disposition' (p370). Just as the figure of Ivanhoe in Scott's novel, which was much admired by Eliot, is postioned between Rebecca and Rowena as the embodiment of European masculinity, Deronda ponders on the relative merits of Mirah and Gwendolen with respect to his 'utopian' ideals (p370). But, although Deronda is represented as an idealised European, in the following chapter Eliot makes him explicitly identify with what Henleigh Mallinger Grandcourt calls the 'beastly sort of baptist Caliban' (p376). (It is the 'baptist Caliban', or local black population, who caused the anti-colonial uprising in Jamaica which was so viciously repressed by Governor Richard Eyre). Deronda, we are told, had 'always felt a little with Caliban' and it is worth remembering, in this context, the extent to which Harriet Beecher Stowe's remarkably popular *Uncle Tom's Cabin* (1852) was a major influence on George Eliot's novel. Palestine and Liberia, in these works, enact respectively the simultaneous assimilation and expulsion of the Jewish and black Other with regard to the dominant colonial values of the West. This exclusivist point of closure might well explain why Southern Africa, in Eliot's aside, is crudely denoted to be a realm that 'we all' differ from. To resolve Daniel's ambivalent positioning between a 'barbarian' or 'black' East and a 'civilised' or 'white' West - the indeterminate location of a future Jewish nation-state - blackness becomes a structuring absence, an ultimate Other, onto which is displaced the potentially uncontainable Otherness of Deronda's Jewishness.

To be sure, George Eliot's racialised construction of 'the negroes' as both unassimilable and endlessly enduring was significantly qualified in the light of the impact of Beecher Stowe's *Uncle Tom's Cabin*. This extraordinarily popular novel, it should be remembered, sold more copies in England than in America when it first appeared and George Eliot was only one among many of Beecher Stowe's most ardent English admirers. Rachel Bowlby's reading of *Uncle Tom's Cabin* as an appeal to a 'common humanity rooted in the Christian heart' - which simultaneously disproves and naturalises racial difference - was, I want to argue, replicated in *Daniel Deronda*. By identifying Deronda with those that had caused the uprising in Jamaica, it is clear that he has to humanely transcend a brutal and unjust Empire that gave rise to Governor Eyre in the first place. This latter context is made clear in Eliot's much cited letter to Beecher Stowe which notes specifically the 'spirit of arrogance and contemptuous dictatorialness' which 'we English' have shown 'not only towards the Jews, but towards all oriental peoples'. Eliot intended her novel to, ideally, counter this 'national disgrace'.[8]

Speaking through her rather precious persona in her late essay, 'The Modern Hep! Hep! Hep!' (1879), Eliot contends that the 'Red Indians, not liking us when we settled among them, might have been willing to fling such facts [of our historic rapacity] in our faces, but... their opinions did not signify, because we were able, if we liked, to exterminate them' (p171). Grandcourt has long since been read as an allegory of a potentially exterminatory colonialism in Eliot's novel. The brute ability of imperial power to deform historic memory so that it no longer 'signifies' in contemporary English life is, as many have claimed, a central concern of *Daniel Deronda*, which is made explicit in 'The Modern Hep! Hep! Hep!'. Following this anti-imperial narrative line, Jim Reilly reads Eliot's novel as a 'revisionist historiography of history's excluded' as, in other words, a counter-narrative to the more 'convential' accounts of a spuriously civilising colonialism.[9] Reilly has argued that Gwendolen Harleth's isolation and sense of herself as correspondingly divorced from a historical role is thrown into relief by this 'other' history of Jewish national liberation which attempts to supersede, at home and abroad, the received language of colonising liberalism. By the end of the novel, both Daniel's and Gwendolen's stories have yet to begin and are clearly differentiated from an already 'known' and dominating historical narrative.

The problem, however, with casting *Daniel Deronda's* rejection of Victorian certainties in these unproblematical liberationist terms is that this 'other' post-liberal narrative can just as easily be assimilated into a dominant colonial discourse. Edward Said has argued in his *The Question of Palestine* that the most significant absence in Eliot's novel is that of Mordecai's so-called 'debauched and paupered conquerors', who inhabit Palestine, which Mordecai wishes to transform into an idealised European homeland situated between 'East' and 'West' (p64). As Gillian Beer has shown, the narrative of *Daniel Deronda* is largely defined by the non-occurrence of key events and these unfilled desires turn the novel into a 'wilful and conscious form of negation'.[10] The negation of the inhabitants of Palestine, as the alternative promised land of liberalism, is a stark illustration of this point.

The incommensurable range of progressive and regressive possibilities that are associated with Jewish otherness in *Daniel Deronda* clearly highlights the extent to which such racialised categories are always radically contingent and open to reinterpretation. The problem with Cynthia Chase's well-known 'deconstructive' reading of *Daniel Deronda* is that she fails to recognise that the figure of 'the Jew' is, above all, contested and equivocal and is neither pure 'play' nor pure 'fixity' as she would have it. For Chase, the 'scandal' of Daniel's Jewishness is predicated on a racialised structuring absence, his circumcised penis. Just as 'we all' differ from the 'Bosjesman' of Southern Africa in Eliot's racial hierarchy, a supposedly stable and masculine European centre differs unequivocally from Deronda's 'circumcised penis'. When observed as one of the 'circumcised' Deronda is 'black', but when this absence is left unrecognised he is infinitely malleable and, thus, transfigured into an undifferentiated 'white' European. The abiding problem with Chase's influential analysis is that it simply reproduces the split, in the novel, between the supposed certainties of Deronda's racial identity and his uncertain 'fusion' or assimilation into a dominant imperial culture.[11]

My criticism of Chase's unambivalent reading of *Daniel Deronda* can also be applied to Said's understanding of the negation of the desire for Palestinian national self-determination - as opposed to Jewish national self-determination - in the novel. His unequivocal critique, I believe, is at once entirely correct and entirely reductive. At one point in *The Question of Palestine*, Said argues that liberal hopes in *Daniel Deronda* are: 'restricted to Europeans and Jews, who are themselves European prototypes so far as colonising the East is concerned' (p65). This blunt positioning of Jews as unambiguously European and colonial is, however, immediately undercut in Said's next sentence: 'There is a remarkable failure [in *Daniel Deronda*] when it comes to taking anything non-European into consideration although *curiously* all of Eliot's descriptions of Jews stress their exotic, "Eastern" aspects' (p65). The use of the word 'curiously' here, which I emphasise, indicates once again the dangers of a too easy assimilation of 'the Jews' into a dominant Western culture. For, as Said notes, at the same time as Eliot constructs Jews as ideal colonialists, she also constructs them as fixed racial Others (which is why they can not be assimilated into British liberal culture in the first place). This ambivalence, and not an easy 'fusion or extermination', severely disrupts Eliot's text and helps us to more effectively challenge the racialisation of culture within Western liberalism.

I will now re-examine George Eliot's gestures of inclusion and exclusion, with regard to the equivocal figure of 'the Jew', in the context of Frantz Fanon's anti-colonial *Black Skin, White Masks*. My argument is *not* that George Eliot's essentially abstract and ultimately diminished liberal anti-Imperialism is somehow equivalent to Fanon's passionately involved anti-colonialism. Any crude notions of equivalence here would, unforgivably, fail to take account of the different political readerships - one metropolitan, one colonial - that Eliot and Fanon wrote for. With this proviso in mind, Fanon's conflicted account of 'the Jew' and post-Holocaust antisemitism, in relation to anti-black racism and colonialism, does relate interestingly to Eliot's novel. Both texts, that is, are pointedly equivocal with regard to a 'white' European Jewishness which, in radically differing terms, is also perceived to wear a 'black mask'. Whereas the figure of 'the Jew' lays bare the limits of Eliot's anti-imperialism, I want to show that the partial incorporation of Jean-Paul Sartre's *Anti-Semite and Jew* (1946) into *Black Skin, White Masks* exposes wider ambivalences and divisions in Fanon's writings.

One final proviso. All that I have to say about Fanon is not meant, in any way, to detract from his all important insight, as Said puts it in *Culture and Imperialism*, that he helped the colonised realise that they were 'prisoners in their own land' (p258). Fanon's sense that this consciousness of oppression should not merely lead to a form of Africentric chauvinism partially resulted in him bringing together the history of Western antisemitism with his account of Western colonialism in *Black Skin, White Masks*. As Jock McCulloch has shown, this form of double consciousness was primarily aimed at the work of Octave Mannoni who argued, in his *Prospero and Caliban: The Psychology of Colonization* (1950), that colonial racism was, above all, essentially unique. Fanon's critique of Mannoni in chapter four of *Black Skin, White Masks* and his subsequent incorporation of Sartre's *Anti-Semite and Jew* is, in other words, part of the wider tension in Fanon's writings concerning the relationship between a particularist anti-colonial nationalism and more universalist or transnational theories of racial oppression.[12] Whereas Sartre's *Anti-Semite and Jew* could reveal, in part, a generalised anti-racism, his universalising *Black Orpheus* (1948) was to be famously resisted by Fanon until he published *The Wretched of the Earth* (1961). Sartre's *Black Orpheus* 'destroyed black zeal' (p135), according to Fanon's earlier work, by placing black cultural nationalism in the context of a supposedly all-encompassing Hegelian dialectic. This fear of being assimilated back into a set of 'pre-existing' (p134) Eurocentric paradigms - however ostensibly progressive - also plays itself out in relation to Sartre's *Anti-Semite and Jew*.

Just as there are, in general, what Benita Parry calls 'persistent instabilities' in Fanon's writings, there are two simultaneous but utterly incommensurate narrative strands that he uses in relation to antisemitism in *Black Skin, White Masks*.[13]

The first of these strands explicitly brings together his own history of anti-Black oppression with the history of European antisemitism and is often written in an experiential, as opposed to a philosophical, mode. The second strand, however, wishes to draw an absolute theoretical distinction between anti-Black racism based, according to Fanon, entirely on skin colour and anti-Jewish racism which Fanon believed was a product of an altogether different social psychology. Not unlike Mannoni, Fanon argued that because Jews were apparently an integral part of a distinct European culture and history, they were ultimately distinguished from those who were denied such historical or cultural possessions by colonialism. I'll begin my reading of Fanon by giving what appears to be a rather straightforward example from the first inclusive or universalising narrative strand.

Towards the beginning of chapter five, which is called 'The Fact of Blackness', Fanon speaks of listening to a drunken Frenchman on a train who, after spouting some antisemitic vitriol, turns to Fanon and states: 'let's face up to the foreigners... no matter who they are' (p121). His conclusions from this incident are echoed throughout the following chapters:

> At first thought it may seem strange that the anti-semite's outlook should be related to that of the Negrophobe. It was my philosophy professor, a native of the Antilles, who recalled the fact to me one day: 'Whenever you hear anyone abuse the Jews, pay attention, because he is talking about you'. And I found that he was universally right - by which I meant that I was answerable in my body and in my heart for what was done to my brother. Later I realised that he meant, quite simply, an anti-semite is inevitably anti-Negro (p122).

This process of working through the acknowledged strangeness of associating antisemitism with Negrophobia - which culminates in the simplicity of his eventual conclusion that anti-semites are inevitably anti-Negro - is slightly more troubled than at first appears. Does his final self-confident sentence mean that he is no longer 'answerable in my body and in my heart for what was done to my brother'? Presumably not, but this uncertainty is repeated on a larger scale in the subsequent pages of *Black Skin, White Masks*. What is more, this paragraph also gives a clear indication of Fanon's uneasy intimacy with Sartre's *Anti-Semite and Jew*. Sartre ends as follows: 'what must be done is to point out that the fate of the Jews is [our] fate' which clearly echoes Fanon's philosophy professor: 'whenever you hear anyone abuse the Jews, pay attention, because he is talking about you'. But, just as Fanon resists the universalising dialectic of *Black Orpheus*, he resists similar gestures in *Anti-Semite and Jew*. After all, the main conclusion of Sartre's work is that antisemitism can only be defeated in a classless society. Unlike Fanon, Sartre relies upon an all-embracing dialectic, and not particularist acts of resistence, to defeat racism. But, as McCulloch notes, Fanon pointedly chose to ignore the Marxist tenor of *Anti-Semite and Jew* in his early writings.[14]

At his best, Fanon makes it possible to run together both black and Jewish oppression in relation to the 'manichean delirium' of Western metaphysics which divides the world into: 'Good-Evil, Beauty-Ugliness, White-Black' (p183). There are a number of telling moments in *Black Skin, White Masks* when the implications of this broader, inclusivist analysis are dramatically brought home by Fanon. At his most inclusive, Fanon can argue that, 'what others have described in the case of the Jew applies perfectly in that of the Negro' (p183). Earlier in the chapter, Fanon is quite explicit about what he calls the 'one point in common' that Jews and blacks have: 'both of us', he says, 'stand for Evil' (p180). But this facile point of identification is quickly qualified as he goes on, 'the black man more so, for the good reason that he is black'. It is the difficulties of such too easy forms of identification that Fanon grapples with throughout his work.

Towards the beginning of Chapter Six, which is entitled the 'Negro and Pyschopathology', Fanon speaks of the oppression of the 'black man' who, when he first encounters a 'white man', is made to feel what he calls 'the whole weight of his blackness' (p150). Immediately after this he goes on to refer, in a footnote, to Sartre's *Anti-Semite and Jew* which cites the example of a young Jewish girl who discovered her Jewishness through being racially abused at the age of fifteen. Sartre draws a more general conclusion from this episode which clearly influenced Fanon:

> *The later the discovery, the more violent the shock. Suddenly they perceive that others know something about them that they do not know, that people apply to them an ugly and upsetting term ['Jew'] that is not used in their own families (p150).*

This statement surely echoes Fanon's chilling and often cited sense, at the beginning of chapter five, of being 'splattered' with 'black blood' as he begins to think of himself for the first time as an 'ugly' object after a child sees him and is immediately frightened by his skin colour. Fanon's over-riding sense, at this point, is of being what he calls 'completely dislocated, unable to be abroad with the other, the white man' (p112). This sense of complete dislocation from so-called 'white' society, however, is precisely what makes it difficult for Fanon to fully identify with the abused Jew, who is always 'white' in his work. But this construction of 'the Jew' as being identified, at one and the same time, with both the abused 'blacks' and the 'white' oppressors clearly creates a good deal of anxiety in *Black Skins, White Masks*. After all, much of Fanon's experiential evidence, taken from his psychiatric case studies, explicitly echoes Sartre's *Anti-Semite and Jew*. Thus, Fanon's belief that the greatest fear of many of his patients is that they will behave 'like a nigger' reinforces Sartre's definition of the 'inauthentic Jew' as someone who fears that they will behave 'like a Jew'. In other words, as Fanon vehemently argues in response to Mannoni's *Prospero and Caliban*: 'it is the racist who creates his inferior' (p93) - whoever happens to be the object of his gaze - and, thus, 'colonial racism is no different from any other racism' (p88).

At this point of absolute identification with 'the Jew', insofar as s/he is created by the racist, Fanon most explicitly disrupts any manichean notions of an essentialised black victimhood by evoking a wider French complicity with the Holocaust that includes himself:

*Antisemitism hits me head on: I am enraged, I am bled
white by an appalling battle, I am deprived of the possibility
of being a man. I can not disassociate myself from the
future that is proposed for my brother. Every one of my acts
commits me as a man. Every one of my silences, every one of
my cowardices reveals me as a man (p88-9).*

This extraordinarily powerful statement confirms Fanon's
common humanity or 'whiteness' precisely at the point where
he is most associated with a European society which collaborated
with the death of millions. His complicity in European oppression
during the Second World War finally makes him, with bitter irony,
'a man'. As he eventually showed in *The Wretched of the Earth*,
Fanon was well aware of the complicity of European humanism
with the worst atrocities: 'leave this Europe where they are never
done talking of Man, yet murder men everywhere they find them'
(p251). This underlying awareness, most crucially, brings
together the histories of colonialism and genocide as ever-present
potentialities within European humanism. Fanon, significantly,
cites Aimé Césaire's refrain in *Black Skin, White Mask* that
'Hitler is not dead' to counter Mannoni's misguided belief that
'European civilisation and its best representatives are not
responsible for colonial racism' (p90). In *The Wretched of the
Earth*, Fanon also uses the example of Jewish reparation monies
from Germany to back up his claim that the colonial powers
should compensate those nations that have gained independence
only after centuries of exploitation (pp80-1). These all-important
connections were taken up by Sartre, in his Preface to *The
Wretched of the Earth*, who rightly expanded on Fanon's
fundamental understanding of the role of Western humanism
in relation to both colonialism and the Holocaust: 'liberty,
equality, fraternity, love, honour, patriotism and what have you.
All this did not prevent us [Europeans] from making anti-racial
speeches about dirty niggers, dirty Jews and dirty Arabs. [T]he
European has only been able to become a man through creating
slaves and monsters' (p22). Sartre's constitution of European
'civilisation' through the creation of inauthentic 'Jews', 'niggers',
or 'Arabs' is, nonetheless, prefigured in Fanon's *Black Skin,
White Masks*.

At the same time, the construction of a dominant racialised European identity was given a disturbing, less inclusive, interpretation by Fanon when applied to his more immediate circumstances. Let us return again to the incident on the train, already cited from *Black Skin, White Masks*, where we have an incredible statement before Fanon's seemingly untroubled sense that an 'anti-semite is inevitably anti-Negro'. Immediately after encountering the antisemite on the train, Fanon comments as follows:

> *An outrage! The Jew and I: Since I was not satisfied to be racialised, by a lucky turn of fate I was humanised. I joined the Jew, my brother in misery (p122).*

Once again Fanon is arguing that when he is brought together with 'the Jew', as part of the brotherhood of the racially abused, there is a fateful, if paradoxical, form of humanisation because 'the Jew' is 'white'. This supposed humanisation is then opposed to the experience of being 'racialised' which is associated, in Fanon's mind, exclusively with anti-black racism. Much of Fanon's exclusivist or particularist rhetoric, I will now show, revolves around this distinction. Whereas the Holocaust and colonialism can be brought together as prime examples of the potentiality for genocide within European humanism, these distinct histories can just as easily be split apart. At this point, racially constructed 'niggers' begin to be conflated with a particularist or authentic 'blackness' which is evoked as the only effective means of opposing 'white' colonial racism. As Paul Gilroy has shown, there is a very real danger that an anti-racist politics, defined largely in relation to the Second World War, can reproduce a spurious ethnocentricism that gave rise to anti-black racism in the first place.[15] That Fanon, at times, does not want to be in any way subsumed by a European humanism, however constituted, is made clear in those sections of *Black Skin, White Masks* where 'the Jew' ceases to be a neutral or 'inauthentic' object of the racist gaze. Just as 'the nigger' can achieve an authentic 'blackness' by resisting colonialism, inauthentic Jews can also be misguidedly specified as authentic products of an essentially 'white' history.

As well as bringing together Jews and blacks in relation to a spurious European humanism, Fanon also counters this welcome inclusiveness at a great many points in his text. I will cite a number of examples of these counter-narratives to show the extent to which anti-black racism was also seen as the polar opposite of antisemitism. I will begin with a rather lengthy quote which usefully covers a good deal of ground:

> *In* Anti-Semite and Jew *Sartre says...that [Jewish] conduct is perpetually over-determined from the inside.*
>
> *All the same, the Jew can be unknown in his Jewishness. He is not wholly what he is ... He is a white man and, apart from some rather debateable characteristics, he can sometimes go unnoticed. He belongs to the race of those who since the beginning of time have never known cannibalism. What an idea, to eat one's father! Simple enough, one has only not to be a nigger. Granted, the Jews are harassed - what am I thinking of? They are hunted down, exterminated, cremated. But these are little family quarrels. The Jew is disliked from the moment he is tracked down. But in my case everything takes on a* new *guise. I am given no chance. I am over-determined from without. I am the slave not of the 'idea' that others have of me but of my own appearance' (pp115/6).*

It is differentiating statements such as these that, to put it at its kindest, begin to expose the limits of Fanon's inclusive vocabulary and anti-racist rhetoric. References to 'little family quarrels', especially when left unqualified, clearly show the dangers of the absence of a more universalising vocabulary that, as Said puts it in *Representations of the Intellectual*, can give 'greater human scope to what a particular race or nation suffered' (p33). Perhaps understandably, Fanon seems to be continually struggling with the implications of a too easy humanism when, as we have seen, it can be absolutely complicit with colonialism. However, the logic of Fanon's more exclusivist argument - that Jews are over-determined from the inside and blacks from the outside - means that he is able, eventually, to reduce anti-Jewish and anti-black racism to the following formula: 'The Negro symbolises the biological danger; the Jew, the intellectual danger' (p165). The refusal to universalise, in these epigrammatic formulas, results in a spate of absolute distinctions throughout *Black Skin, White Masks*.

Versions of such oppositions abound, and it is worth reflecting on some of the conceptual and political consequences of these fixed splittings which are constructed around the essentialised 'whiteness' of Jews and the equally essentialised 'blackness' of blacks. I'll first of all just quote a few more examples of this particularising logic to show the extent to which Fanon relied upon it. The mind and body or inner and outer are rewritten metonymically to oppose 'inauthentic' Jewishness and blackness throughout chapter six: 'In the case of the Jew, one thinks of money and its cognates. In that of the Negro, one thinks of sex. Anti-semitism can be rationalised on a basic level. It is because he takes over the country that the Jew is in danger' (p160). Or, again,

> *no anti-semite would ever conceive of the idea of castrating the Jew. He is killed or sterilised. But the Negro is castrated ... The difference between the two attitudes is apparent. [E]very time that a Jew is persecuted, it is the whole race that is persecuted in his person. But it is in his corporeality that the Negro is attacked. It is as a concrete person that he is lynched. It is as an actual being that he is a threat. The Jewish menace is replaced by the fear of the sexual potency of the Negro (pp163-164).*

At this point, Fanon can be clearly related to George Eliot who makes her Jews 'white' by unequivocally opposing them to the South African 'bushmen'. In Fanon's case, there is a further twist as 'the Jew' is 'white' only in so far as he represents the spurious 'humanism' of European culture.

But, even within their own terms, such oppositions between a visceral anti-black racism and a cerebral antisemitism are unsustainable. When Fanon states that 'anti-semitism can be rationalised on a basic level. It is because he takes over the country that the Jew is in danger' (p160), he is referring worryingly *both* to the supposed actions of Jews as well as the 'idea' of Jewish behaviour. There is, more generally, a wider slippage in this work between conceptual or 'inauthentic' Jews and blacks and their 'authentic' or 'real' counterparts. To say that anti-black racism can not by definition be rationalised, however spuriously, makes it impossible to think of colonialism as a form of power-knowledge within European humanism and racism as anything other than a visceral hatred. At these times, anti-black racism is understood simultaneously as both a function of European 'civilising' discourse and as a function of individual psychopathology. Whereas the 'inauthentic' Jew and black can be brought together in relation to the oppressive potentiality of European humanism, they are irrevocably separated in relation to Fanon's particularising theories of racial pathology and colonial resistence.

One obvious but, ultimately, limited reaction to Fanon's fixed oppositions, or to George Eliot's attempt to construct Jews as ideal 'white' colonialists, is to cite the historical evidence which runs counter to these misguided certainties. The work of Sander Gilman, in recent years, has shown the extent to which the masculine 'Jew's Body' was constructed as disease-ridden, feminine and, above all, as irrevocably different from his 'aryan' counterpart in Central and Western European societies in the nineteenth and mid-twentieth centuries. This ubiquitous rhetoric of difference also applied to the Jew's skin colour which was often represented as black and which was also associated with the kind of fixed corporeal and sexualised fantasies that Fanon emphasises in relation to anti-black racism.[16] But, although Gilman's work is important and rightly influential, it does not seem enough of a response to Fanon or Eliot simply to say that Jews have been, historically, represented in the same way as blacks and that these writers are therefore historically inaccurate. The problem with Fanon's thinking about antisemitism in *Black Skin's White Masks*, and Eliot's idealisation of Daniel Deronda, should surely extend far beyond the question of historical accuracy and is specifically related to the unambivalent construction of 'the Jew' as 'white' within a dominant imperial culture.

What is at stake here, however, is less to do with Jewish history as such - nor even with the belated acknowledgement that antisemitism is also a part of the Western Judeo-Christian tradition - but much more to do with challenging the fixed binaries of black and white, Jew and gentile, East and West. These racialised categories too often reinforce notions of an essentialised victimhood, which in turn exclude those not deemed to have entered this particular sanctifying pantheon. The point is not that Jews were unequivocally victims or 'other' or 'black' in Western liberal culture but, as I have argued in my book, that they were ambivalently positioned as both black *and* white; self *and* other as both inside *and* outside Western culture.[17] Both Fanon and Eliot register, however inadvertently, the possibility that their 'white' Jews might at times also be 'black'. My contention is that the ambivalence of 'the Jew' within the West can be mobilised to expose the tensions at play between the fixed antitheses that define 'the West' which Eliot dubbed 'extermination or fusion'. By reinforcing the unambivalent readings of, in our case, Fanon and Eliot, we lose this subversive possibility to rethink 'the West'.

Gillian Rose, in her recent *Judaism and Modernity* (1993), confronts the 'mutual ignorance between general philosophy and modern Jewish thought' and has rightly and severely qualified the commonplace misconstruction of otherness as absolute, unchanging 'alterity'. She argues that to 'denounce [Western] reason and exalt its abused Other is to replace one mistake by another', as it disempowers, depoliticises and mutates into nihilistic dogma any understanding of *both* the 'freedom' *and* 'unfreedom' inherent within 'the West'.[18] By excluding Jewish history and the history of antisemitism from 'the West', we reinforce both an orthodox unchanging otherness, as well as an orthodox essentialised history of Jewish victimhood. This latter history, in turn, learns to narrate itself as the ultimate, because separate, form of unchanging otherness. My fear is that by excluding this historical formation from within imperial culture, many post-colonial theorists help to replicate the very oppositions that they are working against. By making Jews unambivalent - fixed in their whiteness and dominance (or, for that matter, their blackness and victimhood) - it becomes that much harder to historicise the kind of 'unstable' and 'promiscuous' identities and multiple and impure national traditions that all agree are needed to rethink the certainties of 'the West'. In the end, one can only hope that Said's consistent plea for an explicitly universalising response to suffering - so that it can be related to the suffering of others - is a lesson that both post-holocaust and post-colonial writers will eventually learn.

I am grateful to Griselda Pollock, Adrian Rifkin and Max Silverman for comments on an earlier draft of this essay.

Notes

1. I will be referring to Edward Said's corpus, in parenthesis, in the body of the text. The Penguin edition of George Eliot's *Daniel Deronda*, the Blackwood edition of Eliot's *The Impressions of Theothrastus Such* (1879), the Pluto Press edition of Frantz Fanon's *Black Skin, White Masks* (1952), and the Penguin edition of Fanon's *The Wretched of the Earth* (1961) will also be referred to in the body of the text.

2. James Young, *The Texture of Memory: Holocaust Memorials and Meaning*, Yale University Press, New Haven 1993.

3. Paul Gilroy, *The Black Atlantic: Modernity and Double Consciousness*, Verso, London 1993, chapter 6; and Cornell West, *Race Matters*, Beacon Press, New York 1993. See also Henry Louis Gates, 'Black Demagogues and Pseudo-Scholars', *New York Times*, 20 July 1992, and the misguided response to this article in *Black Books Bulletin*, vol. 16 nos, 1 and 2, Winter 1993-94.

4. Robert Young, *White Mythologies: Writing History and the West*, Routledge, London 1990, pp125, 139.

5. Letter to John Sibree, 11 February 1848, in Gordon S Haight (ed), *The George Eliot Letters: Volume 1, 1836-51*, Oxford University Press, Oxford 1954, pp246-47.

6. Cited in Martin Bernal, *Black Athena: The Afroasiatic Roots of Classical Civilization, Volume 1*, Free Association Books, London 1987, pp240-41 and chapter 5.

7. Bernal, *Black Athena*, p340 and chapter 8.

8. Letter to Harriet Beecher Stowe, 29 October 1876, in Gordon S Haight (ed), *The George Eliot Letters: Volume VI, 1874-77*, Oxford University Press, Oxford 1956, pp301-02; and Rachel Bowlby, 'Breakfast in America: *Uncle Tom's* Cultural Histories', in Homi Bhabha (ed), *Nation and Narration*, Routledge, London 1990, p200 and chapter 11.

9. Jim Reilly, *Shadowtime: History and Representation in Hardy,*

Said

Conrad and George Eliot, Routledge, London 1993, pp26-7 and p39; and Katherine Bailey Lineham, 'Mixed Politics: The Critique of Imperialism in *Daniel Deronda*', *Texas Studies in Language and Literature*, vol. 34, no. 3, Fall 1992, pp323-346.

10. Gillian Beer, *Darwin's Plots: Evolutionary Narrative in Darwin, George Eliot and Nineteenth-Century Fiction*, Routledge, London 1983, p243.

11. Cynthia Chase, 'The Decomposition of the Elephants: Double-Reading *Daniel Deronda*', *PMLA*, vol 93, 1978, pp215-27.

12. Jock McCulloch, *Black Soul, White Artifact: Fanon's Clinical Psychology and Social Theory*, Cambridge University Press, Cambridge 1983, p214 and Appendix; and Benita Parry, 'Resistance Theory/ Theorising Resistance, Or Two Cheers for Nativism', in Francis Barker et al (eds), *Colonial Discourse, Postcolonial Theory*, Manchester University Press, Manchester 1994, pp186-87.

13. Parry, *op. cit.*, p186.

14. McCulloch, *op. cit.*, p80; and Jean Paul Sartre, *Anti-Semite and Jew*, Schocken Books, New York 1948, p153.

15. Paul Gilroy, *There Ain't No Black in the Union Jack*, Hutchinson, London 1987, chapter 4.

16. See especially Sander Gilman, *The Jew's Body*, Routledge, London 1991.

17. Bryan Cheyette, *Constructions of 'the Jew' in English Literature and Society: Racial Representations, 1875-1945*, Cambridge University Press, Cambridge 1993.

18. Gillian Rose, *Judaism and Modernity: Philosophical Essays*, Blackwell, Oxford 1993, p3 and chapter 1.

HYBRIDISM AND THE ETHNICITY
OF THE ENGLISH

Robert J.C. Young

One of the most arresting aspects of *Orientalism* was Said's contention that seemingly impartial, objective academic disciplines had in fact colluded with, and indeed been instrumental in, colonial subjugation and administration. *Orientalism* provided powerful evidence of the complicity between politics and knowledge. Yet in all the work that has developed out of *Orientalism*, the charting of the collusion of Western academic knowledge with the history and ideology of European colonialism remains relatively neglected. We are only learning slowly the extraordinary extent to which European culture and, particularly academic knowledge, was implicated in the racial ideology of its time - and equally, how much that racial ideology came to define the terms of European culture. We are also only slowly discovering how much we remain implicated in that past.

Today it is customary to portray the racialism of the nineteenth century as 'pseudo-scientific', and to assume that it was mostly designed to denigrate colonised peoples. While such denigration was clearly central to racial theory, we tend be struck by what was said about Africans or other non-Europeans without noticing that in fact much of the work on race, certainly from the 1860s onwards, was devoted to analyses of European ethnicity. Of this only anti-semitism is widely known, but it was part of a much wider project of analysing European races.

Nowadays we tend to think of white English culture as relatively homogeneous, and to celebrate its challenge and diversification by ethnic minorities in Britain. In the work of contemporary cultural theorists, the term hybridity has become widely used to characterise the ethnic diversity of contemporary

British culture. What is less often recognised is that this emphasis on hybridity repeats the very way in which English culture itself was discussed according to the racialist paradigms of the nineteenth century. A recent book called *The Times Guide to the Peoples of Europe*, which seems to have been capitalising on the re-emergence of ethnic nationalism after the break up of the Soviet Union and Yugoslavia, offered itself as a piece of anthropology in which sophisticated modern Europe was startlingly represented as a collection of ethnic groups. In fact this phenomenon is part of a long and obviously still virulent tradition.

THE RACIAL PAST OF ENGLAND

If nineteenth century anthropologists such as E.B. Tylor were obsessed with the question of how much the primitive past survived in European culture, British historians were equally preoccupied with the national past, and the question of the origin of the English nation - thus betraying the extent to which 'Great Britain' has always functioned as a metonymy to mask England's domination of Wales, Scotland and Ireland. To ask who the English were inevitably moved to the question of where they came from. Broadly speaking, as MacDougal shows in *Racial Myth in English History*, there have been two myths of racial origin developed for the English.[1]

The first, put forward by Geoffrey of Monmouth in the twelfth century, and subsequently elaborated by Malory in the fifteenth, was that Britain had originally been peopled by Celts, and led by the heroic King Arthur. Eventually the conquering Arthur came to be seen as the hero of 'a composite people', uniting the Celtic Britons with the Saxons and Normans and drawing them together into a single nation. His myth was used actively by Plantagenet, Tudor and Stuart monarchs, to suggest that they were the legitimate heirs of the early British kings, and to link them to romantic British history.

However, the power of this Arthurian Celtic myth began to wane in the sixteenth century and was effectively eliminated by the so-called Glorious Revolution of 1688. It was replaced by an alternative myth: that the real British had arrived with Hengist and Horsa and the Saxon invaders who landed at Ebbsfield, Kent, in 449, and that the native Celtic Britons had subsequently been either exterminated or pushed back to the Celtic fringes of Wales, Scotland and Ireland. The subsequent arrival of the Normans in 1066 was regarded as an infringement of the true racial identity of the Saxon English: historians therefore developed the thesis of 'the Norman yoke', the best known example of which within popular culture was the struggle of Robin Hood against the Sheriff of Nottingham.[2] The significance of Magna Carta was magnified to emphasise the political liberty supposed to be intrinsic to the Saxon race, with the rest of British history portrayed as a question of freeing itself from the shackles of the Norman yoke. The apogee of this view was developed by the historian E.A. Freeman, said never to have recovered from the happy accident of his name, who developed most fully the popular ideology that intrinsic to the Anglo-Saxon character were the qualities of protestantism, freedom and liberty.[3]

The real ideological kernel of this Saxon supremacist myth of English origin was to legitimate the Reformation, and to provide a historical genealogy for the Church of England. The Saxon affiliations with the Teutonic Germans perfectly encapsulated a protestant solidarity against the wiles of Catholicism and the French. Saxonism, therefore, was always closely identified with English protestant values, which accounts for its popularity among protestant whites in the United States.[4]

This Teutonic Saxon model became dominant from the time of the Reformation onwards. What is perhaps most extraordinary about it is the way that a single remark by the early historian Gildas that the Britons had been exterminated allowed the English to claim a pure Saxon lineage for themselves. Although today this smacks of recognisable racism, up to the mid-eighteenth century at least, race was still generally thought of in terms of lineage, of an aristocratic family line, a relic of which lives on in the way some American men still embellish their name with a patriarchal 'Sr' and 'Jr', or I, II, and III, in an anxious attempt to evoke the impression of a powerful, even monarchical, family genealogy. In Britain, lineage was associated with 'stock' and 'pedigree', and thus by analogy with the breeding of domestic animals. Doubtless British pride in their racial stock connected for many with the idea of the thoroughbred animals that were the constant focus of attention in their day-to-day country life.

The first famous challenge to the Saxon supremacist view came in 1701 from Daniel Defoe. In 'The True Born Englishman', he satirised the pretensions of the Englishman to have a pedigree as pure as his horse and cattle:

> *Thus from a Mixture of all Kinds began,*
> *That Het'rogeneous Thing,* An Englishman:
> *In eager Rapes, and furious Lust begot,*
> *Betwixt a Painted* Britton *and a* Scot:
> *Whose gend'ring Offspring quickly learnt to bow,*
> *And yoke their Heifers to the* Roman *Plough:*
> *From whence a Mongrel half-bred Race there came,*
> *With neither Name nor Nation, Speech or Fame.*
> *In whose hot Veins new Mixtures quickly ran,*
> *Infus'd betwixt a* Saxon *and a* Dane.
> *While their Rank Daughters, to their Parents just,*
> *Receiv'd all Nations with Promiscuous Lust.*
> *This Nauseous Brood directly did contain*
> *The well-extracted Blood of* Englishmen.[5]

Defoe's extraordinary poem seems to have had little success in challenging the dominant Saxon ideology of English origins at the time. His satirical suggestion that the English were really a mixed race, even 'a mongrel breed' was, however, to be revived as a serious thesis in the latter part of the nineteenth century.

In 1850 the Saxon Celt rivalry was given a new twist by the publication of Robert Knox's *The Races of Men*.[6] Knox combined the new racialism of comparative anatomy with the European idea of the racial determination of history. In the *Races of Men* Knox argued that it was the violent animosity between races - an idea derived from natural history of a natural repugnance between different species - which determined the course of history; for him, as for many others, the revolutions of 1848 subsequently proved this thesis. Within a general theory of conflict between the fair and the dark races, Knox proposed a fundamental racial antagonism between the Celt and Saxon, the former of which he saw as a usurper of the superior Saxon's rightful territory. The Celt, he declared, must therefore 'be forced from the soil' (p379).

HYBRIDITY: W.F. EDWARDS

The increasing emphasis, from 1848 onwards, on the permanence of racial types, and their inalienable difference from each other, led to an ever-greater preoccupation with the implications of racial mixture. Polygenesis, or the belief that the different races should be described as different species, was first widely considered in the eighteenth century. But there was an apparently insuperable barrier to its general acceptance, in as much as the generally accepted definition of species was that the product of any sexual union between different species was infertile. The mule, the product of a horse and a donkey, was the central example of this principle. The widespread appearance in the colonies of *mulattos*, the product of unions between white and black, apparently refuted the argument that human beings were made up of different species. Monogenists such as the great English anthropologist J.C. Prichard argued for the correctness of the Biblical account in which all humans are portrayed as descended from a single source; they claimed that the variety of features of the different races were the product of climactic difference and of racial intermixture which could produce new races with new physical and mental characteristics.

The prolificness of inter-racial unions did not, however, stop other writers such as Edward Long of Jamaica from claiming that mulattos were indeed mules, if not in the first generation, then definitely by the second or third.[7] This argument was put on a more scientific footing in 1829 by another white Jamaican, by then a naturalised Frenchman, whose own life was a history of migration and transformation of cultural identity, W.F. Edwards. Edwards proposed a more sophisticated version of Long's argument which came to be called the law of decomposition.[8] His interest in the racial composition of whole nations enabled him to side-step the more or less impossible question of whether individual unions over several generations had produced fertile off-spring (anthropologists such as the American Josiah Nott argued that apparent continuing fertility between mulattos was not itself proof because their alleged licentiousness meant that it could never be assumed that they had not had a liaison with someone of pure race). Looking at populations as a whole allowed Edwards to formulate the question in a different way. He pointed out that at a national level it was never the case that two populations of exactly the same numbers came to mix; historical and geographical factors meant that in general intermixture took place only between a large population and a small alien group (for example the Norman conquerors in Britain), in which case the smaller would be absorbed by the larger, unless it remained isolated for political or religious reasons, as in the case of the Jews. For Edwards the Jews were a crucial example of the permanence of racial types. Not only, he argued, were portraits of Jews in Egyptian wall illustrations or in Renaissance paintings still recognisable as Jews, the Jewish diaspora provided crucial evidence that climate did not change human physical features, as Prichard and the monogenists had claimed. It is one of the ghastly ironies of history that the example of the Jews provided both the evidence and the model for a racial theory that was eventually to end with the attempt to exterminate them. Edwards also pointed to other examples of the fixity of morphological types such as the case of domestic animals taken from the Old World to the New. Others admiringly invoked the Indian caste system. As De Quincey put it in 1822: 'Even Englishmen ... cannot but shudder at the mystic sublimity of *castes* that have flowed apart, and refused to mix, through such immemorial tracts of time...'.[9]

Edwards' interest in the role of race in national history meant that his own sphere of interest was focused particularly on Europe. This was particularly problematic for tracing a racial genealogy. It was all very well to claim permanent difference between Europeans and Africans, with mixed-race unions becoming infertile and eventually dying out. Europe, by contrast, was historically documented as made up of a composite of races who had successively invaded and colonised the European landmass, and was frequently used by the monogenists as a refutation of permanent racial differences. Edwards' decisive move was to differentiate between different kinds of racial intermixture: he distinguished between what he considered absolutely different races and what he called closely allied races ('distant' and 'proximate'). Unions between radically different races, he argued, produced half-breeds whose progeny would eventually die out. But with similar races, the case was very different. Here Edwards cited the experiments of a Swiss scientist named Colladon who had researched into the laws of hybridization. Colladon had crossed white and grey mice, and reported that the product of these unions was not a indistinct mousey colour but mice which were definitively either grey or white. This led Edwards to claim by analogy that when European races were crossed with each other, the children similarly preserved intact the exact characteristics of just one of the parental races. Although he allowed the possibility of the production of intermediate types, Edwards suggested that these would in time revert to one or other of the original types. In what was to become the dominant theory of hybridity in the nineteenth century, racial fusion was thus impossible: it was a theory of permanent separation, of a natural apartheid between the races.

What is noticeable in this context is that Edwards used his science in order to substantiate a ready-made thesis about race that had been developed by contemporary historians. Science came to the aid of history, which meant of course that science itself was already ideologically determined. Since the Restoration it had become customary among anti-monarchical French historians to interpret the French revolution as the historical product of racial antagonism: in the *Histoire des Gaulois* (1828), Amédée Thierry argued that the ancient conflict of the Celts (or Gauls) and Belgae was still being played out in French history. Edwards was clearly attracted to the assumption in this argument that the two races, far from merging one into another, had continued in their separate ways, with the tension between them accounting for the dynamics of French history. His contribution was to suggest to Thierry that this racial difference was still discernible at a physical level in the population of France. The idea of the enduring and permanent nature of these different racial types was predicated on the Colladon thesis.

Edwards' book, *Des caractères physiologiques des races humaines, considérés dans leur rapports avec l'histoire* (1829), though little known today, was widely credited by French anthropologists and raciologists in the nineteenth century as being the founding text of French ethnology. The distinguished anthropologist Paul Broca called him 'the first author who clearly conceived and formulated the complete idea of race'.[10] Edwards' importance was the result of the fact that he succeeded in combining the purely physiological analysis of human difference (which had been well established in France since Cuvier) with the contemporary historical accounts of the moral, intellectual capacities of different nations evident in their histories and cultures. If race became the general explanatory category of nineteenth-century analysis in the humanities and social sciences, it was the result of this particular combination of physical and cultural difference. Edwards' contribution was to combine these new features in a decisive way by allying physiology and anatomy to history; to do this he produced an apparent solution to the problem of how racial difference could be combined with a history of racial fusion - a solution which by the 1860s was widely accepted throughout Europe and America as received scientific knowledge.

The tendentiousness of Edwards' evidence for the origin of this thesis is striking. The widespread acceptance of the idea throughout the nineteenth century leads one to ask how it could have been taken as fact by even the most reputable scientists such as Darwin or Tylor. Edwards' work was substantiated in 1860 by Broca's full study of hybridization among animals (including humans), a work which became the standard reference for the subject.[11] It is worth noting that Darwin's discussion of hybridism in *The Origin of Species* and *The Descent of Man* did not really arrest the Edwards thesis, because he himself used the idea that there were different degrees of interfertility between different plants and animals.[12] In his discussions of hybridity, even Darwin allows analogous evidence from plants and animals, just as the raciologists did, and it was this that appeared to substantiate the distant and proximate races theory of humans. Darwin used this evidence to undermine the distinction between species and varieties. But others invoked the notion of racial 'types' to avoid this, and by characterising types as distant or allied, utilised the idea of species difference, a difference and distinction of kind rather than merely of degree, while circumventing the problematic term. The phenomena with which this science was trying to deal were in fact outside the scope of its technical capacity, and were only understood with the advent of genetics in the twentieth century. Edwards' thesis of human hybridity was not seriously attacked until the 1930s.

His work was not only influential in Europe. It became the standard reference point for the new American Anthropological School developed by S.G. Morton and Josiah Nott. The attraction of the thesis in the United States was that it allowed apologists for slavery to claim that blacks and whites were entirely distinct races that would never succeed in intermixing, and that the white race would remain predominantly Anglo-Saxon despite the arrival of other European immigrants. Nott and Gliddon, in their *Types of Mankind* (1854), the most influential work of American anthropology of the nineteenth century, cite Edwards' work as the authority for their thesis of the permanence of racial types.[13] In Britain, probably his best-known admirer was Matthew Arnold. Said cites Matthew Arnold as one of many liberal cultural heroes who 'had definite views on race and imperialism, which are quite easily to be found at work in their writing';[14] this racialism also provided the basis for his views about English ethnicity.

MATTHEW ARNOLD AND ENGLISH ETHNICITY

Arnold's *On the Study of Celtic Literature* (1867) is now probably the best-known attack on the English-as-Saxons supremacists. In the first place, Arnold had to argue against the Saxonist view that all the Celts had been exterminated on English soil. In order to claim that the English population was still preserved as a mixture of Celt and Saxon, he invoked the work of the first person to link history with ethnography: W.F. Edwards. Arnold remarks that the book 'attracted great attention on the Continent; it fills not much more than a hundred pages, and they are a hundred pages which well deserve reading and re-reading'.[15] Arnold's comment suggests that he was unaware that Edwards was also generally acknowledged by contemporary anthropologists in Britain as the source of a racial theory based on a notion of hybridity that represented not a form of amalgamation but rather one of permanent separation. Arnold cites Edwards for the thesis that Europeans, though physically mixed, continue to bear the physical, psychological and moral characteristics of their particular racial forbears. He does not mention its corollary of allowing the idea of a polygenetic difference between black and white.

In his essay, Arnold develops a version of the older historical myth that the English were made up of a composite of Celtic and Saxon races. But his version differs from the standard Arthurian account: instead of an integrated fusion of the Celts, Saxons, and Normans, Edwards allowed him to argue that the English were made up of a dialectic of still distinct Celts and Saxons. In Edwards' theory, between allied races such as these the progeny would revert to type. If you crossed a Celt with a Saxon, you didn't get a mixed race child, for the child would turn out to be either a Celt or a Saxon. Unlike the Arthurian myth which represented the English as a composite people, an amalgamation of Celt, Saxon and Norman, Arnold's version of British history argues for a continuing racial dialectic. Edwards' thesis allows him to suggest that there has been no racial fusion, only mingling and mixture. It was only in the realms of English literature that a cultural fusion took place between the Celt and Saxon; the task of the literary critic was to detect and chart the harmonious literary resolution of this racial dialectic.

Arnold's argument that culture is generated by a racial antipathy recalls Knox's thesis of a racial antagonism between Celt and Saxon. But in so far as literature and culture resolves the antagonistic dialectical alternation between them, Arnold's model could be seen to be effectively incorporating and subsuming the two incompatible historical myths of origin of British history. Even in *Culture and Anarchy* (1869), where Celt and Saxon give way to Hellene and Hebrew, Arnold has simply extended the race-character associations of Celt and Saxon into the cultural origins of the English - classical civilisation and the bible. Only culture offers a harmonious and aesthetic resolution to the fractured historical genealogy of the English nation.[16]

In suggesting this cultural synthesis, Arnold seems to have accepted the arguments of Knox and Renan that the races themselves were antagonistic. But why did he not suggest a racial as well as a cultural amalgamation? One reason why he would have been attracted to the apartheid thesis of racial separation was that at this time mixed races had a common political connotation with something that was not dear to Arnold's heart: anarchy.

HYBRIDITY AND ANARCHY

While it was convenient to argue that, in political terms, a fusion between the different races of Britain towards a common good was desirable, Arnold's terms such as mingling or admixture always implied a physical mingling without a physical blending. His attraction to the idea that the different races could maintain their distinct racial characteristics can be allied to the fact that contemporary commentators argued that racial hybrids, as a chaotic form of 'ethnic commotion', produced political anarchy. By the 1850s it was a commonplace to point to the racial anarchy (i.e. racial intermixture) of South America and identify the political instability of its states with the 'raceless chaos' of its population. Correspondingly, the political stability of Britain was associated with the constancy of its racial type, with the high pedigree of the English breed. A forthright article in the *Anthropological Review*, reviewing J.S. Mill's *Principles of Political Economy, On Liberty* and *On Representative Government,* makes it clear that this anarchy of racial mixing was associated with the 'doing as one likes' philosophy of liberalism, which forms the object of Arnold's attack in *Culture and Anarchy*. Mill's error is specified as his 'unwise rejection of the racial element' in his political philosophy, and his lack of consideration of the differing aptitude of 'the various races for political liberty'.[17] Mill's 'deficiencies and misconceptions', in the reviewer's eyes, are augmented by his lack of reference to:

> *hybridism, as an obstruction to the formation and maintenance of a stable government. It is, of course, quite legitimate in logic, for the man who does not believe in race, to deny or ignore the existence of half-castes. But, unfortunately nature will not so ignore them, as Mexico and the South American republics have found to their cost.*

Where the parental elements are very diverse, the hybrid is himself a fermenting monstrosity. He is ever a more or less chaotic compound. He is in conflict with himself, and but too often exhibits the vices of both parents without the virtues of either. He is a blot on creation, the product of a sin against nature, whom she hastens with all possible expedition to reduce to annihilation. He is not in healthful equilibrium, whether mental or physical, and consequently cannot conduce to the stability of anything else. He is ever oscillating between his paternal and maternal proclivities. His very instincts are perverted. He unites the baseness of the negro with the aspirations of the European; and while the creature of ungovernable appetite, longs for that liberty which is only compatible with self-command. Such are the many-coloured many-featured 'curs' that abound in most of the colonial populations of modern times, produced ... by our having overstepped the boundaries of nature in the mixture of races. (p129)

As in the United States during the Civil War, where racial mixing was always associated with the liberal amalgamationists, liberal attitudes towards race were associated by those on the right with racial and political anarchy. Arnold's affiliation to the work of Edwards shows that he shared with both Edwards and Knox the same basic presuppositions about the permanence of racial types, as a natural mechanism preventing racial mixing, a guarantor of political stability and counter to working class and Irish disorder. Edwards' theory of a natural mechanism preventing racial mixing avoided the political problems associated with hybridity.

THE CELTIC CHALLENGE

Even if the Saxon myth had been able, to 'forge' the nation, by the 1860s a more substantial challenge was being mounted. During the course of the nineteenth century, the claims of the Saxon supremacists were increasingly put to the test of an empiricist history which sought to determine ever more accurately the exact details of the origin of the English. It

was the development of scientific racial theory that enabled
this project. As ethnography and the classification of racial
difference developed as a science, the possibility became
apparent that the population of Britain could be scientifically
analysed to discover the real racial composition of the British.
The historical claims of the British stock became subject to
modern, scientific ethnographic analysis. Although those who
challenged the Saxon supremacists tended to espouse the
Celtic alternative, they made their arguments by charting in
some historical detail the successive waves of invasions of the
British Isles by different European peoples. From this they
argued that the English were, after all, basically Celtic, with
some later racial admixture. This counter ethno-history was
so successful that by 1885 the ethnographer John Beddoe was
to write

> *It is not very long since educated opinion considered the*
> *English and lowland Scots an almost purely Teutonic*
> *people. Now the current runs so much the other way that I*
> *have had to take up the attitude of an apologist of the*
> *'Saxon' view.*[18]

In Britain this was the result of the fact that, from the 1860s,
attempts had been made, particularly by Beddoe himself, to test
or prove history by ethnic monitoring of the living population of
Britain.

Arnold provided only one of a series of challenges to Saxon
supremacism in the 1860s. All shared with him the assumption
that the survival of the Celt could be based on Edwards' theory
of the workings of hybridity. Critics have claimed that Arnold
himself was unaware of the contemporary ethnographic context
of Celtic challenges.[19] This is unlikely, not only because the
question of race was so well developed in *The Times* and the
quarterlies after 1848, and not only because of the extreme
racialism of Renan, Arnold's major source, but because Arnold
himself tells us of how he went to the Eisteddfod at Llandudno
and heard the recitation of the prize compositions.

These compositions were written in answer to the offer in
1864 of a prize of one hundred guineas for the best essay on

'The Origin of the English Nation' in English, Welsh, French or German. One of those written in response to this competition was by Luke Owen Pike and became the basis of his book, *The English and Their Origin: A Prologue to Authentic English History* (1866), in which he advances the thesis that the English can be shown by historical, linguistic and ethnological argument to be largely Celt.[20] Pike's work was augmented and developed two years later by Nicholas in *The Pedigree of the English People*, although its argument about the mostly Celtic character of the English was so close to Pike's that the latter successfully took him to court for plagiarism.[21]

In one significant way, Arnold himself was oddly close to Pike. In an unexpected twist, Pike argued that the Celts were actually physically descended from the ancient Greeks. When in *Celtic Literature* Arnold sets up his argument for British culture as a dialectic of the Celt and the Saxon, he himself also alludes to the similarities between the Celts and the Greeks - a connection that would be developed fully in *Culture and Anarchy* when Celtic culture is replaced by Hellenism. In that book the Saxons are also supplanted, in this case by the Jews. Arnold, I have suggested, has moved from a literal discussion of the origin to the English to metaphors of their cultural filiation. When we consider that at this time Pike was arguing that the Celts were really descended from the Greeks, it may have been that Arnold also meant it literally. Even with respect to Hebraism, it will be recalled that the very vigorous British Israelite movement in this period was also claiming that the Anglo-Saxons were actually the true descendants of the Jews.

Arnold's *On Celtic Literature* therefore, far from having a tangential relation to such discussions, was central to them and indeed was quickly picked up by contemporary ethnologists.[22] But he was not the first to offer a harmonious resolution to the racial antagonism advocated by Knox. In fact, despite the deadly seriousness of its racism, it is remarkable that Knox's book, and the new science of physiognomy, immediately called forth a number of mocking ripostes. The most striking of these is Richard Massy's *Analytical Ethnology: The Mixed Tribes in Great Britain and Ireland, and the*

Political, Physical and Metaphysical Blunderings on the Celt and Saxon Exposed (1855).[23] Massy somewhat paradoxically attempts to counter Knox with a defence of the Celts, praising them particularly for their poetic imaginative spirit, while at the same time 'casting shame upon the reckless abuse of race' (p162). Massy concludes by arguing for the integration of the British people on non-racial grounds:

> *Sprung originally from one stock, men may yet be led onwards and upwards towards one standard of perfection. But ere this can be done that jealousy of race, which had made one man an oppressor and another a slave, must be destroyed (p198).*

Massy's anti-racism shows us, pace Trilling's apology for Arnold's racialism as being excusable because so typical, the degree to which there were alternatives to Arnold's position. Arnold by no means rejected racialism, even if he was to offer a relatively benign version of it. Massy, by contrast, mocks the distinctions based on physical characteristics, for example with his wonderfully pointless comparisons between the Celtic and Saxon hand, and further, the Celtic and Saxon foot.

THE COMPARATIVE ANTHROPOLOGY OF ENGLAND AND WALES

The degree to which Arnold was participating in a culture of ethnological enquiry can be surmised from the publication the year before *Celtic Literature* of Mackintosh's 'Comparative Anthropology of England and Wales', first given as a paper to the Ethnological Society in 1861.[24] Mackintosh argued 'that distinct, hereditary, and long-persistent races or types can be traced in different districts of England'(p2). The living population literally embodied the signs of their hereditary descent and thus manifested signs of their 'typical distinctions'. We can see the degree to which Edwards' theory of hybridity had become generally accepted by this time from Mackintosh's short statement affirming the endurance of types even after some interblending or crossing of races:

Among men there would appear to be types which have become sufficiently hardened to resist amalgamation, and even in England many phenomena would seem to indicate that hybridity is followed by extinction or reversion to the original. In some parts, where interblending has occurred to a great extent, we still find distinct types identifiable with those which may be classified in remote and comparatively unmixed districts; and very frequently two or more types may be seen in the same family. In many cases, typical amalgamation does not apparently take place at all, but the children of two parents of distinct types follow or 'favour' the one or other parent, or occasionally some ancestor more or less remote (p7).

Mackintosh therefore announces that he feels justified in 'classifying the types which come under our notice as if they were unalterably fixed' (p8).

He begins by classifying four separate Welsh or Cymrian types, together with their individual 'mental characteristics' - one of which, suitably enough, is *'extreme tendency to trace back ancestry'* (p9) - and their 'moral condition', which he announces for the working class at least is higher than that in England - 'at book and music shops of a rank where in England negro melodies would form the staple compositions, Handel is the great favourite; and such tunes as *Pop goes the Weasel* would not be tolerated' (p12). The first of these Welsh types is described in notably ambiguous language as

stature various, but often tall - neck more or less long - loose gait - dark brown (often very dark) and coarse hair - eyes sunken and ill-defined, with a peculiarly close expression - dark eye-lashes and eye-brows, eye-basins more or less wrinkled. The face was long, or rather long, narrow or rather narrow, and broadest under the eyes. There was a sudden sinking in under the cheek-bones, *with denuded cheeks. The* chin was rather narrow and generally retreating, though sometimes prominent. The nose was narrow, long or rather long, much raised either in the middle or at the point, and *occasionally approaching the Jewish form (p8).*

After elaborating on the four Welsh types, Mackintosh then moves on to South Wales, where the Cymrian type gives way to what he calls the British and Gaelic types. The gaelic physiognomy is described as being characterised by a bulging prognathous upper jaw with receding chin, turned up africanoid nose with 'yawning nostrils' (p15). The Gaelic mental characteristics are characterised in terms which anticipate Arnold's: '*quick in perception*, but deficient in depth of reasoning power; headstrong and excitable; tendency to oppose; *strong in love and hate*; at one time lively, soon after sad; vivid in imagination; extremely social, with a *propensity for crowding together*; forward and self-confident; deficient in application to deep study, but possessed of *great concentration in monotonous or purely mechanical operations* ... want of prudence and foresight...' (p16). In the South of England, by contrast, lives the Saxon type. Here it is noticeable that Mackintosh becomes much more sure of himself in his description. The Saxon has regular features, 'mouth well formed ... chin neither prominent nor retreating, nose straight, neither long nor short ... general smoothness and roundness'; his mental characteristics are 'extreme moderation; absence of extraordinary talents, and equal absence of extraordinary defects, mind equally balanced; character consistent, simple, truthful, straightforward and honest... not brilliant in imagination, but sound in judgement ... tendency ... to have limited intercourse with neighbours' (p17).

THE RACES OF BRITAIN

As Mackintosh's study shows, the problem for a proper scientific analysis was how to survey people with scientific accuracy rather than impressionistically. By the 1860s however some ethnographers were beginning to take a more scientific approach. The eventual winner of the Eisteddfod prize, John Beddoe, spent a lifetime attempting to chart the exact ethnicity of the population of the British Isles. He spent almost twenty years developing his Eisteddfod prize essay into *The Races of Britain* (1885).

The book begins with an historical account of the different racial invasions, after which Beddoe reveals his detailed findings of the racial composition of Britain. His own method was not to measure skulls, in the manner of his contemporaries Davis and Thurnam (who also employ the Edwardsian hybridity thesis), but to register racial signifiers that could be observed without the subjects being aware of it.[25] Clearly the skin colour used to determine the differences between European and non-European races was of no use here, but the science of modern physiognomy required complex anthropometric measurements and appropriate machines. So Beddoe analysed instead the specific signifiers of hair and eye colour which he considered 'so nearly permanent in races of men as to be fairly trustworthy evidence in the matter of ethnical descent' (p297). These, he argued, allowed him to determine the exact racial characteristics of the inhabitants of the British Isles. To conduct his investigations, he went round the country concealing in his palm small cards, on which he marked the characteristics of those walking in the streets about him.

Beddoe's work was designed to produce an exact scientific analysis of the racial composition of the British Isles. However, it was not possible to demarcate the different areas with any exactitude. Beddoe's solution was to produce a composite portrait of the racial composition of the area. He did this primarily by colour.

> *A ready means of comparing the colours of two peoples or localities is found in the Index of Nigrescence. The gross index is gotten by subtracting the number of red and fair-hairedpersons from that of the dark-haired, together with twice the black-haired. I double the black, in order to give its proper value to the greater tendency to melanosity shown thereby; while brown (chestnut) hair is regarded as neutral*
> ...
> *[D+2N-R-F=Index.]*
> *From the gross index, the net, or percentage index, is of course readily obtained' (p5).*

Beddoe reckoned that this method was 'more apt to represent ethnological truth' than the rival German method of 'separating and estimating the pure blond and pure brunet types' (p86). It allowed Beddoe to construct maps of Britain and Europe that showed the relative comparative 'nigrescence' of each district. As well as simply tracking the alleged ethnic origins and proportions of the various parts of the British Isles, Beddoe also suggested the increasing nigresence, that is darkening, of the population as a whole, though he was reticent in his conclusions about why this was happening.

Some, such as Thomas Price, had argued that this alleged darkening of the population had simple explanations, such as the proximity of people's houses to coal mines. As a man of science, Beddoe was less speculative. However, a single paragraph is revealing:

> *That in the absence of trustworthy evidence as to a change of colour-type in Britain, in the direction of light to dark, it is best to rest upon the undoubted fact that the Gaelic and Iberian races of the west, mostly dark-haired, are tending to swamp the blond Teutons of England by a reflux migration. At the same time, the possible effects of conjugal selection, of selection through disease, and the relative increase of the darker types through the more rapid multiplication of the artizan class who are in England generally darker than the upper classes, should be kept in view (p298).*

Here Beddoe summarises his overall thesis of the increasing nigrescence of the British, covertly implying their degeneration as a result of industrialisation. At the same time his thesis of a 'reflux migration' suggests that the Celts have returned from their fringes to 'swamp' the English. As Grant Allen put it five years before in his essay, 'Are We Englishmen?': 'since the rise of the industrial system the Kelts have peacefully recovered their numerical superiority. They have crowded into the towns and seaports.'[26] In Beddoe this idea is extended to the observation that the working class in general tend to be darker than the upper classes. The exact extent of this would, however, never be known. Beddoe was involved in a later attempt of the Anthropometric Committee of the British Association for the Advancement of Science to carry out a systematic survey of the British Isles, comparable to Risley's Census of India. But it collapsed from lack of funds and from the impossible complexity of the precise anthropometric scientific data demanded. Many people, apparently, also objected to having their heads measured. Despite many efforts, a proposed Imperial Bureau of Ethnology for Greater Britain was never established.[27]

RACE AND CLASS

If we ask what all this ethnographic policing was really about, its real object seems to have been as much an inquiry into the ethnographic origins of the English as an anxious surveillance of the new industrial working class formed through emigration from the countryside and mass immigration from Ireland. The Celtic alien wedge motif goes back to the image produced by Carlyle in *Chartism* of the manly Saxon Briton being assaulted by the flood of Celtic Irish into the manufacturing towns, by way of revenge for five centuries of English abuse: 'Ireland pouring daily in on us ... deluging us down to its own waste confusion, outward and inward'. [28]

The return of the Irish seems to sparked off the dynamics of the Saxon Celt antagonism, as well as the concern about the real ethnicity of the English. At the same time, it quickly enabled the ideological assimilation of the entire industrial working class to the darker Celts. So in *Chartism*, Carlyle writes:

> *But now on the whole, it seems to us, English Statistic Science with floods of the finest peasantry in the world streaming in on us daily, may fold up her reticulations on this matter of the Working Classes; and conclude, what every man who will take the statistical spectacles off his nose, and look, may discern in town or country: That the condition of the lower multitude of English labourers approximates more and more to that of the Irish (p20).*

Five years later, in *The Condition of the Working Class in England*, Engels makes the same point:

> *For when, in almost every great city, a fifth or a quarter of the workers are Irish, or children of Irish parents, who have grown up amid Irish filth, no one can wonder if the life,*

habits, intelligence, moral status in short, the whole character of the working class, assimilates a great part of the Irish characteristics' (p126).

And by the end of the book, Engels goes even further:

Irish immigration has degraded the English workers, removed them from civilization, and aggravated the hardship of their lot; but, on the other hand, it has thereby deepened the chasm between the workers and bourgeoisie, and hastened the approaching crisis ... the working class has gradually become a race wholly apart from the English bourgeoisie (p149-50).[29]

Class division itself becomes identified with the racial difference of Saxon and Celt. This distinction is most brazenly suggested by Knox's illustrations of the Saxon and Celt in *The Races of Men*. The Irish Celts are portrayed as impoverished and overfertile, spilling out of the edges of the picture. The Saxon on the other hand is not represented directly at all, but rather through his comfortable mansion, which Knox describes as 'Standing always apart, if possible, from all others'. The bourgeois Saxon thus embodies his instinctive racial purity, freedom and love of liberty not only in his physiognomy but also in his property and home.

What is striking about the development of the discourse of racial difference in the nineteenth century is the extent to which its writers are quite up-front about the extent to which class is transformed into race. The permanence of racial type was quickly extended to class differences. This provides clear historical corroboration of the traditional Marxist argument that race is simply an ideological screen term for class. The question for today's culture and its self-conscious hybridized identity is to what extent the new ethnicities of contemporary Britain have broken out of this traditional contestatory model, and to what extent ethnicity continues to provide a means of redefining and displacing attention from the exploitation of economic power embodied in the British class system. Forms of exploitation are not uniform: as in the case of Carlyle and Knox on the Celts, ethnicity can be a means of structuring a group in a particular situation as an underclass - or, in today's parlance, an 'ethnoclass'. Though there is no longer explicit antagonism between Saxon and Celt, the conflict between fair and dark races may have simply been displaced.

Isolating different racial groups, with particular emphasis on the Irish, and attaching moral qualities to them, allowed nineteenth-century commentators to suggest a fundamental racial determinism for their condition rather than address the social and economic conditions under which they lived. Something similar happens today with the characterisation of ethnic minorities who are often only characterised as ethnic minorities because their position of special economic deprivation differentiates them from others. This allows them to be considered as both different and as a particular culture which is somehow intrinsically like that, rather than as a group that suffers an unusual degree of economic exploitation. It is no coincidence that we have reverted to the racial terminology of hybridity as the appropriate description of this characteristic of contemporary British culture.

Notes

1. Hugh A. MacDougal, *Racial Myth in English History: Trojans, Teutons, and Anglo-Saxons*, Hanover 1982.

2. See Christopher Hill, `The Norman Yoke', in *Democracy and the Labour Movement*, J. Saville (ed), London 1954.

3. Edward Augustus Freeman, *The History of the Norman Conquest of England: its Causes and its Results*, 6 vols, Oxford 1867.

4. See Reginald Horsman, *Race and Manifest Destiny: The Origins of American Racial Anglo-Saxonism*, Cambridge, Mass, 1981.

5. Daniel Defoe, `The True-Born Englishman', in J.T. Boulton (ed), *Daniel Defoe*, London 1965, pp63-4.

6. Robert Knox, *The Races of Men*, London 1850.

7. Edward Long, *The History of Jamaica. Or, General Survey of the*

Antient and Modern State of that Island; with Reflections on its Situation, Settlements, Inhabitants, Climate, Products, Commerce, Laws, And Government, 3 vols, London 1774, Vol II, p336.

8. W.F. Edwards, *Des caractères physiologiques des races humaines, considérés dans leur rapports avec l'histoire, lettre à M. Amédée Thierry, auteur de l'histoire des Gaulois*, Paris 1829.

9. Thomas De Quincey, *Confessions of an English Opium-Eater, and Other Writings*, G. Lindop (ed), Oxford 1985, p73.

10. Cited by Claude Blanckaert, 'On the Origins of French Ethnology. William Edwards and the Doctrine of Race', in George W. Stocking Jr (ed), *Bones, Bodies, Behavior. Essays on Biological Anthropology*, Madison 1988, pp18-55.

11. Pierre Paul Broca, *On the Phenomena of Hybridity in the Genus Homo [1860]*, trans. C. Carter Blake, London 1864.

12. Charles Darwin, *The Origin of Species by Means of Natural Selection, or the Preservation of the Favoured Races in the Struggle for Life [1859]*, J.W. Burrow (ed), Harmondsworth 1968, pp264-90; and *The Descent of Man and Selection in Relation to Sex [1871]*, London 1901, pp257-308.

13. Josiah Nott and George R. Gliddon, *Types of Mankind: or, Ethnological Researches, Based upon the Ancient Monuments, Paintings, Sculptures, and Crania of Races, and upon their Natural, Geographical, Philological, and Biblical History*, London 1854, p93.

14. Edward W. Said, *Orientalism: Western Representations of the Orient*, London 1978.

15. Matthew Arnold, *On the Study of Celtic Literature, in Lectures and Essays in Criticism*, R.H. Super (ed), Ann Arbor 1962, p339.

16. Matthew Arnold, *Culture and Anarchy, with Friendship's Garland and Some Literary Essays*, R.H. Super (ed), Ann Arbor 1965.

17. F.W. Farrar, 'Race in Legislation and Political Economy', *Anthropological Review* 4 1866, p113-35.

18. John Beddoe, *The Races of Britain: A Contribution to the Anthropology of Western Europe*, Bristol 1885, p297.

19. Frederic E. Faverty, *Matthew Arnold, the Ethnologist*, Northwestern University Press, Evanston 1951.

20. Luke Owen Pike, *The English and Their Origin: A Prologue to Authentic English History*, London 1866.

21. See 'The Origin of the English. Pike v. Nicholas', *Anthropological Review* 7 1869, pp279-306.

22. Thomas Nicolas, *The Pedigree of the English People*, London 1868; and J.W. Jackson, 'The Race Question in Ireland', *Anthropological Review* 7 1869, pp54-76.

23. Richard Massy, *Analytical Ethnology: The Mixed Tribes in Great Britain and Ireland, and the Political, Physical and Metaphysical Blunderings on the Celt and Saxon Exposed*, London 1855.

24. D. Mackintosh, 'Comparative Anthropology of England and Wales', *Anthropological Review* 4 1866, pp1-21.

25. J.B. Davis, and J. Thurnam, *Crania Britannica. Delineations and Descriptions of the Skulls of the Aboriginal and Early Inhabitants of the British Isles: With Notices of their Other Remains*, 2 vols, London 1865.

26. Grant Allen, 'Are We Englishmen?', Cornhill, 1880, p253.

27. See James Urry, 'Englishmen, Celts and Iberians. The Ethnographic Survey of the United Kingdom 1892-1899', in George W. Stocking Jr (ed), *Functionalism Historicized. Essays in British Social Anthropology*, Madison 1984, pp83-105.

28. Thomas Carlyle, *Chartism [1839]*, London 1889, p20.

29. Friedrich Engels, *The Condition of the Working Class in England*, Victor Kiernan (ed), Harmondsworth 1987.

SECULAR CRITICISM AND THE POLITICS OF RELIGIOUS DISSENT

Gauri Viswanathan

DISSENT AND THE STATE

'Secular criticism', Edward Said's term to characterise intellectual work opposed to prevailing orthodoxies and mainstream ideologies, conceives of dissent from established principles as essentially a form of resistance to religious authority. Said points to Orientalism as an outstanding example of religious discourse in that 'each serves as an agent of closure, shutting off human investigation, criticism, and effort in deference to the authority of the more-than-human, the supernatural, the other-worldly.'[1] One of the most powerful associations that Said makes in these formulations, which carry over forcefully into the final chapters of *Culture and Imperialism* (1993), compels the recognition of both culture and religion as systems of authority which operate in parallel ways to establish criteria for membership, command allegiance, and substitute shared values for individual critical consciousness. Indeed, scepticism and questioning, which are activities properly associated with intellectual work, are considered heresies in a religious order, and it is Said's particular brilliance to show how readily cultural criticism acquires a heretical cast even in a supposedly secular climate wherever revered cultural icons are challenged; the slide from criticism to heresy, his work suggests, is a function of the prevailing hold of a cultural discourse that evokes the authority of religion to establish its own norms. Therefore, when Said urges the practice of 'secular' criticism, he seeks to recover the oppositional quality of contemporary scholarship from the guild mentality that enjoins unreflecting obedience to abstract notions like 'nation', 'community', and 'culture'.

Said's careful positioning of secular criticism within an interpretive community tightly governed by ruling orthodoxies is all the more striking because it replicates an historical move, not just from a religious to a secular culture as might be supposed, but from an established to a dissenting ecclesiastical tradition, and it is in the latter transition that the full complexities of Said's understanding of secular criticism can be most sharply discerned. The articulation of religious dissent is of special significance by the mid-nineteenth century precisely because it coincides with national and state formation on emancipatory, legislative principles of tolerance and inclusiveness - a process that might be expected to produce a seamless transition from an exclusionary, monolithic religious culture to a more open, pluralistic one, obliged by law to desist from deciding theological truth and leave matters of faith to private judgment. As long as a dissenter's beliefs were basically compatible with the doctrines laid down in the church's articles, the question of heresy did not arise: what might have been an opinion contrary to accepted doctrinal meaning was non-heretical by the standards of compatibility. Accentuated by the spirit of secularisation, the new tolerance may have been the first step towards separating religious belief from social, or legal, identity.

But if the historical choices for the determination of individual identity have been either religious authority or legislative reasoning, what if the place of private judgment in relation to public doctrine, be it about divinity or the nation? Or, as John Henry Newman asked in *Loss and Gain* (1848), can independence of judgment ever be reconciled with party affiliation and system-building? In societies where the concept of heresy still prevails as a religious concept, it is assumed that private belief has no place whatsoever, its potential expression effectively usurped by public doctrine. On the other hand, in a disestablished society where 'truth' is a function of what is codifiable and administrable, private judgment definitionally has no legal standing because it falls outside the codified precepts of secular civil society.

Even within the terms of Said's analysis, the difficulties of the intellectual vocation are embedded within a series of competing affiliations - between what Said describes as culture and system; but this can be extended further to refer to other contrastive pairs of affiliations, such as nation and religion, tradition and belief, or collective memory and experience. Historically, these competing affiliations are constitutive of the inclusive discourses of the modern secular state, since the dual allegiances that an individual may theoretically hold in a state self-constituted as liberal and tolerant (e.g. one may be both a member of a minority group or religious sect *and* a member of the national collectivity) produce the necessary tension that enables a certain type of critical activity in the first place. Said's larger point is that what is often at stake in dissent is resisting the transformation of criticism into either an act of citizenship - a performative gesture of membership in a self-selecting guild - or an act of withdrawal into a self-enclosed space of particularism or separatism. So that while Said seems to be polarising terms like secular/religious, critic/cleric, human history/sacred time, worldly/mystical, his insistence that culture is a site for hegemonising tendencies, open to co-optation by the state for its own purposes (with regard to both the colonial and the postcolonial state, Orientalism, of course, is its most egregious example), places dissent in a much more complex, adversarial relation not only to religious orthodoxy but also to state hegemony.

In the great movements of secularisation since the nineteenth century it is possible to discern, if not the origins of modern religious and ethnic strife, at least prototypical enactments of the drama of citizenship - a drama which unendingly complicated itself by questioning and rethinking the possibilities of dual allegiances brought on by such things as, in England for instance, legislation to enfranchise religious minorities in the wake of national union and disestablishment: could an Englishman be both English *and* Catholic, or Jewish, or Nonconformist, without undermining the historical progression towards a secular, national identity which resisted invoking religious difference?

If nationalism can be defined as the total set of representational practices that establish the grounds of nationality, then terms like 'cultural nationalism' or 'religious nationalism' already assume a seamless unity of aspirations, a selection and filtering that irons out the contradictions embedded in the construction of national identity from the fragments of religious, racial, cultural, and other forms of self-identification.

Peter van der Veer cautions us against this totalising approach and urges that 'we should take religious discourse and practice as constitutive of changing social identities, rather than treating them as ideological smoke screens that hide the real clash of material interests and social classes.'[2] However forcefully allegories of the nation constituting the history of modern secularism might draw attention to the teleology of its own formation, the narratives produced in the crucial space of negotiation between national and religious identity yield the most visible light on the strains and stresses in community self-identification.

If the historical role of dissent has been not only to question church orthodoxies but also to unbuckle the consolidating ambitions of the secular state under which former religious orthodoxies are subsumed, it is also at this juncture that criticism comes dangerously close to slipping into a separatist, sectarian mode while resisting a citizenship function. This particular turn reveals a dramatic gap between private belief and the ideology of nationhood, that can only be closed by an effective mediation between religious and national identity.

It is precisely this awareness of the critical nature of dissent to succumb to the fatal alternatives of citizenship or separatism that shapes the career of the nineteenth century's most celebrated convert, John Henry Newman, and conducts him from pure theological exposition towards literary and philosophical criticism. His *A Grammar of Assent* (1870) works through a number of carefully considered critical moves that retrace the stages of his own conversion, ultimately to posit Catholicism as a transreligious, transnational force, which, far from being separatist or sectarian, appeared to Newman to perfect the idea of the English nation. The universalism underlying this formation is won by translating the terms of assent to the existence of 'One God', narrowly conceived in terms of Catholic dogma, into a grammar of dissent from all forms of rational, codified systems of thought that exist to induce membership into an interpretive community framed in terms of national belonging. Newman's universalism seeks to go *beyond* the nation, and in that sense aspires to bypass both citizenship and separatism. However, it turns out to be a universalism that works regressively, not only by re-introducing religious identity as both contained in and transcending national identity, but also by locating in the authority of Catholicism the foundational structure of true Englishness. In short, Newman's transnational solution, while enabling philosophical criticism to continue its worldly engagement and, at the same time, resist both affirmative and rejectionist positions, cannot effectively disentangle belief from structures of authority, despite the privileging of popular imagination and intuition over rationality and elite modes of intellectual apprehension.

I should state at the outset that by drawing on Newman to illuminate Said's notion of secular criticism I do not mean at all to suggest a direct correspondence between Newman and Said or to place them both within a single paradigm, but rather to locate an historical moment of such rapidly shifting power bases that, with disestablishment, the notion of existing power structures itself becomes destabilised, and an original defence of Anglicanism turns into a dissent from it, as it was for Newman and other Tractarians. Newman's conversion encapsulates the contradictions of this historical moment, where authority shifts from religion to the legal rationality of the state. The question that interests me is what the idea of 'received notions' means in moments of historical change, such as during the move towards national union. Conceived in response to such historical change, Newman's transnationalism is riddled with contradictions, because by positioning popular Roman Catholicism as a point *outside* established structures he believed he was disentangling authority from state power and separating real assents (involving independent judgment) from notional assents (based on received notions). What Newman's conversion demonstrates so powerfully is the very instability, the shifting ground, of concepts like 'radical', 'authority', and 'existing power structures', which, when historicised, fully reveal their re-orientation in dissent.

The most striking feature of the emergence of a culture of conversion-as-dissent is its contrast to a monolithic, exclusionary culture in which conversion functions as a sign of assimilation to the dominant group - a gesture of acquiescence, a capitulation to the pragmatics of survival, where individuals either adopt the religion that will admit them to certain rights and privileges or otherwise accept the consequences of being made outcasts. Indeed, it would be fair to say that conversion in an era of religious tolerance functions as an expression of resistance to the centralising tendencies of national formation. The blurring of differences between religious groups simultaneously produces a defiant reaction to preserve difference even while acknowledging the need for national identification. As a mode of preserving heterogeneity against the homogenising impact of the state, conversion acquires an oppositional character that conflicts with its customary description as assimilative or adaptive.

Yet I shall also argue that the central paradox of conversion as an oppositional gesture reveals that its assumption of individual identity and autonomy is a fiction produced by the state, which, as the source of the legal enfranchisement of religious minorities, is also the origin of the resistance to the pressure of a threatening homogenisation. Not only is conversion as a mode of resistance enabled by the pluralistic possibilities of legal emancipation, but the ideology of individualism celebrated in conversion narratives does far more to affirm the liberal, tolerant, and pluralistic foundations of the modern secular state than civil enfranchisement itself. The climate of religious tolerance highlights the operations of free will with which conversion becomes inextricably associated. Conversion testimonies, even those set against an unlikely background such as the civil courts, unfold as a drama of subjectivity - of an emerging individual identity confronting the classificatory machinery of state apparatuses, a subjectivity produced not as a function of epiphanic awakening but in the intersections of law, nation, and sectarian society.[3]

At this juncture I want to return to a point made earlier about the sobering possibilities of modern criticism being reduced to an act of either citizenship or separatism, to emphasise, once again, that the nature of religious dissent is no less subject to these twin perils. Furthermore, it is equally crucial to recognise that the ways dissent cuts a path between and beyond acts of either total participation or total withdrawal is as pertinent to the articulation of a radical brand of secular criticism, as Edward Said conceives it, as it is to the mediation of sectarian tensions, particularly where, as in Ashis Nandy's work, these tensions are reductively represented as existing between the state and the people, or between secularism and popular religion.[4] While Nandy makes a significant contribution in demonstrating that the colonial state is one of the primary historical causes for prioritising, national identifications at the expense of local affiliations, and while he is certainly correct to suggest that secularism has so far polarised religious belief as to reduce the latter to religious ideology, his analysis suffers from the very tendency he critiques, for he fetishises the popular faith of the masses in much the same way that secularism, in his view, fetishises the state. Furthermore, though Nandy tries to provide a corrective to the dismissal of religion as belief, he provides too neat a scheme whereby secularism in its ideal manifestation must be essentially syncretic, 'non-monolithic and operationally plural', whereas, he argues, all other forms of secularism that require national identification are inherently flawed because they can treat religion as nothing other than ideology.[5]

Ashis Nandy is probably right to challenge the secular identification of religious tolerance with the separation of private and public spheres and with economic and legal rationality, and his attempt to demonstrate the ideological underpinnings of such identifications has produced one of the most uncompromising anti-state critiques in the discourse of contemporary Indian politics. But in dissenting from the state's refusal to concede the autonomy of popular belief, Nandy comes perilously close to endorsing a sectarian stance that privileges 'the people' and treats people's beliefs as uncontaminated by ideology or elite manipulation. His undiluted faith in the continuing vitality of religion as a 'living reality' in the lives of people, independent of the state's secular character, re-asserts the split between private and public spheres and treats people's beliefs and state ideology as essentially non-interactive. Nandy's idea of religion revives a romanticised image of 'the people' as the true but unacknowledged repository of belief.

By contrast, in exploring the paradox that, though beliefs were necessarily private, sectarian allegiance in mid-nineteenth-century Britain was nonetheless highly public, Hugh McLeod's important work on working-class religion forces a re-evaluation of the effect of popular dissent on secular authority, particularly as it is seen in the intertwining of religious belief and the ideology of the secular state - a focal point that Ashis Nandy evades in his own account. Indeed, McLeod goes so far as to suggest that in nineteenth-century England sectarian allegiance ranked next to class as the most important source of social identity, an observation that takes issue with E.P. Thompson's contention in *The Making of the English Working Class* (1966) that Methodist conversions were made in the 1790s to offer solace to the economically depressed working classes of industrial English towns.[6] But in making this assertion, McLeod is clearly not seeking to endorse sectarianism as a legitimate public ideology or a superior alternative to identification with the nation, or even to claim a separate and privileged status for popular belief. Rather, he appears to be arguing that sectarian identity was a popular mode of dissent to reconstitute a public space for the legitimate assertion of working-class aspirations, including the demand for the franchise. In McLeod's reading of working-class radicalism, dissent has less to do with recovering the autonomy of popular religion than with making the state answerable to its deliberate exclusion (through its legislative apparatus) of the self-definitions of its various constituent members, especially self-perceptions that cannot be accommodated by the classificatory system of the state. (In this connection, the onslaught on Parliament by the anti-Catholic masses in Dickens' *Barnaby Rudge* introduces an extraordinarily subversive note into the novel, particularly because the work appears to espouse the cause of the tolerant state against the encroachments of militant Protestantism, even as it sympathises with the working-class demand for equal representation in Parliament.)

But the more important question still remains fundamentally unchanged: how does dissent secure a critical position for itself from which it resists both the blandishments of a citizenship function and sectarian tendencies? For even in the case studies provided by McLeod, sectarianism is still an instrument for the attainment of working-class ends and the mode through which dissent is expressed. The horrifying reality of a work like *Barnaby Rudge* is that Dickens confers an overpowering agency on sectarianism as the only effective means available to the English poor to press their demands for the franchise. Their bigoted cries of 'No Popery!' slide indistinguishably into equally vehement calls of 'No Property!', an obvious reference to the property qualification for parliamentary representation. The search for an adequate critical position for the articulation of dissent, which eschews the extremes of total membership or total retreat, is obviously complicated by the history of English working-class radicalism, which employs separatist, sectarian strategies to seek accommodation within the public structures of English democracy. One of the most powerful images in Dickens' novel is that of the rampaging English mobs taking over the streets of London to converge on the most public of English national symbols - the Houses of Parliament - in a bid to reverse the exclusionary character of the English political process, a process that is willing to alleviate restrictions against religious minorities but cannot extend its tolerant arm to eradicate class distinctions.

All this is by way of saying that the simplified opposition between militant religious fundamentalism and the secular state fails to establish the extent to which the public sphere continues to remain a contested terrain for the reclamation of belief. 'Belief' can now be more precisely defined against the backdrop of nineteenth-century social history as a reference, not to doctrinal authority, but to the aspirations, understandings, expectations, needs, and goals that constitute the self-definitions of people, the very content of which is denied or suppressed in the construction of their legal or social identity. John Henry Newman clearly saw that what was at stake in his conversion at an immediate level, and in philosophical criticism at a larger level, was the recovery of belief not as private epiphany but as worldly activity. In the popular demand for the franchise, viewed as the carrier of people's self-definitions, Newman found the most coherent expression of that belief, the full acknowledgment of which by the state would establish its own claims to tolerance. That Newman saw the potential anarchy of the masses' total enfranchisement as being offset by a return to a foundational authority - that of Catholicism - overtly compromised the populist cause that he espoused, and revealed that at the base of his desire for a strengthened and fully enfranchised England lay the expectation of a fully restored ecclesiastical authority.

NEWMAN AND THE NINETEENTH CENTURY BRITISH STATE

Legal emancipation and enfranchisement, in opening up a different perspective to analyse conversion experiences and histories, are thus the starting-point for any productive discussion of John Henry Newman that does not limit itself to finer points of theology. Newman's conversion to Roman Catholicism can be read, not simply as progressive spiritual awakening, but as a passionate reaction against the absorption of religious sects and denominations into a diluted form of Anglicanism, stripped of its ecclesiastical influence. Suspicious of tolerance as a real aim of parliamentary reform, Newman at an earlier point in his career strenuously opposed the proposed Catholic emancipation bills as part of a progressive strategy to erode the authority of the Church of England. But, influenced to some extent by Richard Whately's writings on disestablishment, Newman later changed his position and began to subscribe to the course of national developments in limiting the reach of the Anglican church. In 1845, he converted to Roman Catholicism partly out of a recognition that narrow sectarian interests were no longer politically tenable. Thereafter, Newman proposed the 'stark alternative' of Roman Catholicism as the only bulwark against the infidelity towards which all other forms of Christianity tended.[7] If Newman's conversion was deeply motivated by a fundamental urge to restore unity of religious opinion, it was substantially assisted by his gradual acceptance of disestablishment in order, as he claimed, to 'fight the enemy on better ground and to more advantage'.[8] Personally he believed that 'the most natural and becoming state of things' was for the 'aristocratic power' to be the upholder of the Church: and yet he could not deny 'the plain fact' that 'in most ages the latter has been based on a popular power'.[9]

Newman's populist turn gave him the necessary cover to launch a blistering attack on 'crypto-infidelity' - his pejorative term to describe the dismantling of the established church - which, he declared, was hiding behind the screen of parliamentary and civic reform; further, it enabled him to argue that the reforming party's aim of removing civil disabilities against religious minorities obscured its resistance to what should have been an equally pressing parliamentary cause, the extension of the franchise to all social classes. Newman's position is exceedingly difficult to characterise, because while he was indefensibly reactionary in his support of establishment principles, he was at the same time devastatingly critical of the consolidated wealth of the clergy and the aristocracy and of their exclusive promotion of high bourgeois culture.

Newman's work thus simultaneously embraces contrary positions within a wide spectrum of possible positions, ranging from an identification with aristocratic privilege to an espousal of popular radicalism; and this is largely because his unbuckling of the ideology of tolerance shifts alternatively between a class-based critique, where he freely draws upon libertarian notions, and an orthodox religious position, which seeks to unmask the anti-ecclesiastical impulses of the modern secular state. Stephen Thomas astutely observes that the success of Newman's polemic lay in his use of rhetorical analogies between the fourth-century heresies of the early church and the liberal forces of his own time, which, Newman was convinced, conspired to destroy Christian authority under the umbrella of utilitarian reform. Heresy, remarks Thomas, becomes for Newman rather 'a function within a shifting set of strategies than the object of sustained reflection.'[10] But the real ingeniousness of Newman's argument lay in redefining heresy, not as an action against church and state as it was in an earlier, more unified era, but as a directive *sponsored* by the state. In redirecting the goal of a fully emancipated society instead towards what he considered the lesser objective of absorbing religious minorities, parliamentary reform represented the ultimate subversion for Newman. His conversion of the parliamentary discourse of religious enfranchisement into the language of heresy enabled him to restrict the idea of inclusiveness to principles of social equality, and so preclude religious or cultural relativism as admissible in the tolerant state's incorporative philosophy.

Modern criticism's predilection for analysing religious discourse as disinterested and deliberately disengaged from material conflicts is obviated by the discourse itself, which, I suggest certainly in Newman's case, is *openly* engaged with the

problem of articulating the political aspirations of what
Newman called the uneducated masses, for whom religious
identification is increasingly represented as a means of contesting
the selective logic of legislative reform. In other words, Newman's
religious discourse is much more actively pursuing these
identifications, and their embeddedness in class interests, that
it is displacing them. Re-positioned thus in the politics of
disestablishment and prospective national union, Newman's
conversion is less a private event of sudden spiritual illumination
than an interpretive index of the main currents of contemporary
social legislation and the direction of national consolidation upon
which he imagined it to be premised.

Newman's own dissent from the established church, while
influenced by his increasing interest in ' look[ing] to the people',
was based on an *a priori* reasoning that distinguished between
centralisation and democratisation.[11] In identifying himself with
the people to restore the power of Christian belief to English
society, Newman consciously separated the 'nation' from the
'state' and associated the 'state' with pernicious bureaucratising,
hierarchical, and classificatory tendencies, and the 'nation' with
community-centred local experience. But though Newman did
acknowledge that centralisation, while destroying local
influences, also proceeded simultaneously with the Reform Bill
of 1832, the democratisation that the Reform Bill ideally
embodied appeared to him to represent the autonomous power
of the popular will, which aimed 'to supersede the necessity of a
government, and to make the House of Commons, and so the
people, their own rulers.' Newman's novel *Loss and Gain* makes
a trenchant critique of the English state's alienation from the
masses of people, who remain unaffected by the legislative
reforms leading up to and following the 1832 Reform Bill.[12] In a
passage that erupts unexpectedly out of an otherwise placid
conversation among several Oxford students about contemporary
religious controversies, Newman has Carlton, one of his more
politically observant characters, remark that

> *agitation is getting to be recognised as the legitimate*
> *instrument by which the masses make their desires known,*
> *and secure the accomplishment of them. Just as a bill*

passes in parliament, after certain readings discussions,
speeches, votings, and the like, so the process by which an
act of the popular law becomes law is a long agitation,
issuing in petitions, previous to and concurrent with the
parliamentary process.'[13]

Indeed, Newman's enthusiasm for a recentring of English politics in the people led him to see a disestablished and popular Roman Catholicism as the only credible means of recovering the unified religious culture of the primitive church, lost since the time of the early church fathers.

Newman's syncretic vision, compounded by a nostalgia for an originary community disrupted by the equally sectarian forces of papism and protestantism, expressed a deep revulsion from government in favour of the people. However, it was a vision that was blind to the state as the source of a series of orchestrated political and legal moves that gestured towards emancipation of religious minorities, but ultimately with the objective of forging a common English national identity out of the materials of pluralism and tolerance. For Newman's own developing romance with popular radicalism and cultural universalism was not undermining of the state as he thought it was, which suggests that the hidden meaning of religious tolerance could well lie in its cultivating a sense of a common, or even national, identity, engendered by the *mythos* of the people as the real nation before the nation. Newman's nostalgic yearning for a unified religious culture no longer subject to sectarian struggle is at the same time an expression of the will to national unity emanating from the state, whereby syncretism is the ideological expression of what is presumed to be innate. Newman's radical espousal of Roman Catholicism may have given voice to populist dissent from establishment ideology, but this dissent was also a precondition for the process of centralisation that followed the disempowerment of ecclesiastical authority - a process that Newman, for reasons having to do with his own pronounced, earlier Tory stand against Catholic emancipation, rejected as having the potential to construct a syncretic identity out of the materials of emancipatory civil legislation. Such legislation, in effacing class interests, obscured for Newman the English parliament's continued investment in the absorption of religious minorities, and so he continued to read every parliamentary attempt to relax restrictions against excluded religious groups as an onslaught on truth itself.

'THE WORLDLINESS OF BELIEF'

More than either his celebrated memoir *Apologia Pro Vita Sua* (1864) or his novel *Loss and Gain* (1848), Newman's *A Grammar of Assent* (1870) attempts to resolve the ambiguity of a cultural identity split between religion and nation, by forging a middle ground that might be termed 'the worldliness of belief'.[14] *A Grammar of Assent* could easily be retitled 'a grammar of dissent' in its detachment of Catholic belief from established structures and institutional practices, including the discourses of education, metaphysics, literary criticism, and law.[15] The clear aim of this literary and philosophical work is to turn Newman's own conversion into praxis - the action of belief on the world, or what Newman calls a real assent, to distinguish it from notional assent to abstract propositions that attach themselves to systems. But praxis for Newman also entailed developing a dynamic *critical* practice that negotiates between consensual interpretations and private judgment. Belief-as-dissent refers back to history and to the world by moving beyond the text, and beyond provisional understandings of experience based on abstract propositions. As Edward Norman points out, Newman acknowledged the impact of history and the mutations of ideas and cultures on belief systems, maintaining that 'doctrines and views which relate to man are not placed in a void, but in the crowded world, and make way for themselves by interpenetration, and develop by absorption.'[16] In setting down as a condition for belief a disembodied subject severed from an interpretive community, Newman attempted to pry his readers away from the cumulative history of assents embodied in abstract propositions and move them, by examining the grounds of the notional, to the level of 'real assent'. Newman's worldly project is an attempt to re-insert belief into history by a disruptive technique of questioning all previous assents.

By 1845, the year of his conversion, it was clear to Newman

that the Anglican church was too hopelessly mired in its own troubles to provide a creative solution to problems of authority and identity. He made no effort to conceal his alarm that Anglicanism was tending towards the status of secular law, a set of prescriptions by which the nation was to be governed rather than a set of living principles or ideas providing the defining strokes of cultural identity: 'I confess to much suspicion of legal proceedings and legal arguments, when used in questions whether of history or of philosophy. Why am I to begin with taking up a position not my own, and unclothing my mind of that large outfit of existing thoughts, principles, likings, desires, and hopes which make me what I am?' (*GA*, p329). But simultaneously Newman also recognised that one of the ironic effects of the privatisation of belief was that individual faith, by definition, lay beyond the interpretive net of state power, and he saw in this condition fresh possibilities for the articulation of dissent. The freedom opened up by a position lying outside the legislative functions of the state pushed Newman to explore the role of what he called 'personal knowledge' in the construction of the world, even as he simultaneously sought the legitimation of belief in the public sphere. If the turn towards re-centring faith in the subjectivity of knowledge-production often occurs in periods of crisis and cultural change, Newman's critical practice as revealed particularly in *A Grammar of Assent* must be considered a barometer of the deep-rooted intellectual crisis of his time brought on by the paradigmatic shifts in relations between religion and nation.

Newman's extreme conservatism where religious authority is concerned often showed up points of unexpected transformation: for instance, his qualification of received church dogma and his turning to a form of belief that he equates with 'personal knowledge'. The terms in which he presents his theory of assent gradually turn backwards on themselves, so that what appears to be about assent is really descriptive of *dissent*. Even while making the assertion that he 'wished to trace the process by which the mind arrives, not only at a notional, but at an imaginative or real assent to the doctrine that there is One God' (*GA*, p108), Newman distances himself from the 'notional apprehension' of theology and allies his project with the revival of religion which, in its characterisation as 'imaginative', allows him to establish a case for the legitimacy of aspiration, goals, and thoughts expressed by the uneducated masses.

The stress on the imagination, which commits Newman to a theory of the materiality and immediacy of image and sense-objects perceived 'as we might map a country which we had never seen' (*GA*, p95), suggests that he was less interested in propounding orthodox Catholic doctrine than in showing how the *ordinary* person gains an image of divinity and gives a real assent to the existence of divinity. If reason creates a confined circle that defines the parameters of English nationhood, then imagination expands that circle to allow for an identity that transcends nation. A form of Catholicism that is pre-Anglican in its spirit becomes for Newman a focal point for the dissolution of all class differences, embodying a transnationalism in the service of which his own anti-statism is employed. Yet the inevitability of submission to some form of authority remains unchallenged by Newman, though he was continually plagued by how that authority was to be defined.[17]

But in the long run, what promises to be a work that attempts to guide cultural criticism towards the realm of action - the action of belief-as-dissent - turns into a mere protocol of possible critical strategies, a description of mental phenomena that outlines a dynamic critical practice aimed at disempowering notional assent to foundational premises, yet really never manages to enter the realm of action nor remains engaged with the materiality of historical change. In *A Grammar of Assent* an epistemology of critical practice replaces, rather than complements as its possibilities originally suggested, the historical project of realising the 'worldliness of belief'. An ethics of withdrawal, which Newman names 'a state of repose', or 'a tranquil enjoyment of certitude', (*GA*, p166) marks the ultimately non-activist nature of his dissent. The concept of intellectual work and thought as materiality - of the dynamism of mental processes in reconstituting and influencing conduct and perceptions-is abandoned as the gains of personal knowledge become no more than private acquisitions.

In such instances of certitude, the previous labour of coming

*to a conclusion and the repose of mind attendant on an
assent to its truth, often counteract whatever of lively
sensation the fact thus concluded is in itself adapted to
excite . . . Hence it is: that literary or scientific men, who
may have investigated some difficult point of history,
philosophy, or physics, and have come to their own settled
conclusion about it, having had a perfect right to form one,
are far more disposed to be silent as to their convictions,
and to let others alone, than partisans on either side of the
question, who take it up with less thought and seriousness*
(GA, p143).

In these lines Newman argues against the motive-force of
intellectual work as essentially proselytising in nature: that is,
if one has been won over to a proposition by an arduous process
of dissent, one will seek to spread that 'truth' among others. In
fact, Newman insists on equating such an impulse with a lack of
commitment to convictions and locates its treacherous source
in tolerance, which, with its too ready openness to contrary views
and unthinking relativism, encourages people to thrust their
half-baked views on others (*GA* p165). 'Intellectual anxiety', he
surmises, underlies the need to disseminate far and wide the
half-truths that pass off as deep conviction (*GA*, p167). While
commanding a certain respect for the refusal to universalise the
products of mental labour, statements of this kind revert to the
idea of conversion as an intensely private experience, which,
when truly grasped, leads to the withdrawal of the individual
from a larger collectivity. Newman's own investment in the
worldliness of belief is considerably eroded by this unexpected
shift of perspective, signifying his own retreat into a rhetoric of
self-fashioning.

But even this shift would be acceptable were it not for the
fact that Newman's narcotic view of 'repose' does not extend to
the dogmatic, proselytising role he has already pre-assigned
Catholicism, which is invested with such aggressive authority
as to discountenance all dissent.

*Suppose certain Bishops and priests at this day began to
teach that Islamism or Buddhism was a direct and*

immediate revelation from God, she [the Catholic Church] would be bound to use the authority which God has given her to declare that such a proposition will not stand with Christianity, and those who hold it are none of hers; and she would be bound to impose such a declaration on that very knot of persons who had committed themselves to the novel proposition, in order that, if they would not recant, they might be separated from her communion, as they were separate from her faith (GA, p100).

What is remarkable about this passage is how swiftly Newman has detached personal knowledge from the formalised, rigid system of institutional Catholicism, which is given as timeless and immutable and totally unresponsive to the exigencies of history, circumstance, or experience. The dynamism of belief has no place here, and Newman's categorical imperiousness confers an autonomous power on orthodox Catholicism as religious system, in stark contrast to Newman's otherwise historical engagement where he could write about 'great events happening at home and abroad, which brought out into form and passionate expression the various beliefs which had so gradually been winning their way into my mind.'[18]

The stasis of development reached by Newman's critical practice replicates the undifferentiated experience of conversion as this experience is represented in Newman's work. In reducing conversion to a form of change that is *not* real change, Newman neutralises the radical characterisation of dissent and renders it into a discovery of what is already present: a universal, transnational Catholicism that is both the method and the endpoint of all world religions. Newman's inability to realise the radicalism of his initial moves is a measure of his own difficulties in negotiating a viable relation between religion and nation. The pressure to achieve compatibility between two contrary affiliations was more easily resolved in a critical epistemology of belief-as-dissent than in praxis. The sustained and unresolvable tension between Catholicism and Englishness inevitably diluted the efficacy of Newman's dissent from Anglicanism and rendered it homogeneous with assent to prevailing secular norms - in short, to the construction of English nationhood, in the service of which his own conversion is then sacrificed.

Newman's call for reinstituting structures of authority that are not derived from the nation-state (i.e. from Catholicism) proves nothing other than that he wanted to dissolve the state altogether. The Catholicism that Newman affirms, which is much closer to the faith of pre-Reformation England, is a diluted version of the ultramontanism (a movement advocating papal supremacy) that was then fashionable in Roman Catholicism, but with which Newman was by and large uncomfortable. Embedded in the universalist affirmation is a return to origins that prescribes a specific agenda for the English nation, which is resituated globally not as the renegade nation that broke away from Rome but as the imperial centre of what is posited by Newman as the only true world religion. Newman's vision for English Catholicism readily incorporated England's colonial ventures as a logical and inevitable part of its own self-definition as global in reach.

Newman's ultimate purpose, it would seem, is to show that an English Catholic, far from being 'a member of a most un-English communion', is in fact more English than is an Anglican, because he is more in touch with his national and religious origins.[19] Newman's painstaking exertion to prove his patriotic credentials, of course, may have a great deal to do with the suspicion with which his own conversion was received by his peers, most of whom believed that he had either been duped by foreign agents or always been a latent Catholic and therefore anti-nationalist. It is equally pertinent to infer that Newman had also to ward off charges of effeminacy and celibacy, with which Catholicism was notoriously identified, and assert his heterosexual English manliness by proclaiming allegiance to those most English of virtues - scientific objectivity, rationality, and evolutionary progress.[20] Newman's struggle to demonstrate his Englishness against the hostile scepticism of his contemporaries ironically reflects the extent to which belief itself was marginalised in nineteenth-century England, even as his more accommodating Catholic position caused him to be regarded as 'the most dangerous man in England' by both Anglicans and Catholics.

Given the fact that change of any kind is regarded as subversive and threatening, it is understandable that Newman would have sought to convince his suspicious English readership that he had not changed at all. But that raises a far more unsettling question about the representation of his conversion: if it is true that he had not undergone significant change, how then can he persuade his readership of the need for reform of both the English church and the English political process, and to make both truly incorporative? Is he caught on the horns of a dilemma where his eagerness to be accepted as English *and* Catholic makes him finally reduce reform, which must involve change after all, to a lesser priority? The accent on continuity is basically incompatible with the primacy of historical change, which is so crucial to Newman's fastidiously developed notions of assent and belief. For Newman to declare that he has merely rediscovered what was always present might make sense at a level of personal experience, but that knowledge does not automatically transfer to the restructuring of institutions, and it marks a severe limit to Newman's dynamic model of criticism, disengaging his conversion from the critical activity with which it is so closely allied.

The hybrid identities or modes of difference that Newman sees as crucial to the historical progress of secularisation - to be both English and Catholic, 'Caliban and polite', as he puts it - are not discarded as irreconcilable opposites but embraced as syncretic possibility. But that very syncretic ambition erases the relativity of the terms 'assent' and 'dissent' (after all, an assent to a proposition is a dissent from another, and vice versa), and there is only the confirmation, or what Newman calls the *certitude*, of what is already known. Caught between the demands of secular national identity and local religious differences, Newman turns his back on conversion as a dynamic principle of change - the action of belief upon the world - to one of self-confirmation and discovery of what is already latently present as religious teleology. The radical revisionist possibility of conversion is reversed, as achieving a point of compatibility between Catholicism and Englishness replaces the earlier challenge to the desirability of nationhood posed by his conversion. For after all, when assent is reinscribed as political dissent, it changes the terms of reference, and England does not have to be bound by concepts of nationhood or nationalism, nor does being 'English' necessarily have to be the goal of reconstructing religious identity.

Notes

1. Edward W. Said, *The World, the Text, and the Critic*, Harvard University Press, Cambridge 1983, p290.

2. Peter Van der Veer, *Religious Nationalism*, University of California Press, Berkeley 1994, pix.

3. The public assertion of belief in the civil courts is an idea I explore in further detail by drawing on actual court testimonies, in 'Coping with (Civil) Death: The Christian Convert's Rights of Passage in Colonial India', Gyan Prakash (ed), *After Colonialism: Imperial Histories and Postcolonial Displacements*, Princeton University Press, Princeton 1994.

4. Ashis Nandy, 'The Politics of Secularism and the Recovery of Religious Tolerance', Veena Das (ed), *Mirrors of Violence*, Oxford University Press, Delhi 1990.

5. *Ibid*, p70.

6. Hugh McLeod, *Religion and the Working Class in Nineteenth-Century Britain*, Macmillan, London 1984, p36.

7. Stephen Thomas, *Newman and Heresy*, Cambridge University Press, Cambridge 1992, p4.

8. *The Letters and Diaries of John Henry Newman*, Charles Stephen Dessain (ed), Clarendon Press, Oxford 1978, vol 2, p128; also quoted in Ian Ker, *John Henry Newman: A Biography*, Oxford University Press, Oxford 1988, p34.

9. *Ibid*, p103; quoted in Ker, p83.

10. Thomas, *op cit*, p3.

11. John Henry Newman, *Historical Sketches*, vol 1, p340; quoted in Ker, *op cit*, p82.

12. *Letters and Diaries of John Henry Newman*, *op cit.*, p339; quoted in Ker, p109.

13. John Henry Newman, *Loss and Gain*, 1848, Oxford University Press, New York 1986, p121.

14. 'Worldliness', of course, is a concept central to Said's thought, and the textural engagement with history that Said emphasizes as a way of resisting both critical systems and dominant orthodoxies has its counterpart, I might suggest, in Newman's concept of belief as interactive with history.

15. John Henry Newman, *An Essay in Aid of A Grammar of Assent*, University of Notre Dame Press, Notre Dame 1979, p330. Hereafter cited in the text as *GA*.

16. John Henry Newman, *An Essay on the Development of Christian Doctrine*, p186; cited by Edward Thomas, 'Newman's Social and Political Thinking,' in *Newman after a Hundred Years*, Ian Ker and Alan G. Hill (eds), Clarendon Press, Oxford 1990, p165.

17. Edward Said, in a response to an earlier version of this paper, addressed the question of authority in terms of Newman's own biography. Said proposed that Newman was so driven by anarchic, egotistical impulses that authority constituted for him the stable structure that would both contain and shape those impulses in more creative ways.

18. John Henry Newman, *Apologia Pro Vita Sua*, 1864, Doubleday, New York 1956, p146.

19. *Ibid*, p120.

20. I am indebted to Sarita Echavez See for these insights.

THE WEST AND ITS OTHERS

Bhikhu Parekh

Thanks to the great geographical explorations from the sixteenth century onwards, Europeans came into close contact with non-European societies. They could have responded to the latter in a variety of ways, such as leaving them alone, quietly settling down among them as newly arrived immigrants, establishing regular trade relations and returning home, rejoicing in the diversity of human life, learning about the native ways of life and using that knowledge to acquire a better understanding of their own, killing the natives, conquering and ruling over them, and so forth. Without exception Europeans took over the countries they had 'discovered', and in some cases exterminated or uprooted those already settled there. They were largely motivated by the desire for wealth and domination, and took full advantage of their technological and material superiority.

Although the violence and the physical and moral suffering involved make painful reading, this is in no way peculiar to Europe. Within societies as well as between them, strong and powerful groups have always taken advantage of the weak and vulnerable, and found ways of justifying their actions to themselves and sometimes even to their victims. In this respect 'civilised' groups are no better than 'barbarians'. Their methods and aims might be more humane and restrained, but their pursuit of self-interest is just as, if not more, single-minded and ruthless.

During the period of colonial expansion Europe had at least three influential traditions of thought that were committed to the ideals of human unity, equality, freedom and the inviolability of the human person, and which were in principle hostile to the violence and exploitation inherent in the colonial enterprise. They were Christianity, liberalism from the early decades of the eighteenth century onwards, and Marxism from the last few decades of the nineteenth century onwards. It is striking that with only a few exceptions, the three bodies of thought approved

European colonialism. From time to time they did, no doubt, condemn its *excesses*, but rarely the colonial enterprise itself. In this paper I intend briefly to explore how they reconciled their basic moral commitments with their approval of colonialism, and were able to approve of colonialism yet condemn its excesses.

CHRISTIANITY

When Spaniards arrived in South America, they encountered long-established 'Indian' communities. The latter differed greatly among themselves, spoke different languages, practised different religions and followed different social practices. But these differences were inaccessible to the insensitive outsiders who saw them as a homogenous group. Spanish explorers were struck by two things. First, in some respects Indians were like them. They had a human shape, possessed the gift of speech, enjoyed music and dance, offered prayers, had families and a social structure, and so forth. Second, Indians also differed from them in several respects. They had no script, no system of exchange, wore scanty clothes, were sexually uninhibited and worshipped strange gods, and so forth. Spaniards were particularly struck by the fact that they made human sacrifices and in some cases ate human flesh.[1]

Spaniards, almost all of whom were devout Christians, had to decide how to treat the Indians, and that depended on how they conceptualised them. As Christians, they were committed to the view that since human beings were made in the image of God, they were all inviolable and entitled to equal treatment. What needed to be decided was whether Indians qualified as human beings. They were neither animals nor belonged to an intermediate species between animals and humans, an increasingly current description of Africans that informed much contemporary art and was frequently used to justify black slavery. Some Spaniards concluded that although Indians had a human 'shape', they had the 'nature' of beasts and were really 'savages', a term widely used at the time to refer to human beings displaying such an ambiguous identity. As Christians, Spaniards defined humanity in religio-moral rather than rationalist terms. They therefore concentrated on Indians' religious and moral practices, and concluded that since Indian made human sacrifices, ate human flesh, were 'mad', 'fierce', etc., they were children of Satan, governed by an evil spirit, and could not be said to have been made 'in the image of God'. They were not human beings in the full sense of the term, did not belong to the same species as the Spaniards and the rest of civilised mankind, and their lives, liberties and property lacked moral immunity.

Caines de Sepulveda put the difference starkly: 'There is a great difference between them [and us] as there is between *savagery* and forbearance, between violence and moderation almost - I am inclined to say - as between *monkeys* and men'.[2] Like others he was convinced that war against Indians was a holy duty:

> *The greatest philosophers declare that such wars may be undertaken by a very civilised nation against uncivilised people who are more* barbarous *than can be imagined, for they are absolutely lacking in any knowledge of letters, do not know the use of money, generally go about naked, even the women, and carry burdens on their shoulders and backs like* beasts *for great distances.*[3]

The view that Indians were not human beings proper, which was dominant during the early years of conquest, was effectively challenged by a large number of Christians both in Spain and in Mexico. Their style of reasoning was the same, but it stressed different aspects of Indian life. They started with the basic Christian premise that human beings were made in the image of God and necessarily had an intuitive knowledge of Him, which manifested itself in religious and moral life. If Indians could therefore be shown to possess religious and moral sensibilities, they could be proved to have been made in the image of God, and hence to be human. Accordingly several Christian theologians argued that although Indians worshipped strange and even evil gods, they did thereby display an awareness of the existence of a transcendental being, and that although they had many vices, they also possessed several virtues, thus demonstrating that they were endowed with a moral sense of 'natural light'. Indians therefore were human beings, flawed and grossly imperfect but nonetheless members of the human species, possessing not only a human shape but also human 'nature' or 'essence'.

An order of Charles V dated 1530 commanded the 'No one must dare to enslave any Indian, on the pretext of having acquired him through a just war, or repurchase, or purchase, or barter ... even if these Indians be considered as slaves by the natives.[4] In the papal bill of 1537, Paul III declared that Indians were 'true men', and commanded that they 'must not be deprived of their freedom and the ownership of their property'. For Bartolome de Las Casas, the Dominican Bishop of Chipas, Indians were just as human as Spaniards, and in some respects even better. As he wrote to Prince Philip in 1544, 'All the Indians to be found here are to be held as free, for in truth so they are, by the same right as I myself am free'. Las Casas was one of the most vigorous defenders of Indian dignity and rights, condemning the conquistadors in the strongest possible terms and even demanding their expulsion.

As a Christian, Las Casas believed that salvation was of absolute importance and that *extra ecclesian nulla salus*. Had Indians not been human beings, their salvation would not have mattered. But since they were, it mattered enormously, and could only be obtained by embracing Christianity. Since Indians were human, they *had to be* Christians, and must be converted by persuasion if possible, by coercion if necessary. Since Spanish colonisation was the necessary precondition of missionary activity, Las Casas was not opposed to colonisation but only to its inhumanity and excesses, and wanted it to be led by God-fearing persons of 'good conscience and great prudence' rather than by soldiers. As he grew old, he mellowed and urged that conversion should be the free choice of Indians. However he never relented on the importance of colonisation and conversion. For Las Casas's critics, Indians were not human beings and may be killed. Las Casas accepted their humanity and spared their bodies, but claimed their souls.

In Las Casas' view every man, being made in the image of God, had a natural propensity towards the true knowledge of God, and thus towards Christianity. Every man was therefore an actual or a potential Christian, and all good was ultimately

Christian in its nature and origin. Such Indian virtues as obedience, humility, patience, gentleness and rejection of worldly goods were basically Christian virtues. Since Indians already lived as Christians, albeit unknowingly, their conversion was not an external imposition but intimated by their own way of life and a 'fulfilment' of their deepest aspirations. It was true that Indians had several un-Christian vices and that their virtues lacked discipline, but that only meant that their Christianity, was 'wild' and unsophisticated. His conclusion was predictable.

> *At no other time and in no other people has there been such capacity, such predisposition, and such facility for conversion ... Nowhere in the world are there countries more docile and less restraint, or more apt and better disposed than these to receive the yoke of Our Lord.*[5]

Since Las Casas' deep and genuine concern for Indians arose out of his commitment to Christianity, it suffered from obvious structural limitations. He saw Indians through Christian eyes, and lost sight of all that was distinctive about them. He only saw their virtues and vices and ignored everything else about their way of life. And he defined and judged their virtues and vices in his terms and missed their specificity. It is striking that his *Apologetica Historia* reduces Indians to characters in a Christian morality-play and tells us little about their way of life. Furthermore, since Indians mattered to him not as a distinct people with their own virtues and limitations but as crypto-Christians, he was convinced that he neither needed to understand their way of life from within nor had anything to learn from them. For him their importance lay in being symbols of Christian virtues which the European Christians were in danger of forgetting, and in preserving true Christianity. Since Indians mattered to Las Casas not as human beings but as unconscious Christians, his concern for them did not extend either to Muslims whom he dismissed as 'the veritable barbarian outcasts of nations', or even to blacks to whose slavery his opposition was half-hearted.

Other missionaries rose above Las Casas' limitations. For example, Diego Duran, a Dominican missionary, sought to understand the Indian way of life from within, gave a fairly faithful account of it, and paid generous tributes to it. However his efforts were deeply informed by a desire to highlight Indian analogues to Christian beliefs and practices, and to show not so much that Indians were crypto-Christians as that they had independently arrived at several Christian truths. While he generously acknowledged their originality, he defined and judged it in Christian terms and remained unable to respect their cultural integrity.

Some missionaries, such as Franciscan Bernardino de Sahagun, went yet further. He learned the local language, mastered the local culture, and explored the Indian way of life in its own terms. He respected its integrity and appreciated that it had grown out of and suited Indian 'aspirations and needs'. Although a devout Christian himself, he wondered if conversion was necessarily a good thing. Since it replaced their socially embedded gods with an alien and partially inassimilable Christian conception of God, it disorientated the Indians and sometimes led them to behave in a manner that was 'hateful to God'. Sahagun could not face the full implications of his argument, and ended by suggesting that while conversion should continue, the converted should be allowed to retain some of their religious and cultural practices. For advancing this view, his book was condemned by his superiors, and a royal edict by Philip II in 1577 forbade its discussion and circulation. Although both Duran and Sahagun showed some respect for the Indian way of life, neither saw any reason to disapprove of Spanish colonisation. For them Christianity was a superior religion and did much good to Indians. Since colonial rule had brought it to them and created the conditions of its spread, it was to be welcomed provided that it was humane and did not wantonly destroy the Indian way of life.

Spanish missionary attitudes to Indians then covered a wide range. Some refused to recognise their humanity, but this 'blasphemy' was vigorously challenged by others. Although the latter stood up for Indian rights and dignity, many of them were deeply hostile to the Indian way of life and attempted to dismantle it. Some saw its virtues, but translated them in Christian terms and undermined their integrity. Rare individuals resisted the temptation, respected the specificity of the Indian way of life, and even admired its unique features. However they did not know how to relate it to their Christian way of life and bring the two into fruitful interaction. By and large the vast majority of theologians and missionaries as well as the religious establishment found it difficult to respect the Indian way of life consistently with their belief that Christ was 'the way' to salvation. They already knew the truth and had nothing to gain from a sensitive exploration of and a sympathetic dialogue with other religions. Since Christian knowledge was in the ultimate interest of Indians, and since its dissemination was facilitated by colonisation, they all endorsed colonialism with varying degrees of enthusiasm.

Missionary attitudes in other parts of the world showed the same pattern, albeit with important difference. Take the case of India, the home of several well-developed religions. Initially European missionaries, be they British, French, Dutch or Portuguese, found Hinduism abominable and poured unmitigated scorn on it. Later they mellowed and adopted the Las Casas strategy. They argued that Hindus were 'unconsciously' groping towards Christianity, that Christ was their 'unknown God', that the commendable 'natural reason' of the Hindu sages was inadequate, and that Hindu fulfilment lay in embracing Christianity. This required the missionaries to study classical languages and texts, which they did with considerable skill. It also required them to study the vernaculars, and some of them did the excellent job of providing them with grammars, linguistic structures and scripts, sometimes even recreating the languages themselves. While their secular contribution was immense, their religiously motivated interpretations of classical and popular Hindu religious texts often left much to be desired.[6]

Some missionaries and theologians went further. They read Hinduism in its own terms, found some of its metaphysical and religious insight illuminating, and sought to integrate them into Christianity. By and large their approach to Hindu religious texts paralleled the traditional Christian attitude to the great Greek philosophers or to the Old Testament. The Hindu texts were good first drafts of the Bible, anticipatory of the final truth, incomplete in themselves but suggestive and stimulating. A genuinely open-minded and mutually exploratory dialogue with Indian religions was confined to very few, and never became part of mainstream Christian thinking in India.

Whatever their attitudes to Hinduism, the missionaries were convinced that it was inadequate in varying degrees, and had become particularly degenerate during the recent decades. As such it could not be the basis of a truly moral life, and it was in Indian interest to embrace Christianity. However since Indians were reluctant to convert, and since forcing them was politically unwise, the next best thing was to subject them to Christian values at the hands of politically sensitive Christian rulers. Since the British missionaries and religious leaders justified colonial rule in Christian terms, many of them were anxious that British rulers should behave as good Christians and set good examples of moral rectitude. When the colonial administrators failed to live up to these demands, they were criticised, sometimes in strongest terms, and reported to the government in London. While condemning the un-Christian excesses of colonial rule, the missionaries had no doubt about its 'civilising' value and importance. It was only after the anti-colonial struggle began in the 1920s in India that some of them showed any sympathy for it, and even then only a few actively supported it. The story in other parts of the European empires broadly followed the same pattern.

LIBERALISM

In many respects liberalism was secularised Christianity and reproduced many of the missionary attitudes to non-Europeans and colonialism. This is hardly surprising, for it grew up within a milieu suffused with fifteen hundred years of Christianity, and could hardly avoid imbibing its ethos and ways of looking at the world. Almost all early liberals were Christians. And even those liberals in the eighteenth and nineteenth centuries who were not largely rejected its theology, but neither its morality not its central categories. Although an atheist, Jeremy Bentham deeply admired Jesus' ethics and called him the 'first utilitarian'; the agnostic J.S. Mill thought that Jesus' teachings summed up the basic principles of his brand of altruistic utilitarianism; and while rejecting much of Christian theology, Tocqueville could not see how a liberal society could do without or be built on any other foundation than Christianity, the 'only religion of free men' as he called it. Since almost all liberals aimed to retain some aspects of Christianity, they reinterpreted it along liberal lines, of which Locke's suggestively entitled *The Reasonableness of Christianity* was an excellent early example. In liberalising Christianity, they Christianised liberalism, and took over such beliefs as that mankind constituted a unity and shared a common nature, that a single vision of life was valid for all, that those in the know had a duty to enlighten the ignorant, and that good had a duty to fight evil. The liberal civilising mission was embedded in these beliefs and represented a secularised version of its Christian original; which is why liberalism and Christianity were able to operate in tandem, and the expression 'spreading civilisation *and* Christianity' aroused no anxiety on either side.

When England began to colonise the 'new world' in the seventeenth century, its actions provoked muted criticism. The critics argued that since Indians had occupied and cultivated their land for centuries, it was their 'rightful inheritance' of which they should not be deprived. They also argued that since Indians had established stable societies, the latter were, like their European counterparts, entitled to non-interference by outsiders. Locke, one of the founding fathers of liberalism, took on the critics and advanced an articulate philosophical defence of English colonialism that bore considerable resemblance to that of the Christian missionaries.

For Locke, God created men and endowed them with several basic faculties, including, and especially, reason. They therefore enjoyed equal dignity and rights, and were entitled to the equal protection of their interests. Every man had a right to mix his labour with nature, and to use its fruits to satisfy his needs consistently with a due regard for others. Since God wanted men 'to be fruitful and multiply', every man had a duty to develop the earthly resources to the full and maximise the conveniences of life. As Locke put it, 'God gave the world to man in common, but ... it cannot be supposed he meant it should always remain common and uncultivated. He gave it to the use of the

Industrious and Rational'. Locke's equation of reason with industry is deeply suggestive.

Locke was well aware that some of his contemporaries did not consider blacks, Indians and others human. He knew how they had reached that conclusion.[7]

> *A Child having framed the* Idea *of a* Man, *it is probable, that his* Idea *is just like that picture, which the painter makes of his visible Appearances joined together; and such a Complication of Ideas together in his Understanding, makes up the single Complex Idea which he calls* Man, *where of White or Flesh Colour in England being one, the child can demonstrate to you, that a* Negro *is not a Man, because white-colour was one of the constant simple* Ideas *of the complex* Idea *he calls* Man: *And therefore he can demonstrate by the principle,* It is impossible for the same Thing to be, *and not to be ... that a* Negro *is not a Man.*

Locke rejected this reasoning. All human beings possessed shape, colour, size, etc, but none of these marked them out from animals. Furthermore, colour, etc, varied greatly, and no particular form of it could be considered a necessary feature of man. What distinguished man from the animal and needed to be added to the 'idea of man' was his capacity for 'rational discourse' or reason, which Locke defined as the capacity to perceive similarities and differences, to formulate general statements, to make logical deductions, and so on. All human beings, including Indians and blacks, possessed this capacity and were, as members of the same species, entitled to equal rights.

Since reason was the essence, the *differentia specifica*, of man and the basis of his dignity, he had a duty to lead a rational life. To be rational was to be industrious and energetic, to exploit the earth's resources to the full, to follow rules, to discipline one's passions, and so on. A rational way of life was distinguished by the institution of private property, without which human beings lacked both the incentive to develop the earth's resources and a sense of individuality and freedom. Since the religious duty to be fruitful and multiply 'contains in it the improvement too of arts and sciences', a truly rational society encouraged these as well. As for its political structure, it had a clearly defined territorial boundary, a cohesive, centralised and unified structure of authority, and a will to persist as an independent community.

In Locke's view the Indian way of life did not satisfy these conditions.[8] Indians were lazy, passive, unruly, undisciplined, wild, fierce, unpredictable. They roamed freely over the land, did not enclose it, and lacked the institution of private property. They had no arts, sciences and culture. And although they called themselves nations, they lacked the familiar features of the state. Since Indians had no sense of private property, 'their' land was really empty, free, vacant, and could be taken over without their consent. And since their society was not organised as a state, it enjoyed no immunity from others' interference. The English were not only at liberty to, but also had a duty to take over the 'surplus' Indian land and to interfere with their way of life. God had given man land on condition that he should exploit it to the full, and He had given him reason in the expectation that he would live a law-governed civil life. Since Indians did neither, they were in breach of God's commands and stood in need of discipline and education. English colonisation was indispensable to their transition to civilisation, and hence fully justified. Locke's argument bears a striking resemblance to that advanced by Las Casas a century and a half earlier.

Locke contrasted the English mode of colonisation with the Spanish. The latter was based on 'conquest by sword', violated the natural rights of Indians, and had failed to establish a civilised life among them. It was also contradictory because colonisation was motivated by a desire for economic gain, whereas the right of conquest extended 'only to the lives of the conquered' and not to their property. By contrast English colonisation was humane. It respected the basic natural rights of Indians, used force only when they refused to part with their vacant lands, and both morally uplifted them and drew them into an economically interdependent world. Locke had no doubt that English colonialism performed the moral miracle of serving God, mankind, Indians and, of course, the English themselves. He had no doubt either that when Indians rebelled against it, they forfeited their liberty in an 'unjust' war, and could be legitimately treated as slaves. In taking this view he fell far below the level of the papal bull of 1537 and the anti-slavery arguments of the Spanish missionaries.

For Locke then, Indians were human beings and entitled to the protection of their basic rights and interests, which is why he condemned the early outrageous Spanish treatment of them in the strongest possible terms and took great pains to show that English colonisation was quite different. However, precisely because Indians were human beings, they were expected to live up to the rational and moral imperatives of their human nature. And since they were not doing so, the English were right to dismantle their way of life. For Locke only one way of life was truly rational, and those differing from it deserved no respect. His theory of man accepted Indians as equal *objects* of concern, but not as equal self-defining *subjects* entitled to choose their way of life themselves; that is, it protected them as *individuals* but not as a *community*, and respected their material interests but not their way of life and the moral and spiritual interests associated with it.

During the eighteenth and the early nineteenth centuries, European colonialism entered a new phase. Hitherto the 'empty spaces' of such countries as America, Australia and New Zealand had been subject to colonisation. Now it was the turn of the heavily populated countries of Asia and later of Africa. This new phase of colonialism, which did not involve colonial settlement, and is rightly called imperialism, needed a philosophical defence. Although Lockean arguments were not without value, they needed to be revised to suit the new circumstances. Among the many liberal writers who provided such a defence, John Stuart Mill was the most influential.

Like Locke, Mill divided human societies into two distinct groups, but his principle of classification was different.[9] In some societies, which he called civilised, human beings were in the 'maturity of their faculties' and had 'attained the capacity of being guided to their own improvement by conviction or persuasion'(pp117-8, 125). In his view most European societies had 'long since reached' that stage. By contrast non-European societies were all 'backward', and their members were in a state of 'nonage' or 'infancy'. Mill did not think much of Africa, a 'continent without a history'. And although he thought that

India, China and 'the whole East' had begun well, he was convinced that they had been 'stationary for thousands of years' (p118).

Since backward societies lacked the capacity for self-regeneration, Mill argued that they needed to be civilised by outsiders. He dismissed the likely objection that all societies including the backward had rights to territorial integrity and to develop at their own pace. Like Locke, he argued that the right to non-intervention only belonged to those capable of making a good use of it; as for the rest it was 'either a certain evil or at best a questionable good'. For Mill, as for Locke, backward *individuals* had equal *moral* claims to the protection of their rights and interests, but as *collectivities* they had no *political* claims to the inviolability of their way of life and territorial integrity.

The kind of argument advanced by the British liberals was also to be found in the writings of their French and even German counterparts. Writing to an English friend about the conquest of India, Tocqueville wrote, 'I have ... never for an instant doubted your triumph, which is that of Christianity and civilisation'.[10] He wrote to Nassar Senior after the Indian mutiny of 1857, 'your loss of India could have served no cause but that of barbarism'.[11] Like Sahagun Tocqueville admitted that French rule had unsettled and disorientated Algerian society, and made it 'much more wretched, more disorderly, more ignorant and more barbarian than it was before it knew us'. However he was convinced that colonial rule was in the interest of both France and Algeria: the former because it increased French self-confidence and influence in 'the general affairs of the world', the latter because it civilised the Algerians in the long run. Like Locke and Mill, Tocqueville was anxious that colonial subjects should not be 'exterminated', 'crushed' or 'enslaved', but he was convinced that they could neither be treated 'exactly as if they were our fellow-citizens and our equals', nor be educated except against a background of the 'unfortunate necessities' of violence and even terror. When the troops of M. le Marechal Bugeaud trapped and asphyxiated hundreds of Arabs in the Dahra caves, Tocqueville praised his 'great service to his country on the soil of Africa'.[12]

When Herder challenged the current liberal distinction between civilised and uncivilised societies and attacked liberals for despising the latter, Kant wrote a scathing reply. Mocking Herder's admiration for the happy and carefree inhabitants of Tahiti, Kant asked: 'Why do they exist at all, and would it not have been just as well if this island had been populated with happy sheep and cattle as by human beings happy in mere sensual pleasure'?[13] For Kant, as for Locke and Mill, only the industrious, rational, energetic and purposive life was worthy of human beings. Since Tahitians failed to live up to it, they were little different from 'sheep and cattle' and had no claim to the respect of civilised societies. Kant's question, which goes to the very heart of the liberal view of non-liberal societies, had been asked by the Spanish colonisers. And since they concluded that 'primitive' people had no right to 'exist at all', they saw nothing wrong in following its murderous logic.

Although the general body of liberal thought approved of colonialism, some liberal writers such as Bentham, Voltaire and Diderot did not. They were a small group, and mostly marginal to mainstream liberal thought. Some of them attacked the colonial empires of other countries, but not their own. More importantly they disapproved of colonialism not on moral or cultural grounds, but because it was deemed to be expensive, unprofitable, inconsistent with the principle of free trade, or uneconomic in the long run. They never doubted that the European way of life, and in some cases the European *race*, were superior to the non-European, and thought that commerce and trade rather than colonial rule were the best means of civilising the latter. It was only when anti-colonial struggles gathered momentum, and made colonial rule impossible without considerable violence, that the main body of liberal thought swung against it.

Although liberalism has undergone important changes in recent years, its capacity to appreciate and accommodate cultural diversity remains too limited to restrain its propensity towards cultural colonialism. As post-war literature and government policies on the developing countries show, Western liberal experts cannot see why the latter should not bow to the 'logic of modernisation' and unreservedly adopt the liberal way of life.

They also feel deeply uneasy about the demands of native peoples, minority nationalities and nations, gypsies, tribals, immigrants and others to be allowed to lead their traditional ways of life with such changes as they freely wish to make. Even when liberals are sympathetic to these demands, they have considerable difficulty in making a convincing case on liberal grounds. Will Kymlicka, a sensitive liberal defender of the indigenous communities' right to their cultural integrity, is a good example of this.

Kymlicka advances two related arguments.[14] First, if members of an indigenous, ethnic or any other minority community are to make meaningful choices between their own and the modern ways of life, the former must exist as an option, and since it is under threat, it deserves special help and protection. Second, being culturally embedded, human beings need a secure cultural background to develop their capacity to make choices and appreciate the available range of options. To deprive them of their culture is to cripple this capacity. While Kymlicka's arguments are perceptive, they reveal the tension lying at the heart of liberalism.

Kymlicka sees culture not as an integral part of one's identity as some ethnic minorities do, nor as an ancestral inheritance to be cherished and transmitted as most indigenous communities do, but as a resource whose ultimate value consists in facilitating choices. This is a distinctly liberal view, which he uncritically universalises and imposes on communities who view their culture very differently. Furthermore, for Kymlicka a culture is an option, a contingent and detachable part of one's identity, a matter of conscious and deliberate choice. Accordingly he wants members of indigenous and ethnic communities to decide freely whether to retain or reject their way of life. It is not enough that they retain it out of habit or respect for their history and tradition, for this is presumably irrational; they must step out of it, locate it within a range of options, and choose it as a matter of conscious decision. For Kymlicka deliberate choice is the only proper way to relate to one's culture, and all alike must conform to it. He does not see that different communities might have different modes of conceiving and relating to their cultures, and that the liberal way is neither the only one nor the best. Kymlicka wants

AmerIndians, Inuits and others to become liberals, that is, he liberalises the non-liberals , and is prepared to defend them only when, and to the extent that, they are prepared to behave as respectable liberals. Like the Christian missionaries and the liberal writers discussed earlier, he is unable to understand non-liberal modes of thought in their own terms and to respect their integrity. While genuinely appreciative of diversity at one level, he denies it at another and remains trapped within the parameters of liberal thinking developed by Las Casas, Locke and Mill.

MARXISM

Marxism is one of the most radical and emancipatory projects in Western thought. Few bodies of ideas match its commitment to the cause of the poor and the oppressed, and its concern for human freedom and wholeness. One would therefore expect it to be far more critical of colonialism than the liberals. In some respects it was, for it exposed the exploitative basis, racism and brutality of colonialism as well as the limitations of its familiar liberal defence. However it too found good historical reasons to justify colonialism.

For Marx man was a free and self-creating being whose nature and destiny consisted in creating a society free from non-human constraints. As he imagined it, a truly human or free society was one in which human beings were liberated from the 'tyranny' of God and other transcendental human projections, as well as from most of the constraints imposed by external and internal nature. Human beings enjoyed unmediated unity with their species, and were no longer imprisoned into narrow ethnic, cultural, national and other communities. Marx even thought that, since local languages stood between the individual and the species, they would and should eventually be replaced by a single universal language. The collective life of such a boundaryless society was based not on inherited customs and traditions but on self-consciously formulated rules and careful planning. Marx was also opposed to the division of labour on the ground that it imposed a specific occupational identity on its members and restricted the scope of self-creation, and imagined a society in which people would paint or write without becoming painters or writers.

Marx used this vision of human freedom to judge and classify societies and historical epochs. Since human self-creation was a protracted process and since, except in the communist society, it occurred without conscious human control, it entailed much suffering. Marx insisted that rather than condemn such suffering in abstractly moralist terms, once should judge it in terms of its contribution to the long-term interests of the species. Marx's theory of the nature and historical dialectic of human self-creation formed the basis of his theory of colonialism. Non-European societies were static, restrictive, technologically backward, mired in religious superstitions, lacked individuality, were slaves to nature, and cut off from the world history. Since they offered little freedom in Marx's radical sense of self-creation, they needed to be dismantled. And since they were unable to do so themselves, European colonialism was a historically necessary and progressive force. This was exactly the argument of almost all liberals from Locke onwards.

Marx agreed that the destruction of a long-established social order invariably caused 'terrible' suffering and was often 'sickening ... to human feeling', but insisted that it was in the long term interest of both the societies concerned and mankind as a whole. As he put it in relation to British rule in India:

Now sickening as it must be to human feeling to witness those myriads of industrious patriarchal and inoffensive social organizations disorganised and dissolved into their units ... we must not forget that the idyllic village communities, inoffensive though they may appear, had always been the solid foundation of Oriental despotism, that they restrained the human mind within the smallest possible compass, making it the unresisting tool of superstition, enslaving it beneath traditional rules, depriving it of all grandeur and historical energies ... We must not forget that the little communities were contaminated by distinctions of caste and by slavery, that they subjugated man to external circumstances, that they transformed a self-developing social state into never changing natural destiny, and thus brought about a brutalizing worship of nature, exhibiting its degradation in the fact that man, the sovereign of nature, fell down on his knees in adoration of Hanuman, the monkey, and Sabbala, the cow.

England, it is true, in causing a social revolution in Hindostan, was actuated only by the vilest interests, and was stupid in her manner of enforcing them. But that is not the question. The question is, can mankind fulfil its destiny without a fundamental revolution in the social state of Asia? If not, whatever may have been the crimes of England she was the unconscious tool of history in bringing about that revolution.[15]

Since most Indians did not see British colonialism in this way, they often protested and even rebelled against it. Marx's judgement on their actions was predictable. In so far as they were reacting against the historically necessary suffering entailed by colonialism, their protests, though understandable, were unjustified. In so far as they were reacting against the gratuitous or surplus suffering caused by the mindless brutality and arrogance of the colonial rulers, their protests were both understandable and justified. This is why Marx disapproved of the Indian mutiny in 1857, but condoned some of the excesses of the mutineers.

Although Marx justified colonialism, he was too acutely aware of its brutality and exploitative nature not to appreciate the need for anti-colonial struggle. The point of the struggle was not to end colonial rule 'prematurely', but to sustain the spirit of revolt, to restrain colonial excesses, and to build up a movement until such time as it was both possible and necessary to end colonial rule. After the Russian Revolution in 1917, Lenin, Trotsky and others supported the growing anti-colonial struggles first in India and then in other parts of Asia and Africa. However their support suffered from the limitations of the Marxist theory of colonialism. Their primary concern was not so much to help the colonies regain their freedom to fashion their self-chosen ways of life, as to destabilise metropolitan capitalism by removing its sources of profits and reducing its capacity to buy off internal discontent and to pave the way for a world revolution.

Independence of colonies had largely an instrumental value, and it was hoped that after independence they would all follow the communist path of development. The thought that they might be left free, let alone encouraged to choose an alternative vision of life more consistent with their history and tradition, was dismissed out of hand. Not surprisingly communist anti-colonial struggles often had a colonial air about them, as later became evident in the Soviet attempts to control their post-independence destiny.

A CHALLENGE FOR OUR TIMES

The egalitarian potential of Christianity, liberalism and Marxism was emasculated by, among other things, their monistic vision of the good life. All human beings were endowed with dignity. But precisely because of that, they were expected to lead a truly human way of life. Those who did not were misguided, ignorant, moral and political infants, and stood in need of guidance from those who did. The basis on which the three traditions granted human equality thus contained an inegalitarian thrust. The equality was conditional and required inequality to actualise it. The three traditions could therefore both justify colonialism with a clear conscience, and criticise its excesses. *Qua* human beings, colonial subjects were entitled to a moral minimum. In order to enjoy *full* equality with 'civilised' mankind, they had to become like it under its tutelage.

In recent years all three traditions have begun to reconsider their commitments to their monistic visions of the good life. Many Christian writers and churches acknowledge that other religions are not all wrong and contain important spiritual insights from which Christianity can benefit. However the inter-faith dialogue, first initiated by the World Council of Churches and endorsed after some hesitation by the Vatican, has not proved easy. Many Christian leaders see it as a subtle attempt to deabsolutise Christianity, to 'reduce' it to one religion among many, and to undermine its doctrinal and historical identity. They welcome inter-faith dialogue so long as it aims to improve mutual understanding and to build alliances against the forces of secularism, but not if it involves accepting the equal legitimacy of other religions, let alone opening up Christianity to their influence, as the small group of Christian pluralists advocate. Similar tensions are evident within the liberal and Marxist traditions. Some liberals appreciate the need to enter into a dialogue with and learn from non-liberal ways of life, including the religious and the 'primitive'. Others see this as a cowardly betrayal of the central liberal commitments. Marxism has long remained too rigid to appreciate the need for a dialogue with its 'others', and it is difficult to foresee how it will respond in its current mood of despondency.

In an increasingly interdependent and plural world in which the belief in moral and cultural monism carries little conviction, and is a source of much conflict, all major Western intellectual traditions face an acute problem. Some form of moral and cultural monism lies at their very basis, and several hundred years of western hegemony have done much to reinforce their faith in it. Not surprisingly, a radical reappraisal of their central assumptions with a view to respecting the integrity of other ways of thought and life, and creating the moral space required for an open-minded dialogue with them, is proving extremely painful. But the challenge of finding ways to reconcile equality with difference and integrity with openness is one no major intellectual tradition can any longer avoid.

I am grateful to Judith Squires for her helpful comments on this paper.

Notes

1. Tzvetan Todorov, *The Conquest of America: The Question of the Other*, Harper and Row, New York 1981. Spaniards were deeply offended by the practice of human sacrifice, but apparently it did not occur to them that their killing of the innocent in the name of civilisation and Christianity was no different.

2. *Ibid*, p153.

3. *Ibid*, p156.

4. *Ibid*, p161.

5. *Ibid*, p163.

6. For a good discussion, see Wilhelm Halbfass, *India and Europe: An Essay in Philosophical Understanding, Motilal Banarsideas*, Delhi 1990, ch3.

7. Locke, *An Essay Concerning Human Understanding*, Bk11, ChXXIII.

8. See Locke, *Second Treatise*, §34, 38, 107 and 108.

9. *Utilitarianism, Liberty and Representative Government*, Dent, London 1912, p117.

10. Cited in Tzvetan Todorov, *On Human Diversity: Nationalism, Racism and Exoticism in French Thought*, Harvard University Press, Cambridge 1993, p194.

11. *Ibid*, p195.

12. *Ibid*, pp202f.

13. Robert T Clark Jr, *Herder, His Life and Thought*, California University Press, 1969, p325.

14. Will Kymlicka, *Liberalism, Community and Culture*, Clarendon Press, Oxford 1989, ch8.

15. Karl Marx, *Collected Works*, Lawrence and Wishart, London 1979, Vol12, p132. For the ambiguities of the Marxist and other views on colonialism, see Edward Said, *Culture and Imperialism*, Chatto and Windus, London 1993, pp288ff.

IDENTITY AND VIOLENCE

David Wood

Recently I have been exploring the idea that there is an important connection between identity and violence, and that understanding this connection might, albeit indirectly, enable philosophy to make a contribution to peace. In Yugoslavia and Northern Ireland, for example, it has been hard to believe that such violence could co-exist with (or could follow so closely on the heels of the collapse of) a relatively liberal, well-educated society. Some link between violence and identity is writ large in what is called 'ethnic cleansing', in which forced eviction, terror and genocide are employed to bring about regional racial purity. Ethnic difference is understood as the alien, the other, and such a category then comes to legitimate extreme brutality. It is as if an entire economy of mutual recognition and accommodation collapses into a tribal, and strictly speaking, primitive economy of rigid identification. And it is this sense of the rigidity of community identity and the fanaticism of identification which makes one reflect hard. I put to one side here the possibility that such forms of ethnic fanaticism might simply be ancient myths exploited by evil politicians, though this must play a part. The question I want to answer is this: if the quest for identity, its maintenance and enhancement was, still is, an independent causal factor in bringing about such horrors, what does this tell us about the relationship between personal and group identity, or about the scope of such relationship? More ambitiously, can philosophers say anything distinctive about the conditions under which less rigid identity-constructs flourish?

My ambition here, however, is more modest: to begin to try to conceptualise certain of the looser shapes in which personal identity is increasingly to be found, and some of the consequences that flow from the range of external conditions on which identity depends.

On reflection, everyone agrees that identity is not one thing. When philosophers come to consider the question of identity they enter a scene already populated by forensic scientists, genetic engineers, social psychologists, regional politicians, advertising agencies, and customs officials. We are accustomed to supposing that these senses of identity can all be gathered together under the umbrella of the empirical - but this unreflective homogeneity may well be an illusion. Within philosophy, of course, matters are no easier. Identity figures in different ways in logic, metaphysics and philosophy of mind. And it is commonly thought indispensable to begin by distinguishing, for example, numerical and qualitative identity, not to mention personal, social, political identity, and so on.

A philosopher will then wonder whether underlying all these senses there might not be one basic conception. Perhaps, 'Everything is what it is, and not another thing'. But even in such an innocent formulation, a distinction is already being made. Identity is being defined in opposition to difference. Numerical identity is being identified by distinguishing it from qualitative identity. It would seem that there is an intimate connection between identity and difference. Perhaps the bare fact of such intimacies undermines from the outset any simple sense of identity. And the particular way in which some contemporary philosophers have come to understand difference - as a productive principle, generating chains of connections - would bring identity and difference closer together, even as they are 'opposed to one another'.

Few philosophers today would insist on the status of identity as a logical or metaphysical primitive; they are much more likely to understand it in terms of a symbolic function. Identity has acquired a life beyond its significance for logic, but it always operates at the symbolic level, where it functions as a site of repetition, overlapping, transformation, condensation, etc. And as such, identity has become complex, internally differentiated, suspended in matrices, constituted, derivative, even dispersed, distributed.

It could be argued that this is not so new. Did not even Plato have a tripartite account of the soul? Perhaps what we are trying still to shake off is that sense of the simple self-transparency of the self as subject to which Descartes introduced us. At any rate, it has become clear that no account of identity and selfhood is adequate if it fails to acknowledge: that we try to make sense of our lives, that the ways in which we do this face interrogation and doubt both from ourselves and others, that we are mortal and know it, and that we want our lives to be publicly as well as privately intelligible. But more significantly such an account must also acknowledge that the means available for us to make such sense are becoming increasingly ragged: unreliable, fragmentary, local.

The idea of a soul, an immaterial substance, the essence of me, which never changed, would certainly guarantee identity through time. But even if such a notion were intelligible, it would prove too much, and reveal too little. It would prove too much in that it would make the deepest anxieties about personal identity unthinkable. And it would precisely not tell us how our fragile and contingent selfhood is constructed. Essentialism drives out both doubt and complexity. What, then, is required is an account of personal identity which offers not just metaphysical security, but real ability to articulate the fabric of our lives.

Difference functions as a sign for what we could call a problematising account of the constitution of identity. The difficulty is precisely over whether identity is being compromised (at the extreme, destroyed), or whether it is being thought through more carefully, more critically. I lean towards the second view: the issue at stake is not whether something exists or not, in any straightforwardly decidable way. The issue about identity is whether the forms of intelligible coherence that we can still sustain, will do the work we want of them. 'Is agency still thinkable for a deconstructed self?' is not a question at the level of 'Can a three legged dog still run?'. It is asking what impact certain reflections on the constitution of the self have on the ways we think about agency.

For the sake of argument, I will take for granted that the self must, in one way or another, be thought of as complex, as constituted. I will leave this sufficiently open even to include the idea that such constitution might take the form of an endless deferral of finality. When Kierkegaard reflected on the question of selfhood, he concluded (in *The Sickness unto Death*) that the question was not whether the self was constituted or not. It was clear to him that it was. The question was whether this process of constitution involved the self alone, or whether it had to pass through a relation to another being. He argued that unless we accept that the self is constituted by another, we cannot account for the existence of that form of despair in which we do not simply give up our lives, but carry on, albeit anxiously. We could not understand how doubt and interrogation about its nature could be part of the weave of our lives. Only an original entanglement with something outside of ourselves would transcend the despair of immediacy, and also the despair that such constitution would make us no longer transparent to ourselves.

Our age is characterised by the most profound mistrust of the transcendental, of there being deep conditions of possibility for anything. This mistrust is only partly alleviated by the gradual separation of the transcendental and transcendence, to the point at which we realise that the conditions of possibility may be met by empirical phenomena, without sacrificing their status.[1]

HORIZONS OF CONTINUITY

Are there any 'transcendental requirements for identity'? And if so, how can they be met? I would claim that 'lived-identity-through-time' has to negotiate some form of relation to the conditions of continuity. The connection between personal identity and 'horizons of continuity' may be obvious, but it is worth filling it out just a little. For each of us to be ourselves, we need to be able to project possibilities, to recall the past and to be able to continue to act and make sense of our relation to the world. When any one of these dimensions is weakened, so too is our capacity for selfhood. And each of these dimensions is essentially horizonal. To project possibilities is already to take for granted the continuation of technical means, personal connections, one's own physical and intellectual capacities, desires - all, we might say, within the framework of our assumed mortality, for which, I might add, we have all the evidence we could want, and none at all. Our capacity, and the shape of our capacity, to recall the past will depend on how (adequately?) we experienced it at the time, but also crucially on the continuity (and sometimes on the discontinuity) of our powers of seeing

Said

and understanding. And these powers are not immune from the loss or transformation of public meaning. Some of these considerations are captured in the claim that if you can remember the 1960s, you weren't there. Dramatic changes in conceptual or social space can block or transform our capacity to remember, and, just as interestingly, our capacity to draw on the past as a resource for self-interpretation and motivation. Our capacity to continue to act in particular ways is clearly bound up with both our sense of self, and with conditions that exceed each of us. We desire not just self-images, but the capacity to earn a living, and the whole pattern of our productive engagement with the world, for being able to continue to act in certain ways. This is why unemployment is so devastating, striking at the heart of our being-in-the-world, and often a discontinuity over which we have no control. And it is not surprising that with loss of productive engagement with the world comes loss of self-worth. I would also mention here those possibilities of action and interaction bound up with friendships and loved ones, the loss of which can force a renegotiation of one's self-understanding.

Finally, there is the horizon sustained by our capacity to make sense of our relation to the world. We rely on our grasp of what, in broad terms, is happening out there, and on what it might mean, in being able to define the intelligibility of our behaviour. In an extreme form, religious conversion experiences, for example, can transform the self because they transform the ultimate horizons of significance. And these can of course be positive and revelatory as well as deeply unhinging.[2]

Perhaps I might add to this brief sketch of the essential horizonality of our being, the importance of place. A place is a site of both public and private memory. To dwell in a place is to engage in a continuing exchange of meaning through which one's identity becomes, at least in part, a kind of symbiotic relationship with where one dwells. This is true not just of those places of which people speak fondly, but of bleak, inhospitable places too. Place here is another way of talking about past and future, about opportunities for action and interaction. The more we accept the importance of place (and correlatively 'home') for the construction of identity, the more we will grasp the full significance of 'homelessness', 'loss of nationality', the problem

198

of refugees, around the world. Clearly there are powerful nomadic possibilities of identity construction. While some are simply tied to place in an extended sense, for others, travelling, wandering, 'going places' clearly serves as a rich narrative resource in itself.[3]

To sum up here: self-identity is constituted rather than given and our capacity to construct it depends on all sorts of openness to and being sustained by 'horizons of continuity' - in which material conditions and existential and hermeneutic functions coincide.

If such horizons of continuity do provide the conditions for projection, sustaining meaning, self-worth, self-understanding and self-location in ways I have suggested, it is equally clear that it is impossible to separate the question of continuity from questions about the predictability and guarantees of such continuity. For the greater the dependence of selfhood on these horizons of continuity and intelligibility, the more one has to lose if they are disrupted, and the more one will invest in mechanisms by which such horizons will be guaranteed. Complex social life rests on a mix of legitimate expectations and guarantees of constancy - which generate a kind of 'second nature'. Common language, patterns of civility, a common range of values, laws, a stable currency - these are all interconnected. Some are maintained by habit, some by informal personal interaction, some by market mechanisms, some by strong state management.

If 'lived-identity' is dependent on this whole range of legitimate expectations and guarantees of constancy - horizons of predictability - then the disturbance of these conditions, these horizons, can be expected to create an identity-crisis.[4]

I have implicated a range of institutions from the state downwards in the maintenance of the horizons of performance that make lived-identity possible. This relationship is often indirect and partial. Our capacity to enter into exchange relationships with others depends on a common currency, and on some control over inflation. But how far this is, can be, or should continue to be a state function is a matter of considerable debate, for example in Europe, where questions of national identity are now loudly debated. Equally, those institutions of state and civil society (army, local government, the press, schools, universities) which one might have hoped would buffer state crisis or disintegration, can be so heavily dependent on the state that they fail too. The return to ethnic or religious loyalties is a return to identity-bestowing affiliations that have one vital ingredient - they are reliable, and promise an end to what turned out to be a fragile dispersal of identity-functions. Linking faith and power, such identity-providers guarantee or claim horizons of ultimate significance, and also the stable material conditions by which identity is sustained.

But one might ask - is not the risk of death a serious objection to the claimed reliability of such affiliations, to those young men who join factional armies. The answer, of course, is absolutely not. If anything, the risk of death, as Hegel knew, is precisely what such identification deals with best. At this level, the risk of physical death is wholly secondary to the risk of loss of self. As Nietzsche put it, men would rather will nothing, than not will. And it is no accident that both religious belief and the military ethos give death the highest significance: death with honour; self-sacrifice; through these you can gain not simply identity, but a permanent place in the hall of fame, as a hero or martyr.

There is no doubting a kind of 'logic' connecting death, identity and sacrifice.[5] There is no doubting the logic of Levi-Strauss's account of cannibalism as a symbolic relationship, the only means by which the young man could acquire a name (and hence an identity), by killing and ingesting an existing name-bearer. Strong reviews of books in journals might suggest that such a way of making a name for oneself lives on in a symbolically transformed way.

Now I cannot deny that there have been societies or circumstances in which such patterns of behaviour have made a positive contribution. The transformation of death into sacrifice really does make something out of nothing. But if we can acknowledge that, with all their grotesqueness, such economies are still human, we can still ask - to what problems do they constitute a solution, and what alternative solutions are there? And if we think of them as 'logics', 'economies', or even 'forms of life' - we must not forget that the bright young Bosnian, or Serbian, or IRA soldier's triangulation of death, identity and sacrifice is a badge shining in a wide field of pain and suffering.

Questions of identity are powerfully implicated in the recent politics of Eastern Europe. If anything like the analysis I have given is correct, we would be led to accept that the role of the other in the constitution of identity is far from being a matter of transcendental social psychology, but of the deepest political importance. On our account, the story of the conditions on which we develop a distinct and individuated self is one in which the shape of our bonds to the community and to the state is of crucial significance. It would not be too perverse to treat Kafka's novels as explorations of an identity for whom the state's contribution to his identity has become an overwhelming problem. But what for Joseph K. is a nightmare, and for the peoples of Eastern Europe an unthinkable horror, does not allow us to describe our contemporary position, as bearers of a distributed identity, in the classical language of alienation. If I am right, to say that our developing identities are made possible by their dependence on external guarantees is a description of the human condition; and the fact that, in Western countries, it is an array of state and other apparatuses that sustain this order, rather than a local community bound together by a common faith, creates deep potential instabilities, but also new possibilities of identity and selfhood.[6]

The real justification of Western democracy as a political system is that it promotes and guarantees freedom to its citizens. But there is an obvious gap between formal, legal freedom, and what Isaiah Berlin long ago called positive liberty. To be able to choose is not just a formal condition, but one deeply indebted to other (e.g. material) conditions. If our own society is not to become riddled with pockets of violence, it has to provide, above all, opportunities for selfhood - that is, for recognition, individuation and development.[7]

NARRATIVE AND INTERPRETATION

Suppose we agree that identity, selfhood, is not given, not simple, but constituted, dependent, etc (without necessarily at this stage agreeing on a particular analysis of this); that identity is a distinct, often overriding, human concern; that whether and how such concerns are met can be of enormous political significance.

Given these premises, what can we learn from contemporary

philosophical discussions of identity - particularly those that would deny it or deconstruct it? My view is that deconstruction is quite as easily seen as contributing to the highly traditional philosophical task of interrogation as to the nature of the self, as to any denial of selfhood. And one suspects that some of those most hostile are not philosophers at all, but the very same people who found Socrates's questioning tiresome.

To ask whether constructed selves are adequate substitutes for the genuine variety is of course deeply question-begging. I propose to assume, heuristically, that selfhood is best thought of as constructed, and in some important sense incomplete and relational. We can then return to our question as to what, if anything, contemporary accounts of the self teach us.

First, however, I would like to bring narrative on stage. In recent years there has been a strong sense that narrative could supply for the identity of persons and states what a metaphysical self could no longer supply. And moreover, would do so in a way that was both flexible, open to development, and knitted together the personal and the social, experience and language. One might think, in principle, that narrative would provide a softening of the outline of a viable identity, one that would reduce those grounds, at least, for violence. Matters are not, of course, that simple. And one of the most interesting aspects of Edward Said's *Culture and Imperialism* is that narrative is not so much a way out of the violence of essentialist identity, but rather the plane on which struggles take place. He writes

> *stories are at the heart of what explorers and novelists say about strange regions of the world ... they also became the method colonised people use to assert their own identity, and the existence of their own history ... as one critic has suggested, nations are themselves narratives.*

If the main battle in imperialism was over land,

> *these issues were reflected, contested, and even for a time decided in narrative ... [and] the power to narrate, or to block other narrations from forming and emerging is very*

*important to culture and imperialism and constitutes one of
the main connections between them.*

Before returning to Said, I want to discuss the distinctly different
approaches of both Ricoeur and Derrida to the status of narrative,
looking in particular at those readings Derrida gives of Nietzsche
and Blanchot which probe the silent identity framing, and hence
exclusion, that makes narrative construction possible.

Identity is a product not an origin. And it is important
epistemologically as well as politically to grasp the
constructedness of narrative; it matters that the construction
of narrative intelligibility is a selective process, and leaves things
out. Exclusion from representation, marginalisation and indeed
elimination in the name of a narrative - collectivisation, racial
purification, liberation, westernisation, perhaps even
enlightenment itself - are central concerns on every agenda. But
there is another side to this: narrative is not just a vehicle for
generating silence and forgetting but often an indispensable aid
in the service of memory, commemoration, helping others who
were not there understand what happened.[8]

There are two straightforward arguments for continuing to
take narrative seriously, and for treating the deconstruction of
narrative as what, after Wittgenstein, we might call a reminder.
First there is a strong sense in which what is forgotten or left out
by one narrative calls not for scepticism about narrative but
another narrative, for it to be adequately represented. Much
political activity in both Argentina and the former Yugoslavia has
centred on recording the stories of those whose sons and
daughters, husbands and wives have disappeared. To fit Auschwitz
into the story of Germany may be to destroy its singularity. But
we must not forget that it is precisely because dead men (and
women) don't talk, tell no tales, that they are killed in the first
place. Second, it is arguable that even being forgotten or left out
is itself a status we can understand, and then try to correct because
it too has a comprehensible narrative form. What then would be
the force of the reminder that the destruction of narrative
constitutes for us? It could transform our reading, listening,
understanding. We would begin to see the framing as well as the
frame, just as we have, for example, become able to read

advertising, to be able to see how we are being manipulated. We might simply bear in mind that there are 'always many sides to the story', that a plurality of stories can be told of the same event (think of the film Rashamon, or of Kierkegaard's retellings of the Abraham story in *Fear and Trembling*). We might keep our eyes peeled for squashed marginalia, the failures of history, the things that did not happen, but could have, the awkward facts that remain unaccounted for, the events that cannot be made part of history without having their singularity threatened.

But these suggestions are all compatible with the thesis that narrative in some broad sense is the inescapable space within which even its own failures are represented. Moreover, it would follow that narrative is never itself the problem. The problem is its mode of presentation - how we understand its scope etc.

Ricoeur's position here is interesting. He understands man as a self-interpreting being. Through narrative we configure and, when we apply this to life, refigure this process of self-interpretation. Ricoeur could be said to be offering a solution to the following question: if to be a self is to somehow synthesize, bring together, the private and the public dimensions of the self, then in the absence of the package deal provided by religious community, how is it that through language, myth, fiction - a whole range of public forms of intelligibility - we weave selves?

What is extraordinary about Ricoeur's work - and this appears near the end of both *Time and Narrative*, and *Oneself as Another*, is his recognition that the various dialectical processes that he sets in train - between the reflexivity of the self, the opposition between selfhood and sameness, and filling the self/other relation - are never resolved. Aporia, and indeed tragedy, remains, and he leaves us with a vision of peace marked by the possibility of ineliminable conflict.

We have seen that for Kierkegaard, Hegel and others selfhood required a constitutive relation to an other, a Power. And we can translate Kierkegaard's remarks about despair into Ricoeur's terms: selfhood deprived of the symbolic resources to weave a narrative of self-interpretation will know only desperation. A selfhood for whom such resources are available may still feel despair, but that despair will be mediated by a symbolic engagement with the social. Kierkegaard's despair at willing to be oneself - what I have called desperation - is one in which the horizon of the future has withered away, as the tracks of symbolically mediated self-interpretation have been torn up. Despairingly willing to be oneself - carrying on, albeit in despair - is continuing this process of self-interpretation even if the story seems bleak, or the story line implausible.

What our translation of this problematic into Ricoeur's language opens up is the whole area of what we might call anxiety about the self, and its relation to the forms of temporalising engagement available. For if what narrative self-interpretation offers is an interweaving of the private and the public in a way that fuses both symbolic and temporal horizons, this articulation of what narrative provides also allows us to thematise how it is that less complex or completely satisfying forms arise, and may indeed have become the norm.

Briefly, I am taking it as axiomatic that selfhood requires some sort of identity through time. It is a well-worn position that bodily continuity is not sufficient. Nor is the continuity of memory. One common objection to memory playing this role is that it is question-begging. Whose memory? we might ask. But it is not clear whether that should count as an objection or rather a spur to recognise the necessity of some sort of fundamental hermeneutical circularity. And the kind of questions we have run into would have to be part of those broader considerations. Memory is not simply a private phenomenon. Its public dimension is to be found not just in the importance of its corroboration by others; memory is woven with public symbols - places, names, times, conversations - which locate it in various series and matrices of meaning. I do not have to sustain the clock, the calendar, the map of the earth, the lexicon of names. I freely draw upon these in my weaving. I have suggested, too, that if we take into account the role of economic and institutional factors, there are further orders - such as exchange rates, national boundaries, shared and contested histories, different levels of industrialisation, and access to communication networks. I mention these kinds of 'material' factors again simply to keep them on the agenda, for the capacity of such 'systems' to supplement the traditional resources for identity-construction and maintenance presents philosophical thinking with both a challenge and an opportunity.

If we accept that something like what Nietzsche called nihilism captures, if not the state of things today, at least a pervasive concern, even tendency, and if we accept that what nihilism means is on the one hand the disintegration of all absolute values, and any and all transcendental grounds for identity formations, then what we are faced with is coping with the contingency of identity, as Rorty would put it. For identity will have to be woven from whatever material is available rather than from a kit in which everything is provided. Now this is not simply a problem for philosophy, it is increasingly a problem for humanity. (Within cultural studies, new concepts of multiple and decentred subject formations, dispersed identities, are being forged to cope with the phenomena conceptually.) The final question I would like to pose is what limits, if any, there are to our ability to imagine substitute identities, bricolage identities, rather than those logically engineered, to rework a Levi-Straussian distinction.

Identity is so often treated corrosively, sceptically, not because the young bloods of philosophy have got hold of powerful weapons they don't really know how to handle, but because the shapes that identity takes, or that identities take, today reflect a massive and general externalisation, decentring, dehiscence and articulation of all constituted beings. If there is any longer any sense in talking about the meaning of history, it would be quite as plausible as anything else to treat its latest phase as a ruthless penetration, or at least threatening, of all established boundaries, and their dynamic reconstitution in accordance with diverse economies. I have great sympathy with Gilles Deleuze when he talks of philosophy as having the task of inventing new concepts, and hence, I think, of tracking, as far as this makes sense, the contours of contemporary experience. The truth is no longer the whole, as Hegel would say, or rather the whole has to be understood as diverse, and plural, with many centres of order and significance. When Kristeva suggests in 'Women's Time' that we need to think of women's time as cyclical and monumental, as opposed to the standard linear time - of progressive and end-oriented time - she is in effect talking about alternative local ways in which identity trails are set up. There need be no grand synthesis of how all these fit together.

The thought that we can entirely eliminate what we might call transcendental questions is misplaced. For there is an inevitable tension between new formations of identity - to which I am suggesting we have to respond - and our continuing sense of that of which they are new formations. And this issue is bound up with questions we cannot relinquish - of the possible intelligibility of a human life. We cannot let go of them, because - and here Kierkegaard and Heidegger were I think right - anxiety accompanies us at every stage not just of our reflection, but of our endeavour to make sense of our lives in the absence of *a priori* guarantees. At the very least, we owe ourselves a discourse, a language, perhaps even a conceptual scheme in which to think the very fragmentation we have adumbrated.

To return, then, to violence. While there will always be violence only accidentally connected to identity, my hypothesis is that there is much that is deeply internally connected. The violence referred to in Derrida's discussion of Levinas in 'Violence and Metaphysics' is the violation of the other, the violence of the face of the other, brought about by a metaphysical or ontological neutralisation of all being, which would eliminate the essential asymmetry of human relating. But we need not swallow this formulation whole to see that if identity is concerned with the boundaries and sequencings of the self, threats, or perceived threats, to those dimensions will be threats to our very being. And these will be understood as threats of violence, and will provoke violence in their turn.

It has been recently suggested to me that identity today is just a negotiable commodity, to be bought and sold, that identities are just various forms of investment[9]. When I hear this, I am challenged, because I have already talked about subjects, selves, being located within various economies. It is easy to respond to such a model by asking 'for whom' is identity a negotiable commodity - as Ricoeur asks of Parfit 'for whom' is identity no longer the issue. But if I am honest there is something chillingly premonitory about his suggestion. It may be, for example, as Julia Kristeva suggests, that we are the first civilisation to witness the widespread breakdown of the family, and hence the breakdown of those Oedipal forms of strong identity-cathexes that went with it. I will not speculate. But I do not think that there is an importantly positive rather than hypernihilistic sense in which we can think the negotiability of identity.

One's first reaction to a boundary threat, a continuity threat, can be expected to be a violently defensive one. But it is the rigid form of one's identity, so to speak, which is responding. It is, precisely, a reactive response. But boundaries and horizons are constituted, and can be transformed. The subject of such a reaction may not be the self in its dynamic aspect, but rather a boundary guard. Negotiable identity does not mean that every boundary has its price. But it does mean that the facility of identity-formation and -transformation can plausibly be regarded as a better 'defence' than the maintenance of rigidities come what may. If we apply the principle we offered earlier - that we must will the conditions of what we value, then we must ask under what conditions such negotiable identity could best flourish. There is little doubt in my mind that such conditions would include a rich diversity of stories, languages, cultural symbols, etc. It may be said that this is no substitute for tradition, that one cannot just buy and sell roots, tribal bonds, etc. But one serious response here would be that a culture of dynamic identity modification is a culture, a tradition itself.

My argument, then, is that identity is a construction, that narrative supplies the most powerful forms of such constructedness, that narrative does not eliminate but elaborates and restages the possibilities of violence and confrontation, and that a certain 'deconstruction' of narrative serves to moderate its capacity to be harnessed for violent ends.

If I understand Derrida's readings of Nietzsche and of Blanchot correctly, he is arguing, as did Nietzsche himself, for the fictionality of the identities constructed through (say) autobiographical writing, and the fragility of the narrative unity wrought by a text. And this fictionality operates through the proper name, through the idealising functions of names themselves. What this suggests is something of a double strategy: the affirmation of the move away from essentialism towards narrative, but at the same time, the maintenance of a certain, and interrogative, space within which narratives operate. This would argue for the necessity of Narrative, but also the pitfalls and dangers of taking any one narrative too seriously.

Edward Said emphasises the heterogeneity in every culture. Once spoken, it is obvious, but its huge force as a reminder rests on the fact that the construction of identity also involves positioning oneself within countervailing identities. And at this point the elision of differences within the other culture is almost automatic. A *critical political culture* and surely it is this above all that is needed, would have to think *against the grain*, it would deconstruct these illusory unities, and keep open the dynamic possibilities of narrativising. Such a political culture would not just preserve a multiplicity of narratives, and encourage differential articulations within perceived unities, it would also have to recognise and promote what we could call the critical space of narrative, which is not 'just another narrative'. If it is a narrative, it is a narrative about the limits and scope and significance of narrative. And if the Enlightenment escapes the charge of just being another grand narrative, it is because it can be understood as a principle regulating, moderating, even deconstructing, the pretensions of individual narratives. If Said is right about the intrinsic heterogeneity of every culture, we might perhaps take that a stage further and argue that versions of this recognition of a critical space of narrative, as I have called it, can be found everywhere. It would not, then, be a matter of imposing some Western concept of enlightenment, but of seeking out and encouraging local forms of this space wherever it appears. The argument for this not being just another grand narrative would be that the plurality of narrative *calls for interpretation*, for its possibility to be even intelligible. The explanation we give is in terms of the non-natural constructedness of identity, which opens up the plurality of grounds.

By the critical space of narrative I do not just mean the space of scholarship, but that dimension of any culture which acknowledges and affirms the constructedness of its artefacts, and does so without falling into an ironic consciousness. For it is this fate which haunts every attempt to acknowledge plurality. Once we hold our deepest beliefs in the same spirit as we wear brand-name T-shirts, once our deepest beliefs become mere matters of taste, something essential has been lost.

Notes

1. I am reminded here of an example of Lacan's - the moebius strip - a circular band, cut, twisted and rejoined, which then possesses only one surface, but at every point two sides. The two sides could be used to represent the empirical and transcendental - made of the same material, but performing distinct functions, and at any chosen point, operating at different levels. On such a model, Kierkegaard's references to God's role in helping to constitute a self would be references to the necessity of a transcendental function, which could not, he claims, be provided entirely by the Self alone; but we might come to wonder whether the construction of a wholly discontinuous power was necessary.

2. See, for example, Nietzsche's account of eternal recurrence (e.g. in *The Gay Science* section 341). See also my discussion on the eternal recurrence in *The Deconstruction of Time*, Humanities, 1989, ch. 1, 'Nietzsche's Transvaluation of Time'.

3. Here one could try to think together the diaspora, the songlines of Australian aborigines discussed by Bruce Chatwin (in *Songlines*), Husserl on gypsies, and the American myth of the road, from Jack Kerouac, to road movies and onwards.

4. What we mean by modernity is clearly connected with secularisation, with the displacement of religious belief and religious fellowship as the basis of our sense of self. If lived-identity rests on certain horizons of constancy, and if the maintenance of some of these horizons of constancy has been displaced from religion to the state, and dependent institutions of civil society, then a great deal will hang on the maintenance of state-functions. If these state-functions disintegrate, then, in the absence of surviving buffering institutions, a cascade of consequences follow, and we can expect a return to the war of all against all from which the state had delivered us. It is not difficult to see the extreme and almost unbelievable violence that followed the breakup of Yugoslavia in this light, and the combination of genocidal 'ethnic cleansing' with rape and torture camps suggests a desperate scramble for even the most primitive forms of selfhood. One is reminded of Sartre's dialectical accounts of the variety of concrete relations with others that follow the breakdown of love: sadism, masochism, hatred, etc.

5. See, for example, Bataille, and also Derrida in 'Eating Well' (in *Who Comes After the Subject*, ed. Cadaver).

6. And we must not discount here Jean-Luc Nancy's suggestion (in *The Inoperable Community*) that it is precisely the sense of loss of community that founds our (residual?) sense of community today, however much of a myth that is.

7. At this point, one could begin to develop a philosophy of education -

and indeed develop the consequences for a broader political philosophy - which reminded us that whatever values we espouse, we are committed to valuing the conditions they presuppose. And if a free market does not supply the conditions for real freedom, they must be met in other ways.

8 As Richard Kearney points out in his *Poetics of Imagining*, Harper Collins, 1991, p225, referring to The Shoah, and to Primo Levi.

9 I owe this suggestion to Joe Macahery, of the Law School, at the University of Warwick.

PHILOSOPHY'S PARADOXICAL PAROCHIALISM: THE REINVENTION OF PHILOSOPHY AS GREEK

Robert Bernasconi

In 1738, Bishop William Warburton summarised scholarly opinion on the subject of the debt Greek philosophy owed to Egypt: 'That all the Wisdom and Learning of the *Greeks* was brought or fetched immediately from *Egypt*, is so unanimously acknowledged by themselves, that it is the best established Fact in Antiquity.'[1] He was thinking, for example, of Isocrates's statement about Pythagoras that 'On a visit to Egypt he became a student of the religion of the people, and was the first to bring to the Greeks all philosophy.'[2] Less than one hundred years after Warburton's confident restatement of a view that few observers had thought to put in question, Hegel stated with equal assurance the new orthodoxy that philosophy began in Greece. Hegel dismissed 'the legend disseminated everywhere that Pythagoras brought his philosophy from India and Egypt', as the result of a failure to distinguish philosophy from religious ideas.[3] Hegel also dismissed the old tradition of including Persian and Indian philosophy within the history of philosophy, insisting that there could be no real (*eigentlich*) philosophy in the Oriental world. When, in his lectures on the history of philosophy of 1825, he did offer some remarks about China and India, he prefaced them with the curious comment that 'I have previously passed them over, for it is only in recent times that we have been put in a position to pass judgement on it.'[4] Hegel lets slip here the fact that the decision against Chinese and Indian philosophy was made largely in ignorance and that the justification, such as it was, was provided mainly after the fact. One could say with little exaggeration that scholars had passed with a minimum of debate from one orthodoxy to another simply in the space of a generation. When one considers that the canon of the history of philosophy that has survived largely intact up to our own time was established during that period, it is surprising how little the process of its formation has been studied.

What counts as philosophy? Who counts as a philosopher? These questions are philosophical questions and are most hotly contested when philosophy is at its most vigorous. Any attempt to reopen the question of the origin of philosophy tends to be treated as an attack on philosophy: it threatens cherished conceptions of philosophy and reason. People hold back because they cannot see where it is leading. Even deconstruction, which challenges the notions of both the origin and unity of the tradition of Western philosophy, and constantly questions the account of that tradition that is found in Hegel and Heidegger, never ceases to return to it, as if it could not bear to depart from it. I propose that the questioning of the philosophical tradition has to be rethought as a questioning of the identities in terms of which philosophy has been fabricated. The construction of the history of philosophy in terms of, for example, the Germans, the English, Europe, the West, and especially Greece, must be investigated. I shall try to show why the question of the pure origin of philosophy became important to the extent that that origin could be located in Greece.

In what follows I want to explore the hegemony accorded to the so-called Western philosophical tradition as it is reflected in most of the standard presentations of the history of philosophy. Many philosophers today are quite ready, when asked, to question the claim to exclusivity on the part of 'Western philosophy'. The boundaries are not as tightly drawn as they once were. However, more important than what academic philosophers think are the institutional practices they endorse. Most philosophy departments, and this is not only true of Europe and North America, teach the history of philosophy as a narrative which begins in Greece: attempts to break from this model are at best half-hearted. That is why I believe it is important to re-examine the institutional process by which, in the late eighteenth century, philosophy came to be conceived as a preeminently European or Western enterprise, Greek in origin. The question of the institution of philosophy is also always a question addressed to the institutions of philosophy. What is one to make of the apparent tension between the alleged universality of reason and the fact that its upholders are so intent on localising its historical instantiation? It is this that I call the paradox of philosophy's parochialism.

In this essay I do not intend to re-examine the historical evidence that might allow us to judge whether philosophy began in Egypt, Greece, or elsewhere, although I would underline that most of that evidence tells us relatively little, unless we already think we know what philosophy is, which is, of course, precisely what is in question. I am attempting merely to explore what came to be invested in the question of the origin of philosophy as it was posed at the end of the eighteenth century. Only if one recalls this history is it possible to understand the form taken by the challenge to this orthodoxy by African and African-American scholars, among others, who persist in, or revert to, the longstanding tradition in favour of the Egyptian origins of philosophy.[5] However, the question of the Greek indebtedness to Egypt must always be seen within the larger context of the state of the study of the history of philosophy at any given time.

It seems that in eighteenth century Europe, philosophy reinvented itself specifically as the Western philosophical tradition in order to address a specific problem. The problem faced by Europeans in the late seventeenth century was the existence of something in China that looked sufficiently like what they already knew as philosophy to lead some of them to believe that it was indeed philosophy. Leibniz addressed the questions posed by the discovery of Chinese thought in his *Discourse on the Natural Theology of the Chinese*. Although Leibniz was familiar with the 1687 translation of the Confucian *Analects*, the *Great Learning*, and the Doctrine of the *Mean*, he also relied heavily on Catholic missionaries for his knowledge of Chinese thought.[6] He was persuaded by one of them, Joachim Bouvet, that the basic trigrams of the *I Ching* were a notation for describing scientific truth similar to Leibniz's own work in mathematics. It was an observation that accorded well with Leibniz's own belief in the universality of reason.[7] However, Bouvet also appears to have persuaded Leibniz that, since the Chinese sometimes arrived at the right answers without sufficient reason for doing so, as for example, in astronomy, they must have learned these answers from 'the tradition of the

Patriarchs.'[8] When Bouvet told Leibniz that he considered Hsi to be 'the prince of all the philosophers', he added that the description was not an 'atrocious offence against Europe' because Fu Hsi was not Chinese, but was instead Zoroaster, Hermes Trismegistus or Enoch.[9] It was such a shock to Bouvet's sensibilities to find philosophical acumen among the Chinese that he had to locate its source in his own tradition. Nor should one forget that Leibniz's interest in the Chinese was motivated less by his commitment to the universality of reason, than by his quest to find those philosophical insights that would best prepare them for conversion to Christianity.[10]

Although written during 1715 and 1716, Leibniz's *Discourse* was not published until 1735. It was Christian Wolff who bore the brunt of the controversy about Chinese philosophy, as well as the hostility that many of his contemporaries felt toward the philosophy of Leibniz. In 1721, in his fifteenth year as Professor of mathematics at the University of Halle, Wolff gave a lecture 'On the Practical Philosophy of the Chinese', in which he praised the moral teaching of the Chinese, while at the same time underlining the fact that they had attained their knowledge of moral truth without the assistance of revelation. At that time the primary argument against Confucianism was not that it was not philosophy, but that it was atheist. This is reflected in the fact that Wolff's interest in Chinese philosophy led him to be charged with atheism. The ensuing controversy expanded to cover other controversial aspects of Wolff's thought and in 1723 he was banished from Prussia under pain of death.[11] The story of Wolff was not forgotten by Voltaire who recalled it in the entry on China in his *Philosophical Dictionary*. Voltaire's own opinion was that Zoroaster, Hermes, Orpheus, and the legislators of Chaldea, Persia, Syria, Egypt, and Greece, could not be considered philosophers, but that it was entirely legitimate to recognise Chinese philosophy. Indeed, Voltaire, who was particularly interested in moral philosophy, acknowledged Confucius, not a Greek, as the first philosopher, even if, as he said in a phrase that recalls Bouvet, this was 'a disgrace for occidental nations'.[12] There was in the eighteenth century genuine interest in what today might be called non-Western philosophies. So, when Diderot in 1764 published his *General*

History of Dogmas and Philosophical Opinions, containing
articles drawn from the *Encyclopaedia*, he included, for example,
an essay on the 'Philosophy of the Canadians' detailing the beliefs
Native Americans held about God, the immortality of the soul,
and the nature of human reason.

Certain eighteenth century scholars allowed for a kind of
pluralism in the history of philosophy that, for all its limitations,
is not even close to being matched today. This was particularly
true of Germany, where the importance of Wolff's contribution
was reflected in the widespread adoption of his name for
philosophy: *Weltweisheit*. In the eighteenth century, histories of
philosophy tended to begin with a section describing the variety
of philosophies that constituted worldwisdom. For example,
Schubert's *History of Philosophy* from 1742 began with the
philosophy of the Chaldeans, the Persians, the Phoenicians, the
Arabs, the Jews, the Indians, the Chinese, the Egyptians, the
Ethiopians, the Druids or Celts, the Scythians, the early Romans,
and the Etruscans.[13] Only then did Schubert turn to the Greeks.
The range of these histories corresponds to that already
recognised by Augustine in *The City of God*. Even though
Augustine believed himself to be in possession of the truth, and
even though he had already decided that Platonism was the
philosophy that most closely anticipated that truth, he did not
rule out in advance the possibility that others might have
approximated to it and that Platonism might have been
discovered independently by non-Greeks.

> *There may be others to be found who perceived and taught
> this truth among those who were esteemed as sages or
> philosophers in other nations. Libyans of Atlas, Egyptians,
> Indians, Persians, Chaldeans, Scythians, Gauls,
> Spaniards. Whoever they may have been, we rank such
> thinkers above all others and acknowledge them as
> representing the closest approximation to our Christian
> position.*[14]

By the end of the eighteenth century this sense of the multiplicity
of philosophies was disappearing in favour of a narrative
conception of Western philosophy of the kind that prepared the

way for Hegel. However, narrativity was not the sole issue. If it was, Egypt could have retained the place in the story that had traditionally been assigned to it. The exclusion of Egypt from the history of philosophy - a virtual silence in the case of Hegel - coincided with a sudden investment in the question of the origin of philosophy, and specifically its Greek origin.

When in 1690 Sir William Temple published 'An Essay upon the Ancient and Modern Learning', he may not have had a great deal of information on which to base his speculations, but he was also not encumbered by a sense that there must have been an origin to philosophy. So although Temple began with the standard recognition of Egypt's role, he was not beyond extending the inquiry further afield.

> *There is nothing more agreed than, that all the Learning of the* Greeks *was deduced originally from* Egypt *or* Phoenicia; *but, Whether theirs might not have flourished to that Degree it did by the Commerce of the* Ethiopians, Chaldaens, Arabians, *and* Indians *is not so evident, though I am apt to believe it.*[15]

Temple judged Thales and Pythagoras to be the *two* founders of Greek philosophy and he was ready to believe that both had travelled extensively. This was especially true of Pythagoras, whom he claimed visited Ethiopia, Arabia and India, in addition to spending twenty-two years in Egypt and twelve in Babylon. Using the doctrine of the transmigration of souls as his criterion, Temple was inclined to think that Pythagoras learned more from the Indian Brahmana than from the Egyptian priests. However, there seemed relatively little at stake for him in the discussion. He thought that the Egyptians also drew their learning from the Indians, but probably via the Ethiopians, whom he thought of as a colony that had originally transplanted itself from the area around the river Indus. Clearly Temple, for all his lack of knowledge, was uninhibited either by the presupposition of an absolute origin or by a refusal to admit that non-Greeks, and particularly Indians and Chinese, are capable of philosophy. Temple stated the problem as follows: 'It may look like a Paradox to deduce Learning from Regions accounted commonly so barbarous and rude. And 'tis true the generality of People were always so in those *Eastern* Countries, and their lives wholly turned to Agriculture, to Mechaniks, or to Trades' (p14). However, Temple was aware that it is still possible that in such circumstances 'particular Races or Successions of Men' might be 'turned wholly to Learning and Knowledge': 'Besides, I know no Circumstances like to Contribute more to the advancement of Knowledge and Learning among men than exact Temperance in their Races, great pureness of Air, and equality of Clymate, long Tranquility of Empire or Government' (p15). That, for Temple, the forms of government found in India and China were conducive to philosophy, sets him apart from later scholars who would insist that philosophy began in Greece.

Dietrich Tiedemann was not the first to say that philosophy began in Greece, but his *Geist der spekulativen Philosophie*, which was published in 1791, was apparently the first history of philosophy of the late eighteenth century to begin its account of worldwisdom with Thales. Tiedemann devoted very little attention in *Geist der spekulativen Philosophie* to challenging the account that he displaced. Tiedemann effected this transformation by working with a strong definition of philosophy, which included reference not only to knowledge acquired through reasoning, but also to the individual thinker who originated or authored it. A community or a people does not have a philosophy; it is the individual thinker who has a philosophy. Tiedemann's insistence on the individual thinker is particularly significant because at a stroke it rendered irrelevant the question of the extent of the indebtedness of Greek philosophy to other sources, especially Egyptian philosophy. A similar process is at work in Tennemann's eleven volume history of philosophy that began to appear in 1798. Reading this work one would have no idea that a generation earlier the orthodoxy was still that the Greeks owed a strong debt to the Egyptians and others. So far as Tennemann was concerned, the main benefit Pythagoras derived from his stay in Egypt was a certain enhancement of his fame and his reputation among his contemporaries. The argument is still heard today.

It is worth recalling that there had been Greeks who had sought to diminish the contribution of Egyptian and other non-

Greek or barbarian people to the development of philosophy in Greece. Perhaps the foremost among them was Diogenes Laertius, who, it should be remembered, is nevertheless an important, albeit late, source for our knowledge of the contacts that Greek thinkers had with other peoples. Diogenes Laertius wrote in support of the Greek origins of philosophy:

> *There are some who say that the study of philosophy had its beginning among the barbarians. They urge that the Persians have had their Magi, the Babylonians or Assyrians their Chaldaeans, and the Indians their Gymnosophists; and among the Celts and Gauls there are people called Druids . . . If we may believe the Egyptians, Hephaestus was the son of the Nile, and with him philosophy began . . . These authors forget that the achievements which they attribute to the barbarians belong to the Greeks, with whom not merely philosophy but the human race began.*[16]

Only the reference to the origin of humanity would make these sentiments out of place in Tiedemann, or almost any nineteenth or twentieth century history of philosophy. But the excessiveness of his claim that humanity began in Greece makes it impossible not to ask why it is so important to Diogenes Laertius to exclude the possibility that philosophy was an activity in which so-called barbarians engaged. The same question arises in respect of the rewriting of the history of philosophy that take place in Tiedemann and Tennemann.

What led to the transformation of the history of philosophy into a single narrative, and one from which Egypt was excluded? The most prominent of recent attempts to answer this question is to be found in the first volume of Martin Bernal's *Black Athena*. It is important to remember that *Black Athena* is primarily concerned with what he calls 'the Afro-Asiatic contribution' to the formation of Greece in the Middle and Late Bronze Age and not the question of the origin of philosophy. Bernal announces his interest in the transmission of Egyptian and Phoenician philosophy to the Greeks, but postpones consideration of it to another occasion.[17] If Bernal cannot resist introducing some discussion of Tiedemann's view on this subject, it is largely because he wants to use the latter's attitude to the question of Greece's intellectual debt to Egypt as a measure of German racism as applied to intellectual questions. Bernal believes that it is revealed so clearly in this case that it can then be used to help gauge the bias of other scholars when they address the question of the Egyptian colonisation of Greece, which is his primary interest in *Black Athena*.

Bernal identifies four forces at work in the change in the relative assessment of Egypt and the Orient vis-à-vis Greece: the tension between Christianity and Egyptian religion after hermeticism; the rise of the concept of progress; the growth of racism; and Romantic Hellenism. In *Black Athena* Bernal gives most weight to racism. What renders this claim plausible is the growing belief among Germans that they were a people of poets and thinkers who had a spiritual relationship that they shared uniquely with the Greeks. By focusing on the German proponents of the thesis about the Greek origin of philosophy, Bernal leaves the impression that the dominant factor in the change was the 'German crisis of identity in the 18th century' (p214). In particular, Bernal associates the conviction that philosophy began in Greece with Göttingen University, which he portrays as a seedbed of racism and German nationalism. It is true that Tiedemann was a student there and that Kristophe August Heumann, one of the University's founders, had already in 1715 rejected the claim that the Egyptians were philosophical. However, it is worth recalling that Bernal himself notes that German scholars were more concerned to establish the superiority of the Greeks than they were inclined to disparage the Egyptians whose racial identity was at that time regarded as sufficiently ambiguous for them to be assimilated to Europe. Although it is clear that chauvinism was a powerful force in German thought at that time, Bernal has not yet established his case about the racist basis for the late eighteenth century denial of Egyptian philosophy.

He is on stronger ground when he emphasises the fact that the scholars who rejected the idea of Egyptian philosophy had no additional basis for doing so than their predecessors. The argument is not by itself decisive, however, because theoretically it is possible that it is the previous generations of scholars who should be chastised for failing to recognise the claims of Greek philosophy on the basis of evidence already available to them. Furthermore, Bernal's point that there was not either in 1800 or later a real debate about the Greek origin of philosophy would have been stronger if he had not ignored the debate about the nature of philosophy which inevitably impacts on the way the history of philosophy is written. To that extent the history of philosophy is always philosophical. Bernal is properly suspicious of Kristophe Heumann's distinction between Egyptian 'arts and studies', on the one hand, and Greek 'philosophy', on the other hand, but when he sees that Heumann defined philosophy simply as 'the research and study of useful truths based on reason', he judged that 'its very imprecision made, and makes, the claim that the Greeks were the first "philosophers" almost impossible to refute' (p334). This should have alerted Bernal to the need to address this question. There is always a question - a philosophical question - as to how any specific definition of philosophy comes to be established and exclude whatever might otherwise be regarded as philosophy by displacing it as myth, religion, *Volksgeist* or *Weltanschauung*. It should not go unnoticed that during the time when Egyptian, Chinese and Indian philosophy were being excluded, or at very least diminished in importance, the same thing was happening, for example, to the Cambridge Platonists, as part of philosophy's constant process of redefining itself. The narrowing of the history of philosophy to Greece and its legacy must be understood in relation to a certain narrowing of the conception of philosophy. Not only were Egyptian and other non-Greek forms of wisdom excluded from philosophy, but also much that had passed for philosophy in Europe right up to the eighteenth century. The development of the experimental sciences played an important part in this process, but the conceptual means by which the exclusion was accomplished was a conception of reason authorised in part by the distinction between *muthos* and *logos*. The result was a conception of philosophy that many Greeks - among others - most certainly would not have recognised. Plato did not yet accept the distinction between *muthos* and *logos*. For example, Plato explicitly insisted that 'the myth is still a kind of *logos*.'[18] Indeed, a number of scholars today argue that, for the Greeks, philosophy was a kind of 'art of existing', a conception which also seems to be open to the contributions of other cultures, given the difficulty of establishing that the Greek and European cultures have a monopoly of wisdom on such matters.

Another weakness of Bernal's survey, one that he subsequently recognised, was that he focused almost exclusively on the German contribution to the history of philosophy.[19] There was already in the eighteenth century another effort to explain the originality of Greek philosophy, this time focusing not on the unique linguistic or spiritual affinity that the Germans believed that they shared with the Greeks, but on a more general political affinity that the English believed that they shared with the Greeks, as two democratic peoples. For example, Adam Smith, in a posthumously published essay on the history of astronomy, is quite clear that the first place in the West to attain civilisation was Greece together with its colonies. Smith came to that conclusion, in spite of the fact that, as he conceded, he lacked evidence about the status of learning under the great monarchies of Asia and Egypt. However, he insisted that he did not need direct evidence; he already knew that despotism prevented the growth of philosophy.[20] What makes the argument seem especially arbitrary is the fact that it starts from the argument about law and order as a condition of learning and comes up with the opposite conclusion by adding the premise that despotism prevents the growth of philosophy. In the same vein, Voltaire, in *Essai sur les moeurs*, argued that what contributed to the ingenuity of the Greeks, as opposed to the Egyptians, the Persians, the Chaldeans, and the Indians, was that in Greece 'the avenues to reason were open to everyone: all people gave vent to their ideas.'[21] Voltaire added that, for the same reason, in his own time the English were the most enlightened nation. Whether it be Dietrich Tiedemann at Göttingen or Adam Smith in Edinburgh, the debate was influenced by ideological considerations dominated by the attempt to establish a sense of national identity and endow that identity with a certain character.[22]

It seems, therefore, that a revised version of Bernal's argument, one that refers the paradoxical parochialism of philosophy not to a narrow and localisable German racism, but to a more broadly conceived chauvinism, could be sustained more readily. In this revised form, it would be possible to show that these kinds of considerations have not disappeared. One need only consult Castoriadis's spirited attack in 'The End of Philosophy' (in *Philosophy, Politics, Autonomy*) on both Heidegger and what he calls 'deconstructionist irrelevance'.[23] Castoriadis relies heavily on a conception of 'philosophical democracy' as 'the intertemporal *agora* of living and dead philosophers where they gather over the centuries and truly discuss' (p15). It is, according to Castoriadis, this 'transhistorical *agora* of reflection' that Heidegger and post-modernism generally abolishes. Of course, Castoriadis does not debate with Heidegger whether philosophy began in Greece. Neither of them even pose that as a question. Like Hegel, Heidegger dismissed the idea that there might have been a Chinese or an Indian philosophy.[24] He repeated the claim in favour of Greece in most detail in *What is Philosophy?* where he wrote,

> *The often heard expression 'Western-European philosophy' is, in truth, a tautology. Why? Because philosophy is Greek in its nature; Greek, in this instance, means that in origin the nature of philosophy is of such a kind that it first laid claim to the Greek world (Griechentum), and only it, in order to unfold.*[25]

What is at issue between Heidegger and Castoriadis is, as it was with Tiedemann and Voltaire, two different conceptions of Greece, and of philosophy, one focusing on the spiritual relation of the Greeks with the Germans and the other on democracy.

It is perhaps worth noting in concluding this survey that both conceptions are operative in Hegel's *Lectures on the History of Philosophy*. When Hegel tried to explain why the history of philosophy did not, like world history, begin in the East, he appealed to the universal connection between the political freedom of the individual and freedom of thought.[26] The relation of substance to subject that allows for philosophy is the same that allows for freedom (p269). Furthermore, just as Germanic philosophy inherits and completes Greek thought, so the principle of freedom is only realised among the Germans (pp196-7). It should be noted that Hegel often used the term 'German' in a broader sense than is usual, so that in some contexts it is equivalent to 'European'. For example, 'The European peoples, insofar as they belong to the world of thought are to be called German' (p175).

It might seem that by juxtaposing the chauvinistic narrative history of philosophy that became popular in the late eighteenth century with the more pluralistic model that I have found exemplified earlier in the century, I am advocating the latter as an alternative to the former. This is not the case. While it is certainly true that I have highlighted this contrast in order to bring into relief the genesis of the practices and prejudices that still dominate the writing of the history of philosophy, a straightforward plurality closes off options as much as it opens them. For example, such a pluralism would probably treat Egyptian philosophy and Greek philosophy as discreet units and say nothing about their relation, let alone the possibilities that might emerge if, for example, philosophers in Europe and America would more readily allow themselves to be challenged by philosophers from, for example, Japan or Africa.

One cannot understand why there has never been a serious debate about the origin of philosophy, unless one understands what is at stake in the question. The debate sparked off by this aspect of Bernal's *Black Athena* has largely focused on his claim that race has determined the way the history of philosophy has been written for almost two hundred years. I have partially qualified his thesis by suggesting that, even if chauvinism was clearly at work, more argument is needed before it can be established that the history of philosophy as a modern academic discipline was from the outset dominated by racist considerations. But that makes matters worse, not better, for the contemporary philosopher. If the history of the discipline and the conception of the discipline that history supports was not racist in its design, the question still must be addressed as to whether it has not become racist in its effects. Whole peoples experience themselves as excluded, in part because of the systematic diminishment of the achievements of their group. Philosophers almost everywhere are implicated. The problem must be addressed not just in research, but also at the institutional level in each and every department.

Notes

1. William Warburton, *The Divine Legation of Moses Demonstrated*, Garland Publishing, New York 1978, vol I, p326.

2. *Busiris* 28, in *Isocrates*, vol 3, trans. Larue van Hook, Harvard University Press, Cambridge 1945, p119.

3. G.W.F. Hegel, *Vorlesungen über die Geschichte der Philosophie. Einleitung*, Felix Meiner, Hamburg 1993, p68.

4. *Ibid.*, pp266 and 268.

5. For example, George G. M. Jones, *Stolen Legacy*, United Brothers Communications Systems, Newport News, VA 1989; Theophile Obenga, *Ancient Egypt and Black Africa*, Karnak House, London 1992, and the extensive works of Cheikh Anta Diop.

6. David E. Mungello, *Leibniz and Confucianism. The Search for Accord*, University Press of Hawaii, Honolulu 1977, p6.

7. Henry Rosemont, Jr. and Daniel J. Cook, Introduction to G. W. Leibniz, *Discourse on the Natural Theology of the Chinese*, University Press of Hawaii, Honolulu 1977, pp14-16.

8. G. W. Leibniz, *Discourse on the Natural Theology of the Chinese*, pp107 and 116.

9. Bouvet to Leibniz, 4 November 1701. See *Discourse on the Natural Theology of the Chinese*, p94, n79 and D. Mungello, *op cit*, p54.

10. Daniel J. Cook and Henry Rosemont, 'The Pre-established Harmony between Leibniz and Chinese Thought', *Discovering China*, Julia Ching and Willard Oxtoby (eds), University of Rochester Press, Rochester 1992, pp94-95.

11. Thomas P. Saine, 'Who's Afraid of Christian Wolff?' in *Anticipations of the Enlightenment in England, France, and Germany*, Alan Charles Kors and Paul J. Korshin (eds), University of Pennsylvania Press, Philadelphia 1987, pp118-127.

12. Voltaire, *Oeuvres complètes*, Vol 20, Garnier Frères, Paris 1879, p496.

13. Joanne Ernesto Schubert, *Historia Philosophiae*, pars prima, Jena, 1742.

14. Augustine, *The City of God*, Penguin, Harmondsworth 1972, p311.

15. Sir William Temple, *Essays on Ancient and Modern Learning and On Poetry*, J. E. Spingarn (ed), Oxford University Press, Oxford 1970, p8.

16. Diogenes Laertius, *Lives of Eminent Philosophers*, vol 1, trans. R. D. Hicks, Harvard University Press, Cambridge 1972, Book I, Prologue, 1-3, pp3-5.

17. Martin Bernal, *Black Athena*, Vol 1, Free Association Books, London 1985, p22.

18. *Republic*, 501E.

19. M. Bernal, 'The British Utilitarians, Imperialism and the Fall of the Ancient Model', *Culture and History* 3, 1988, p98.

20. Adam Smith, *Essays on Philosophical Subjects*, Vol 3, Oxford University Press, Oxford 1980, p51.

21. Voltaire, *The Philosophy of History*, Citadel Press, New York 1965, p116.

22. The study of the Greeks in Britain during the nineteenth century focused on democracy in a way that has led one scholar to emphasise the political character of the study of classics during that period. Frank M. Turner, *The Greek Heritage in Victorian Britain*, Yale University Press, New Haven 1981, pp187-264, and 'Martin Bernal's *Black Athena*: A Dissent', *Arethusa* Special Issue, Fall 1989, pp106-107.

23. C. Castoriadis, 'The End of Philosophy,' *Philosophy, Politics, Autonomy*, Oxford University Press, Oxford 1991, p17.

24. M. Heidegger, *What is Called Thinking?*, Harper and Row, New York 1968, p224.

25. M. Heidegger, *What is Philosophy?*, Vision Press, London 1956, pp29-31.

26. G.W.F. Hegel, *op cit*, p266.

NARRATING IMPERIALISM: NOSTROMO'S DYSTOPIA

Benita Parry

If we are to discuss narratives of imperialism, then we must disclose our understanding of what imperialism was, and what, in its late form as transnational corporate capitalism, it is; and we need to make known how we perceive the complex and disjunctive ways in which the cultural text reconfigures received representations of the material world and invents new ones.

Let me begin with the multivalence of the term 'imperialism'. Its interchangeable usage with colonialism and empire is by now so entrenched in literary and cultural studies, that it could appear pedantic to insist on the distinctive significations attached to the term by historians, political theorists and economists. A glance at the indexes of books concerned with the texts of empire, will invariably yield the information: for 'imperialism see colonialism', or vice versa. This suggests that whereas Said's writings have been the most notable inspiration to the proliferation of work concerned with uncovering the overt and hidden role of empire in the making of western culture, its authors have not always been as careful as Said to delineate colonialism as one incarnation of a more extensive and mutable process which he names 'imperialism'. At the same time, in following Said's long view of the modern imperial project as 'the practice, the theory and the attitude of a dominating centre ruling a distant territory', these same critics omit to differentiate between mercantile and plantation colonialism, which stimulated the accumulation of capital in Europe, and the subsequent industrial-military interventions and aggressive investment programmes implemented by the expansionist social orders of western nation-states.[1]

It will already be apparent that the connotations of the word are variable, referring not only to the whole or part of the west's programme of overseas conquest, occupation and rule, but also to the institution of dependencies where no military or administrative presence was or is installed, a mode perfected by the United States in its role as the predominant force of a contemporary imperialism. Given that its significations continue to be debated, I will be using the word to designate the radically altered forms to capitalism's accelerated penetration of the non-capitalist world, a process that gained momentum in the late nineteenth century and issued in the creation of a world economic system. This uneven realignment of geographically and socially diverse territories under western hegemony brought further dimensions to the west's old exploitation and management of the other hemisphere, vitalizing altered modes of apprehending time and space, and engendering new tropological ruses to validate a global reterritorialisating project.

Within the discussion of culture and imperialism, Fredric Jameson, who denotes imperialism as the 'dynamic of capitalism proper', rather than defining it as coextensive with empire's duration, is singular in associating transformations in novelistic practice at the turn of the nineteenth century, with the cognitive effects of expansionism on metropolitan social forms and experiental modes.[2] This has not been the path taken by the contemporary discussion, where critics concerned to make known empire's ubiquity in the mainstream of metropolitan literature eschew periodisation, conceiving of the imperial experience as one discernibly continuous event, presumably begetting recurrent cultural articulations. The tendency to conflate the different imperial regimes has fuelled the preoccupation of discourse analysts with the reprises of topoi in colonial texts, rather than with the innovation of rhetorical themes and figures. This is evident in a study like Sara Suleri's *The Rhetoric of English India*, where texts distant in time (from Edmund Burke to Naipaul via Kipling and Forster) are discussed as sharing 'an idiom of dubiety ... inherent in any narrative of colonial possession' - a predication where discursive form is in advance disconnected from its inconstant social conditions of possibility.[3] This is not to deny repetitions in the construction of difference and reiterations of legitimating devices; nor to overlook that a method concerned with continuities in the vast library of empire, does facilitate reading its multiple signs, whether conspicious or ghostly, written across the body of metropolitan literature.

The loss, however, is the possibility of studying the iterations and improvisations of particular rhetorics underwriting imperialism's triumphalist modernising project, and attending to the stylistic modernism of the counter-narratives these ideological inventions provoked. Here it should be noted that whereas the predominant mode of configuring the imperial connection and of representing other cultures remained overwhelmingly atavistic in form and ideologically complicit in substance, the modernist writing of empire was not intrinsically productive of a negative critique, since it could also serve to narrate an imperialist vision. Kipling's imperial anxieties were not moved by recoil from an imperialist ethos, while his requiems for empire intoned the failure of the nation's will to pursue an austere aspiration and sublime mission. We could also note that Gissing's revulsion at the vacuous pomp of the Jubilee year coexists with the hope that a population fallen into degeneracy would find spiritual renewal through participation in faraway imperial ventures.[4]

As a consequence of Said's work it is now widely recognised that metropolitan culture has for long been permeated by an imperial consciousness. And, despite the very real problems attendant on this undertaking, the search for literature's often concealed and hitherto unacknowledged filiations with empire has significantly enhanced the discussion of canonical British writing. Where once the fictions were narrowly construed as insular moral critiques of domestic manners, mores and social existence, critical attention is now directed at disclosing the ways in which knowledge of the slave trade, slave plantations, indentured labour, colonialist invasions and subsequent colonial rule expanded the novels' intelligence and impinged on the dramatisations of local social inequalities and power relationships.[5]

Although there are hazards in positing linkages by way of analogy, allegory and reenactment, it can be argued that by tracing metonymic displacements and metaphoric recastings, such, often brilliant, work succeeds in articulating colonialism together with metropolitan oppressions, thereby affording an understanding of how tropes of domination inflect each other and can be transposed from one situation to another. The problem is that these interpretations not only divert attention from the singularities of colonialist and later of imperialist enunciations, which did not necessarily replicate or resemble the strategies of metropolitan class and gender oppressions, but they also serve to obscure the literal circumstances of specific historical conditions.

The work of materialist geographers like David Harvey, Neil Smith and Edward Soja, where imperialism is understood as a complex and differential temporal order vitalised by the dynamics of industrial capitalism and implementing a transcontinental programme of reterritorialisation, has drawn attention to its self-presentation as a rational and modernising project.[6] Consider the treatise of Frederick Lord Lugard defending the appropriation of food supplies and raw materials which 'lay wasted and ungarnered in Africa because the natives did not know their use and value ... Who can deny the right of the hungry people of Europe to utilise the wasted bounties of nature, or that the task of developing these resources was ... a "trust for civilisation" and for the benefit of mankind?'[7]

If this mitigation recalls the warrant devised by Locke and reiterated by successive colonisers, for appropriating the territories of peoples amongst whom there was no system of private property and who did not properly use the land, then it is also apparent that contemporary registers are brought to the old recital. Declamations on the west's urgent need to accumulate distant territories confirm the arrival in colonialism's received representational system of a vocabulary vindicating the western nations' right and duty unilaterally to pursue a global project in the interests of 'international utility', and without regard to the desires and aspirations of the indigenous populations whose natural assets and human-labour power were to be exploited.

Not until the late nineteenth century and the massive land expropriations in Africa, intensified capitalist interventions in Asia, and the incorporation of Latin American republics as economic dependencies of western capital, did imperialist rhetoric invent an exorbitant and anomalous idiom of messianic utilitarianism and bellicose mysticism, where the positivist and

aggressive phraseology of compulsory universal modernisation
is joined with the anachronistic and chimerical lexicon of chivalry,
'a mandate of destiny', and 'a high and holy mission' serving as
ideological pillars of the west's planetary ambitions. The very
stridency of proclamations declaring other cultures to be
irredeemibly defective and entreating western guidance can now
be read as suppressing the challenge of alternative traditions
and erasing signs of colonial recalcitrance and resistance. For
cutting across the vainglorious enunciations were troubled
apprehensions of the competing social forms and cognitive modes
of the colonised worlds, intimating that the barriers erected
against dialogue were infringed by glimpses of alternatives which
could not be fixed, named and possessed in the language available
to imperialism's explanatory system. A triumphalist rhetoric
veined with uncertainty is given virtuoso performances in fictions
collusive with imperial goals, while dissident texts in registering
recoil from imperialism's vauntful self-representation and alarm
at empire's deletrious effects on metropolitan morality, parody,
distance, contest and undermine the authorised version.

Before proceeding to my discussion of *Nostromo's* singular
and subversive reworkings of imperialist rhetoric, I want very
quickly to consider how Fredric Jameson and Edward Said in
differen ways, but with equal nuance and refined attention to
the literary text and the historicity of textual form, perceive the
ways in which the imperialist moment effected radical stylistic
changes in the substance and structure of the novel. The dynamic
transcodings in narrative form of the various stages of capitalism
is one which Jameson has examined in *The Political Unconscious*.
From the 'magical narratives' of pre-capitalist society, which are
seen as social products embodying the collective experience of
comparatively unified communities, Jameson, following Lukács,
looks at the novel as the privileged form of an individualist
capitalist society, and the appropriate mode for the expression
of a relatively coherent bourgeois identity. With the passing of
capitalism's heroic age, later novels disclose the disintegration
of this subjectivity, Conrad's fictions offering key articulations
of the fragmentation and reification of experience in an age of
growing commodification and brutal colonisation.[8]

Jameson's subsequent discussion in *Modernism and*

Imperialism, in which more recent novels are considered, is concerned with 'the representational dilemma of the new imperial world system' (p19), where the structural coordinates binding the subjective life of the metropolitan individual to empire are no longer accessible 'to immediate lived experience'. Arguing that fiction must therefore invent modes which 'inscribe a new sense of the absent global colonial system on the very syntax of poetic language itself', Jameson directs attention at the marks imperialism makes on inner forms and structures. An innovative reading of *Howards End* elaborates the proposition that where the worlds beyond the metropolis remain 'unknown and unimaginable for the subjects of the imperial power' (p11), the expanded spatial perceptions of far-flung empire brought into being by imperialist expansion are transformed into radically altered apprehensions and representations of the local socially-produced geography. Jameson's grasp of how intimately metropolitan fiction domesticated the new global consciousness offers limitless possibilities for discerning the refractions of imperialism in modernism's Great Works. All the same, by locating imperialism's traces in 'stylistic or linguistic peculiarities' or formal innovations, Jameson's schema excludes those few but significant modernist texts within the largely non-canonical literature of empire, whose representational structures did encompass an apprehension of the world-system, or where a traditional referential mode conforming to an imperialist world-view was interrupted by linguistic eccentricities and self-reflexible narrative modes.

In *Culture and Imperialism*, overseas empire is perceived by Said as infiltrating metropolitan culture neither as displaced referent, resonant void or return of the repressed, but by way of 'a structure of attitudes and references' designed and perpetuated in a range of textual and other representational media that drew support from and nourished the imperial ideology and imagination. Said associates the preeminence of the novel, which functions as a 'quasi-encyclopoedic cultural form', and was 'a major intellectual voice' within British cultural life, with the dominance of the British Empire, observing that although the novel has for long been recognised as an artefact of bourgeois society, no attempt has been made to examine the 'convergence between the patterns of narrative authority constitutive of the novel ... and ... a complex ideological pattern underlying the tendency to imperialism.'[9] For Said, then, inscriptions of empire are located in the very entrails of the nineteenth century realist narrative, and because he conceives of colonialism's trajectory as a geographical and reterritorialising project culminating in the west's global hegemony, his discussion is able to illuminate affiliations between a bellicose social enterprise and the assertions of narrative power.

Said, who makes no explicit link between imperialism and capitalism's dynamics, relates the loss of narrative confidence and the emergence of modernist style to the crisis of empire, connecting the formal dislocations and displacements in the novel with that moment when the colonised's locations and cultures impinged on metropolitan consciousness with greater intensity, enlarging but also fracturing its cognitive landscape. Thus, in his own terms, he detects the turn from 'the triumphalist experience of imperialism', which was justificatory and celebratory, 'into the extremes of self-consciousness, discontinuity, self-referentiality and corrosive irony whose formal patterns we have come to recognise as the hallmarks of modernist culture' (p227). As both Said and Jameson acknowledge, Conrad's writings exemplify this transition within British literature, and in discussing *Nostromo's* narration of imperialism as historical event, ethical idea and social aspiration, I will attempt to examine how the disintegration of imperialism's moral certainties is dramatised by the the novel's representational and formal structures.

Since my assumption is that cultural practices belong to the same universe as material conditions, and because my interest is in the complex and disjunctive reemergence as aesthetic text of discourses generated at the level of the social and institutional, the relationship of fictional form and rhetorical invention to prior and accredited constructions of historical processes is perceived in terms of the mediation or transcoding between the categories[10], and the outcome is understood as the *initiation*, and not the rehearsal of representations. Such reconfigurations, achieved by way of translation, reanimation, displacement, disguise, estrangment and interrogation, may or may not underpin the established ideology, but they are intimately if contradictorily joined, whether as affirmation or subversion, to prescribed interpretations of social forms, cognitive traditions and cultural meanings.

This does not imply that the author brings to fiction nothing but a copyist's skill in producing variations on existing designs; and because I am discussing a book by Conrad, it seems appropriate to cite his views on the novel as a privileged mode of conceptualising the social world:

> *Fiction is history, human history, or it is nothing. But it is also more than that; it stands on firmer ground, being based on the reality of forms and the observation of social phenomena, whereas history is based on documents, and the reading of print and handwriting - on second-hand impression. Thus fiction is nearer truth.*[11]

Here Conrad is claiming the novelist's unique faculty for inaugurating representations composed through an unprecedented experience of already interpreted existential circumstances. The notion of fiction as the performance of an author's subjective vision will be frowned upon in an intellectual environment where critics insist that the excess of connotatative meaning engendered by writing inhibits any text from reaching its intended destination. All the same, and to the extent that Conrad's fictions, whether earnestly or as pastiche, reiterate received versions of historical worlds, *and* critically distance the social modes and events which the novels narrate, I will read these as the fruits of a sensibility nurtured and constrained by the cultural codes from within which it emerges - as well as by a position of cultural and political authority - *and* as the 'free spiritual production' (which is Marx's term) of an imagination animated by singular persuasions and desires, and inspired to vagrancy by unconformable conceptual and sensory perceptions. This, I must emphasise, is not to maintain that the writing is without unconscious signification or ambiguity and contradiction, and these unrehearsed and inadvertent modulations are amongst the aspects which my discussion seeks to address.

Beginnings, Edward Said has written, 'have to be made for each project in such a way as to *enable* what follows from them'.[12] Because I read *Nostromo* as unfolding the arrival of industrial capitalism in Latin America, an apt point of entry is Rosa Luxemburg's characterisation of imperialism as 'the political expression of the accumulation of capital in its competitive struggle for what remains still open of the non-capitalist environment.'[13] Said who now includes *Nostromo* in the canon of 'great imperialist narratives', (*Culture and Imperialism*, p132) once read it as a fiction which although masquerading 'as an ordinary political or historical novel', overturns 'the confident edifice that novels normally construct', to reveal itself as 'no more than a *record* of novelistic self-reflection.'[14] As I see it, the two aspects are inseparable, since the ostentatious disarrangement of the novel form which Conrad inherited, together with the visible erosion through dispersal of narrative authority, constitute the fiction's historiographical demsystification and produce its uncertain politics. Conrad's problem, I suggest, was how to tell *this* story, the substance of which is the precipitate and uneven transformation of a pre-modern world through foreign intervention, and that could be sub-titled 'Capitalism Comes to Costaguana', without underwriting the process as the enactment of the west's historical destiny and the attainment of a telos. But whereas I argue that the novel's deliberated narrative performance subverts received reconstructions of the western imperial mission, my discussion will also consider how the direction of this critique is circumvented by Conrad's meditations on imperialism's 'saving ideas', and diverted by his suspicion of revolutionary energies that would expropriate the expropriators.[15]

Rather than articulate the consensual cognition of the upward development in history exemplified and implemented by the bourgeois west, the novel's storyline follows an errant path that transgresses the constraints of sequence. Hence the retardations, deferrals, digressions and temporal displacements - where significant effects precede any credible explanation of the generative circumstances to the phenomena recounted - both countermand the official recitation of irresistible progress, and refuse the demand of imperialist ideology to map an itinerary of orderly advance.[16] At the same time, Conrad, who had scant regard for Latin American societies, and eschewed enacting any mind-altering encounter with their cultural forms, apprehended and tracked a different order of time appropriate to the turbulent history of 'the revolutionary continent'; and although he dismisses its endemic political upheaval and social disorder as a tragic farce, his writing admits the impossibility of accomodating so aberrant an experience within a linearly-ordered, continuous chronicle.

Thus far I have proposed that the novel's narrative form contradicts imperialism's prescribed version of its ordained and unimpeded route. This distancing stance is compounded by the irony with which both the optimistic remembrances of Captain Mitchell and the teleological annals of Don Avellanos are disclosed; and it is configured by the Golfo Placido, a space that an expansionist west is unable to master, as it does the land and mountains of Costaguana. Absolutely silent and dark, motionless and veiled in tremendous obscurity, this sea represents an unnegotiable obstacle to imperialism's world-conquering aspiration : 'No intelligence could penetrate the darkness of the Placid Gulf' (p231).[17] For the urbane and intellectually self-confident Decoud, the translated Latin American with pretensions to European refinement and sensibility, the passage across its dark and silent waters acts on 'his senses like a powerful drug' (p219, 220). Alone on an uninhabited island in the vast and motionless lake, oppressed with 'a bizarre sense of unreality affecting the very ground upon which he walked' (p253), Decoud 'caught himself entertaining a doubt of his own individuality. It had merged into the world of cloud and water, of natural forces and forms of nature' (p409).

Despite his cynicism and levity, Decoud, as the accidental architect of Sulaco Province's secession and the formation of the Occidental Republic, had become an agent of imperialism's hold on Latin America. Thus, because his existential anguish and disintegration are precipitated by a metaphysical geography signifying 'the immense indifference of things' (p412), and his self-inflicted death occurs 'in this glory of merciless solitude and silence ... whose glittering surface remained untroubled by the fall of his body' (p411), the Gulf, the figure of an insurmountable impediment to a triumphalist social and ideological project, acts in the narrative as the destroyer of the sovereign self cherished by the ascendant west: 'In our activity alone do we find the sustaining illusion of an independent existence as against the whole scheme of things of which we form a helpless part' (p409). It is perhaps significant that Nostromo, the Italian sailor whose element is the sea, and who is an unreliable servitor of imperialism's purpose, is not defeated by the Gulf, undergoing instead a dual transformation when he reemerges from its waters in the guise of one reborn, but mutated in schizoid fashion as the thief who mimics imperialism's (im)morality, and the dubious dissident resentful of its rule and plotting its demise.

A notoriously devious chronology, together with the dramatisation of the barriers to imperialism's supremacist goals, can thus be read as devices serving to distinguish *Nostromo's* narration from the modes of previous and contemporaneous texts valorising capitalism's inexorable momentum. These defamiliarising strategies also confute the fiction's own pretence to mimetism. Jean Franco has suggested that because 'contemporary critics tended to judge his work according to his ability to create plausible characters and situations', Conrad worked under the constraint of verisimilitude.[18] Certainly the novel's representations of Latin America and the attendant gloss are blatantly tendentious in reiterating Europe's disobliging opinion of a mestizo sub-continent whose habits of depravity and perennial disorder inhibit 'the success of anything rational'. Such ideologically saturated 'realism' displays a lawless and incorrigible population passively tolerant of venal dictators given to Ruritanian dress and the extravagant address of pronunciemientos and plesbiscites - a scenario which undoubtedly functions to validate the west's rational and beneficent intervention. It is, however, interrupted by other representations, and in the glances at the old Costaguana with its pristine ravines and waterfalls (p98), its 'simple and picturesque' scenes (109), and its popular festivals (p112), the fiction invokes an environment destroyed by imperialism, and gestures towards the authenticity of the foreign which it also disparages.

A more profound disruption of the fiction's realist mode, and with it the case for western intrusion into other worlds, issues from the fiction's scrutiny of the imperialist ethos. This is elaborated around the notion of 'material interests', an oxymoronic contraction of the substantial and the abstract, identified by more than one critic as a coded phrase for capitalism. The silver, the fiction's overarching trope and 'the symbol of the supreme importance of material interests' (p219), is both a corporeal, indeed an incorruptible substance - as well as being the physical incarnation of the profits yielded by the exploitation of labour - and an abstraction. Its paradox is thus condensed not only in the tropological movement between the tangible and the imperceptible, but in the ascription of purposive life and affect to an inanimate object: the mine is perceived by Mrs Gould as 'feared, hated, wealthy; more soulless than any tyrant, more pitiless and autocratic than the worst Government' (p427-8); while 'treasure' is imbued by Nostromo with the power to fasten upon a man's mind (p379), appearing to him as 'shining spectre ... claiming his allegiance' (p435).

The affinities between Conrad's dramatisations of the corruptions visited on human relationships under capitalism, and Marx's analysis of commodity fetishism, are apparent.[19] It is the wealth-producing silver mine as an 'idea' that Mrs Gould sees turn into a 'fetish', and in which the mine-owner, Charles Gould, had indeed invested not only capital but desire, holding to it 'as some men do to the idea of love' (p207). The critique of reification extends to the perception of persons as commodities: Nostromo's name is both the Italian word for boatswain/bo'sun, which is his occupation, and a contraction of 'nostro uomo' or 'our man'; the President-Dictator Ribiera, candidate of the Spanish oligarchs and the foreign investors, is regarded by the British chairman of the Railway Board as 'their own creature' (p44), and in backing the project of the Englishman Gould to reopen the family mine, the American millionaire Holroyd exults in 'running a man!' (p79).

Yet although the novel enunciates recoil from the ethos of Material Interest, its recourse to other anomalous constructions - 'inspired by an idealistic view of success' (p68), 'prosperity without a strain on its real, on its immaterial side' (p73), and 'unselfish ambition' (p81) - suggests that Conrad, as in other novels, is again circling around the notion of a 'saving idea'. Hence while the invocations of probity and moral commitment as legitimising strategies for the west's pursuit of a utilitarian and self-aggrandising project are derided, the promise of redemption through adherence to visionary goals is, even if tentatively, tendered - consider the much-cited scene of Mrs Gould ceremonially receiving the silver, which is yet another performance of commodity fetishism: 'She laid her unmercenary hands ... upon the first ingot turned out still warm from the mould, and by her imaginative estimate of its power, she endowed that lump of metal with a justificative conception' (p99).

On the one hand there is a surfeit of irony calculated to deflate the pretentions to righteousness and idealism of those pursuing pragmatic and self-interested purposes : 'the only solid thing ... is the spiritual value which everybody discovers in his own form of activity', is the British Chief-engineer's sceptical remark (p266); while the sentimentalist Holroyd, 'the millionaire endower of churches' (p74), is ridiculed for combining devotion to the accumulation of profits with the idea of 'introducing not only justice, industry, peace, to the benighted continents, but also ... a purer form of Christianity' (p203). All the same, the sentimental, the other-worldly and the chivalric are revalued, and no more so than in the slippage of the original meaning attached to 'material interest'. Initially offered as a conflation of base and superstructure, the two are disjoined when the term comes to signify 'the moral degradation of the idea' and the enemy of 'disinterestness', 'rectitude', and 'moral principle' (p419).

The exposure of 'material interests' as 'materialism', the gainful development of material resources, material prosperity, and material advantage, conforms with its usage in contemporary public discussion, where it unequivocally denoted projects for the accumulation of capital. In his frequent pronouncements on imperialist themes, Joseph Chamberlain, a vigorous exponent of Britain's expansion, reiterated precisely this phrase as a synonym for the acquisition of territory, overseas commercial enterprise, returns on investment in the colonies, the garnering of natural and mineral wealth in imperial possessions, and the exploitation of the empire's labour resources. Here the incongruity is located not within the term, but in the misalliance between mercenary ambition and economic gain, and the boast that these constituted devotion to 'national duty', 'high ideals', 'dreams', 'high sentiment', 'imagination', 'mission', 'responsibility', and 'honour'.[20]

Truly there was much to hand in the contemporary rhetoric for Conrad to parody; and whereas the ideologically conformist representations of Latin America, the sentimentalism of allegorising women as keepers of fine conscience, and the dramatisation of ethical dilemmas are brought into being by languages that remain within the conventions of polemic, romance, melodama and moral drama, another and dissonant idiom is invoked when the text alludes to the perfidious objects of imperialist desire. Consider Mrs Gould's derision of Holroyd's preoccupation as 'the religion of silver and iron' (p71); the narrative scorn when reiterating the version of Sulaco's secession as 'the struggle for Right and Justice at the Dawn of a New Era' (p393); the acerbity in attributing to Holroyd 'the temperament of a puritan' joined with an 'insatiable imagination of conquest' (p75); and the sardonic characterisation of the imperialist ambition as 'the misty idealism of the Northerners, who at the smallest encouragement dream of nothing less than the conquest of the earth' (p278).

The disgrace of honourable aspirations tied to predatory purposes is performed by the gracious figure of Mrs Gould, a reincarnation of The Intended in *Heart of Darkness*, who, like her predecessor, embodies the immaculate 'Intentions' Conrad sought to ascribe to the imperialist project - European women in Conrad's fictional universe being allotted the primary function of limiting and symbolically atoning for the brutalism of the secular world. (Hence Gould, as if claiming absolution for the ruthlessless and moral compromise required to secure the successful operation of the mine, tells his wife, 'The best of my feelings are in your keeping'.) But in contrast to the austerity of that other icon, Mrs Gould's representation lapses into the clichés of popular romance and the literature of upliftment when the impeccable heroine is associated with the blue-robed Madonna in the niche of her elegant Spanish House (p68, 414).

That the text should secretly, or perhaps unconsciously, and through the indirection of tropes, come to strip the decorative and decorous Mrs Gould of the garments of virtue in which it has dressed her - once she herself is symbolically clothed in a blue cloak (p210) - is a sign of Conrad's uncertainty about the noble motivation which he contemplated as a possible exoneration of imperialism's will to ascendency. This double-vision is registered when the 'unmercenary hands' of Mrs Gould, in whose character, the text insists, 'even the most legitimate touch of materialism' is wanting (p73), are seen 'flashing with the gold and stones of many rings' (p419), the jewels already designated as 'the hidden treasures of the earth... torn out by the labouring hands of the people' (p413). And it is rehearsed in the cryptic estimates of her fallibility offered by Decoud and Nostromo.

When Decoud derides the idealisation of self-interest, he invokes the very words used to represent Mrs Gould's goodness and grace - images of the fairy-like lady in shining robes of silk and jewels being replicated, but now with negative import, in his scorn for pragmatic undertakings that are clothed in the fair-robes of an idea, and resort to fairy-tale vindications(p103, 187). Even more disturbing than the disbelief of the disillusioned Decoud in Mrs Gould as a figure of redeeming ideas is the clandestine censure of her ethically suspect position spoken by Nostromo, who in conversation with Viola, invariably and sardonically refers to her as 'Thy rich Benefactress'. On his death-bed he responds to her confession that she too hated the silver with the words, 'Marvellous! - that one of you should hate the wealth that you know so well how to take from the hands of the poor' (p458); while by addressing her in the image of the silver as 'Shining! Incorruptible!', he ties her inextricably to the Material Interests which she disavows but before which she had bowed.

The ambiguities of Nostromo's politics are performed on a stage densely peopled by contenders within the newly-created dependency of western capitalism, the alignment of competing forces signifying the contiguity of non-synchronous modes of production and social forms within the uneven process of modernisation: the relics of a pre-capitalist Spanish oligarchy and the feudal structures of haciendas coexist with dispossessed

Indians and peasants migrating to the new centre of capitalist growth stimulated by the mines, and a nascent working class, largely European immigrants, employed in the ports, railways, and telegraph system.

With the secession of the Occidental Republic and the integration of Sulaco Province into the world capitalist system, the populace, which during the civil war with the populist mestizo Monterists had supported the Ribiera regime of the indigenous aristocrats and foreign investors, now turn against their masters, precipitating 'quite serious, organised labour troubles'(p89). In this turbulent situation, disaffection draws in the clergy, the landless agrarian populations, and the insipient proletariat: Father Corbelên abandons the Church Militant to participate in building a Church of the Poor, warning the representatives of Material Interests, 'Let them beware ... lest the people, prevented from their aspirations, should rise and claim their share of the wealth and their share of the power' (p418); Italian and Basque workers join forces with the Indian miners in the socialist Democratic Party, and Secret Societies conspire to reunite Costaguana and redistribute the wealth of Sulaco amongst the population of the Republic. In Dr Monygham remark, 'There is no peace and no rest in the development of material interests' (p419), we have a moralist's view of the permanent revolution set in train by capitalism's dynamics, an observation reiterated with melancholy by the novel as the inevitable consequence of capitalist modernisation: 'Material changes swept along in the train of material interests. And other changes more subtle, outwardly unmarked, affected the minds and hearts of the workers' (p413).

Nostromo is a novel preoccupied with historiographical constructions of temporal orders and transitions in historical consciousness, and what it narrates is not the passage from edenic nature to a fallen world of culture, but from Spanish colonialism via the regimes of countless unstable and tyrannical republics and endemic civil wars, to Anglo-American imperialism. The beginning and end of this process is imaged in the arched gate to the old town of Sulaco, above whose apex is 'a grey, heavily scrolled armorial shield of stone ... with the arms of Spain nearly smoothed out as if in readiness for some new device typical of the impending progress' (p150-1). In the novel's purview, there is neither nostalgia for a colonial past, confidence in an imperialist present, nor hope in the future envisioned by imperialism's opponents. The old order is deprived of all legitimacy by the living witnesses to the afflictions visited on the native peoples by the rapacity of the *conquistadores*: 'The trudging file of burdened Indians ... would lift sad, mute, eyes to the cavalcade raising the dust of the *camino real* made by the hands of their enslaved forefathers ... The heavy stonework of bridges and churches left by the conquerors proclaimed the disregard of human labour, the tribute-labour of vanished nations' (pp83, 85). But nor is capitalism's success-story endorsed; Captain Mitchell's innocently upbeat recital of how '(T)he Treasure House of the World' was saved intact for civilisation (p397) serves as a sardonic repudiation of official affirmations; while Holroyd's confident prediction of his nation's future as the world leader (pp75,76), inauspiciously signals the arrival of late imperialism under the dominion of the United States.

However, *Nostromo's* disdain for Spanish colonialism and modern imperialism is matched by a negative perception of those seeking its overthrow. This is focused on the ambiguous figure of Nostromo, subaltern, proto-proletarian and renegade. His is a language of *ressentiment* characteristic of populist discourse and shared by the venal Montero brothers and the principled Viola. Nostromo castigates the rich to whom 'everything is permitted' (p359), who betray the poor (pp374, 386), keep 'the people in poverty and subjection' (p342), and live 'on the wealth stolen from the people' (p443). But in the ranks of the socialist Democratic Party he learns to speak a new language of opposition to 'capitalists, oppressors of the two hemispheres', which, the text tells us, would have been incomprehensible to the 'heroic old Viola, old revolutionist' (p432), who is unacquainted with the taxonomy of class and admits only the category of 'the people' oppressed by Kings, ministers, aristocrats and the rich (p342).

Thus if these backward glances at the austere republican ideals of 1848 (p39) are in the spirit of regret for a time that cannot be recuperated, they also serve to deprecate a new vocabulary of class struggle, which, furthermore, is mocked because spoken by Nostromo. For not only had he served his masters as overseer of unruly labourers, as intrepid escort to the beleagured Ribiera, and as courier summoning troops to the defence of Sulaco and the foreign investors, but in stealing the silver he had emulated the (im)morality of his opponents. Yet even when Nostromo's deeds contradict his rhetoric, positioning him as a lackey of class enemies he despises, and who misname him as 'their' man, his deportment is never subservient or deferential, manifesting an estimate of himself as his own person, and confirming Viola's view of him as a man *of* the people, 'their Great Man'. That the text should impale Nostromo on the cross of incommensurable positions and desires - the hireling who aspires to be his own man, the orator who publically castigates the rich but who loves riches, the thief whose loyalty is to the dispossessed, and who is possessed by his stolen treasure - suggests that the irreconcilable demands made on him by the fiction are a symptom of Conrad's unease about affirming a figure associated with socialist aspirations.

It could seem that Dr Monygham's perception of Nostromo not as thief corrupted by an icon of capitalism, but as a socialist-conspirator with 'genius...continuity and force', is testimony to his status as a figurehead of the struggle against the rule of Material Interests: 'Nothing', says the doctor, 'will put an end to him'. Yet a novel which inscribes disillusion in the ethos of a triumphant capitalism also refuses to sanction the hopes of those seeking its transcendence; and the misshapen form of a fanatical communist, 'small, frail, bloodthirsty, the hater of capitalists' (p459), serves as a malignant augury of what may come to pass with the victory of a left revolution, thereby negating the allusions to the reach after another condition. Nonetheless, *Nostromo*, which is disingenuously sub-titled *A Tale of the Seaboard*, unfolds as a dystopian narrative of the west's ascendency, and one which proleptically signals disenchantment in imperialist designs.

My thanks to the audiences of the Culture and Imperialism Conference held at Bristol University in January 1994, graduate seminars at SOAS and Queen Mary/Westfield Colleges in the University of London, 1994, and the Annual Meeting of the Conrad Society, London 1994

Notes

1. For an insistence on the necessity of periodisation and differentiation in usage, see Introduction to *Colonial Discourse and Post-Colonial Theory*, Patrick Williams and Laura Chrisman (eds), Harvester, London 1993; Laura Chrisman, 'The Imperial Unconscious? Representations of Imperial Discourse', *Critical Quarterly*, 32:3, 1990, pp38-58 and Michael Sprinker's Introduction to *Late Imperial Culture*, Román de la Campa, E Ann Kaplan and Michael Sprinker (eds), forthcoming Verso.

2. Fredric Jameson, *The Political Unconscious*, Methuen, London 1981, and *Modernism and Imperialism*, Field Day, Derry 1988. See also 'Cognitive Mapping', in *Marxism and the Interpretation of Culture*, edited with introduction by Cary Nelson and Lawrence Grossberg, Macmillan, London 1988, p349-50.

3. Sara Suleri, Univ of Chicago Press, Chicago 1992, pp3, 32.

4. See David Trotter, 'Modernism and Empire: reading *The Waste Land*', *Critical Quarterly*, Vol 28, Nos 1 and 2, 1988, pp143-153.

5. See, for instance, Moira Ferguson, '*Mansfield Park*: Slavery, Colonialism and Gender', *Oxford Literary Review* , 13: 1-2, 1991, pp118-139; Susan Meyer, 'Colonialism and the Figurative Strategy of Jane Eyre', in *The Macropolitics of Nineteenth Century Literature: Nationalism, Exoticism, Imperialism*, Jonathan Arac and Harriet Ritvo (eds), Univ of Pennsylvania Press, Philadelphia 1991, pp159-183; Katherine Bailey Lineham, 'Imperialism in *Daniel Deronda*', *Texas Studies in Literature and Language*, 34:3, Fall 1992, pp 325-346; Tamar Heller, *Dead Secrets: Wilke Collins and the Female Gothic*, Yale Univ Press, New Haven 1992; Jane Marcus, 'Britannia Rules *The Waves*' in *Decolonising Tradition: New Views of Twentieth Century "British" Literary Canons*, Karen R. Lawrence (ed), Univ of Illinois Press, Urbana and Chicago 1992.

6. David Harrey, *The Condition of Postmodernity: An Enquiry into the Origins of Cultural Change*, Blackwell, Oxford 1989; Neil Smith, Uneven Development: *Nature, Capital and the Production of Space*, Blackwell, Oxford 1984; Edward Soja, *Postmodern Geographies: The Reassertion of Space in Critical Social Theory*, Verso, London 1989.

7. Frederick Lord Lugard, *The Dual Mandate in British Tropical Africa* (1922), Frank Cass, London 1965, p615.

8. I am indebted to Douglas Kellner's lucid gloss, 'Introduction: Jameson, Marxism, and Postmodernism', in *Postmodernism, Jameson, Critique*, Douglas Kellner (ed), Maisonneuve Press, Washington DC 1989.

9. Edward Said, *Culture and Imperialism*, Chatto and Windus, London 1993, p82.

10. See Jameson, *The Political Unconscious*, especially pp41-9, 56-7.

11. 'Henry James: An Appreciation' (1905), in *Notes on Life and Letters*, Gresham Publishing, London 1925, p17.

12. Edward Said, *Orientalism*, Routledge, London 1978, p16.

13. Rosa Luxemburg, *The Accumulation of Capital* (1913) trans Agnes Schwarzschild, London: Routledge and Kegan Paul, 1951, pp446, 362.

14. Edward Said, *Beginnings: Intention and Method*, Columbia Univ Press, New York 1975, pp118, 137.

15. An argument I attempt to elaborate in *Conrad and Imperialism*, Macmillan, London 1983.

16. For rereadings of the narrative structure, see Avrom Fleshman who maintains that it reflects a sense of history's unfolding process in a society perceived as a living organism; *Conrad's Politics: Community and Anarchy in the Fiction of Joseph Conrad*, Johns Hopkins, Baltimore 1967; Gareth Jenkins attributes the ideological tensions hidden in the work's 'curious chronological distortions and narrative complexities' to a commentary on its own narrative structure 'which is calculated to deny the possibility for real change and expose history as illusory.' 'Conrad's *Nostromo and History*', in *Literature and History* 6, Autumn 1977, pp138-178.

17. References are to Penguin edition; first published in 1904.

18. 'The Limits of the Liberal Imagination: *One Hundred Years of Solitude* and *Nostromo*' (1975) in *Joseph Conrad: Third World Perspectives*, Robert D. Hamner (ed), Three Continents Press, Washington DC 1990, p201.

19. On the affinities to Marx's analysis, see *The Political Unconscious*, esp p278; and Jim Reilly, Ch 4: 'Stasis, Signs and Speculation: *Nostromo and History*', in *Shadowtime: History and Representation in Hardy, Conrad and George Eliot*, Routledge, London 1993.

20. Joseph Chamberlain, *Foreign and Colonial Speeches*, George Routledge and Sons, London 1897 especially pp78,101,195.

ANNA MARIA FALCONBRIDGE AND SIERRA LEONE: 'THE REALITY OF A COLONISER'

Moira Ferguson

A newcomer to the colonial enterprise of West Africa, Anna Maria Falconbridge recorded her experiences during two visits to Sierra Leone in the late eighteenth century. Her travel account was entitled *Two Voyages to Sierra Leone, during the years 1791, 1792, 1793, a series of Letters.*[1] Seven years earlier, in 1787, several hundred liberated slaves and some white prostitutes had set sail for Sierra Leone after the abolitionist Granville Sharp, had devised a plan for a slave-free, self-governing British settlement there.[2] Subsequently, however, the British government had withdrawn support, and at that point, some well-connected anti-slaveryites assumed responsibility for the project, reorganising the old settlement as a commercial enterprise, and naming it the Sierra Leone Company.

Falconbridge's anti-slavery husband, Alexander Falconbridge, assumed an administrative role in the colony, and she accompanied him there. *Two Voyages* consists of fourteen letters about Anna Maria Falconbridge's experiences in the colony, which conclude with her return to London, disagreements with the Sierra Leone Company, and correspondence by two black settlers, Cato Perkins and Isaac Anderson.[3] Her writing reflects the ambivalence of her response to colonial settlement, which is further complicated by her position as a woman in a largely male domain.

The Falconbridges were aware of earlier problems in the colony. But more pressing matters faced them on arrival. For years Alexander Falconbridge had worked as a surgeon on slave ships crossing the Middle Passage, before coming an opponent of slavery in 1787 and publishing an exposé of his experiences the following year.[4] Consequently, the first night at dinner in Sierra Leone was a tense affair, with arguments about the trade frequently erupting between him and other white residents. As a result, Alexander Falconbridge refused Anna Maria's request that they sleep comfortably on shore at the home of slave traders; complicity in slavery - for him but not for her - repellent. In accord with his decision, they camped on the supply ship, the Lapwing, which she compared to a hog trough:

> *Conceive yourself pent up in a floating cage, without room either to walk about, stand erect, or even to lay at length; exposed to the inclemency of the weather, having your eyes and ears ... offended by acts of indecency, and language too horrible to relate - add to this a complication of filth, the stench from which was continually assailing your nose, and then you will have a faint notion of the Lapwing Cutter (p24).*

Despite annoyance and frustration, however, her discourse about filth aboard the Lapwing parallels the discourse of filth aboard slave ships that informed her husband's famous polemic. She begs the captain to have the Lapwing washed down. Scrubbing the ship restores a form of control and matched ideal feminine behaviour while implicating slavery. Scouring the cabin with vinegar emblematises her harsh and sour surroundings as well as the anger she feels at being stuck in this situation. Acid applied to metonymized slave ships corrodes the plantocracy. But within a day, she finegles a tour on shore in the company of slavetraders.

Less conflicted than her remarks about hygiene are Anna Maria's attitudes toward the royal family of Koya Temne. As wife of the chief British negotiator, she is present on the first day of the two-week-long debate over land - happy, it seems, to witness a massive territorial swindle and to laugh at the attire of the Naimbana (the paramount sub-chief of the Koya Temne Kingdom). As a bribe to secure land and coastline for the British, Alexander Falconbridge offers rum, wine, cheese, and a gold-laced hat to the Naimbana while arguing that the old contract signed by him with a British representative three years earlier remains valid. As Britain's spokesman, Falconbridge claims that Englishmen would never renege on a contract and would hold 'in detestation every person so disposed' (p36). Falconbridge stresses his disdain for 'obtaining wealth', while Anna Maria spotlights the extensiveness of the West African territory at stake and how Africans are being infantilised. She also boldly represents King Naimbana's opinion that 'every white man (is) a rogue' (p37). By now, the Falconbridges are privy to an alternate narrative about a dispute which led to the burning of the settlement, about flagrant baiting of the Africans by British individuals. But that knowledge of the narrative of the colonised cannot dissolve official allegiances. Their bureaucratic presence necessitates cultural distortion.

After the first day of negotiations, Anna Maria Falconbridge feigns sickness and attends no further meetings. Instead she enjoys excursions with a French slaver named Captain Rennieu whose occupation she never mentions. Celebrating adventure was celebrating empire, so she chooses not to stress her complicity.[5] The captain's slave-trading negotiations within and around the community are a resounding textual silence. The fact that her husband is contracting for slave-free territory along the slave coastline while she spends time in the company of slave traders goes unnoted. Also unnoted is any link between public rituals to ward off evil (i.e. slavery) which she observes and evidence of slavetrading around town. In conventional negative ethnographic commentary, she alludes to cultural practices and leaves it at that.

While visiting Bunce Island, home of a French slave-trading station, she unexpectedly glimpses a group of slaves:

> *Judge then what my astonishment and feelings were, at the sight of between two and three hundred wretched victims, chained and parcelled out in circles, just satisfying the cravings of nature from a trough of rice placed in the centre of each circle.*
>
> *Offended modesty rebuked me with a blush for not hurrying my eyes from such disgusting scenes; but ... I could not withdraw myself for several minutes (pp32-33).*

Her distraught response resembles her husband's account in his anti-slavery tract. Yet she quickly recovers and assumes a detached attitude. Her choice of this incident to highlight the presence of slavery is complex. First, *Two Voyages* was published in 1794 when Britain was already at war with France. Hence her discourse of incredulity at this atrocity might inscribe a francophobic dimension. Her rhetoric of discovery about French grossness is also, as Peter Hulme argues in a different context - a 'ruse of concealment' (about British slavery).[6] Second, as a woman, Anna Maria Falconbridge is supposed to forego a masculinist gaze; she is not supposed to look and possess what is seen in the same way. But she does gaze on the slaves nonetheless. She employs, not an 'objectivist discovery rhetoric' but one that is 'resolutely dialogic, seeking out rather than defying local knowledge', a colonial discourse that violates gender codes.[7] And the distance she assumes is a colonial complement to the more active male gaze that does not - as she does - flinch and withdraw. Later, she describes the separation of burial grounds along racial lines without comment and labels indigenous people as lazy (p83), remarking shortly afterwards, without comment, that 'deaths are not frequent' there (p84). She may view Africans as interior - she scoffs that they speak 'broken English' - yet their confined condition vaguely resembles her own. The woeful sight of slaves enhances her sense of personal entrapment. These conflicting discourses occasionally fuse with equally mixed references to gender. After noticing how people stare at her elaborate outfits, she utilises dress to uphold European standards, even to construct a notion of gendered whiteness.[8]

She strains to construct a visible little England that upholds sartorial custom. Exporting prescribed notions of womanhood from Britain to Africa, Falconbridge both accepts and denies the cultural definition of femininity. Although given to bold, unconventional acts - for example, her marriage was an elopement - she does not hesitate to appear lady-like. In striking contrast, the stunned attention her costumes receive and her ridicule of the Naimbana's attire lie side by side. In that case, she returned the gaze that was trained on her own clothes only a few days before, turning the king into her object. High rank notwithstanding, the coloniser stares at the colonised. When the king mentions that no other woman has ever sat down to eat with him, she assumes he is granting her a privilege rather than denoting her inferior status as a woman. Cancelling the king's comment arbitarily, she acts as if imperial status supersedes gender. Differential authorities face off at this point.

Additionally, she tries to talk the Naimbana's daughter, Clara, into wearing cumbersome western attire - deemed 'feminine' - since scanty dress speaks preconceived ideas about allegedly unsophisticated Africans. Falconbridge wants English womanhood to assume/assert its universal form. By mimicking Anna Maria Falconbridge, the theory goes, Clara will replicate her and stress the coloniser's authority. But Clara wisely declines, whereupon Falconbridge petulantly dismisses the princess.

Predictably, the situation of other white females - a remnant of the original settlers - disturbs Falconbridge the most; she condemns their involuntary expatriation as white prostitutes who will become breeders. When she comes upon seven of them who are diseased and unkempt, she undertakes to clean them up; she wants them to copy her own impeccable grooming, just as she wanted Clara and the Lapwing to reflect her sense of propriety. White gendered authority and a veiled patriotism are at stake; but so too is an unsentimentalised sense of solidarity with her white sisters:

I should never have supposed they were born white; add to this, almost naked from head to foot . . . they seemed insensible to shame, or the wretchedness of their situation themselves; I begged they would get washed, and gave them what clothes I could conveniently spare (p64).

Privileging the white woman, exonerating the septet as European women who endure hard times, she reads their condition as a sign that the metropole prefers profits over people. She repeats a description tendered to her by one of the white women:

We were mostly of that description of persons who walk the streets of London; and support themselves by the earnings of prostitution; that men were employed to collect and conduct them to Wapping, where they were intoxicated with liquor, then inveigled on board of ship, and married to Black men, whom they have never seen before; that the morning after she was married, she really did not remember a syllable of what had happened over night, and when informed, was obliged to inquire who was her husband? After this, to the time of their sailing, they were amused and bouyed up by a prodigality of fair promises, and great expectations which awaited them in the country they were going to(p65).

Falconbridge finds this treatment - their sexual exploitation, their reduction to a category usually reserved for black women - untenable since she reserves a status of difference for white women. When sluttishness becomes a sliding signifier attached to white women, things have gone too far. Unconsciously, the Sierra Leone Company has meshed English national identity with ravished white female identity.[9]

Anna Maria Falconbridge refuses to lock herself into a self-perpetuating, traditional colonial-gender grid. Instead, she obliquely invokes a personal situation while challenging the modus operandi of the London administrators. Abolition has trapped her and locked her up, she thinks, as it trapped the unfortunate white female settlers.

This excoriation of the colonial bureaucracies both in London and Sierra Leone is nothing new. From the outset, the type of supplies sent to the colony had incurred her wrath. Instead of food, administrators had sent out tools used by blacksmiths and plantation owners - of scant use in the colony - as well as numerous toy knives and scissors. Shortly after, she mocks the weapons that were exported from England to arm settlers. They could not be fired because their carriages were missing (p68).

There was not a thing on board, but salt beef, so hard, we were obliged to chop it with an axe, and some mouldy, rotten biscuits; however, so great was my hunger, that I could not help satisfying it with some of this beef and bread, uncouth as it was (p58).

With each objection, Falconbridge shifts position, reinforcing the plurality of colonial practices; her authority as a white English lady differs from a gentleman's. She confirms their contesting terrains, the often contradictory axis of power among the English themselves, as a new corporate institution strove to emerge in West Africa. With Anna Maria Falconbridge on the spot, circulating new knowledge about colonialism, *Two Voyages* spells cultural hegemony and recontextualizes Englishness.

The Falconbridges left Sierra Leone for London - for good they thought - in June 1791 to report to the Company Directors. The Naimbana's son (known popularly as Prince Naimbana, and sometimes John Frederick) accompanied them at the Naimbana's request. Intent on initiating a new commercial venture in the colony and hoping to improve relations with the indigenous population, the Directors coaxed the couple to return. A battery of promises won over a reluctant Anna Maria Falconbridge: first, her husband Alexander Falconbridge would probably be governor of Sierra Leone as well as a commercial agent; second, she would be well compensated if he died: 'Though all their rhetoric could not persuade me to revisit Africa, their noble generous actions have effected it' (p223).

In addition to Falconbridge's appointment, the directors hired one hundred and nineteen white Company officials, who arrived in Sierra Leone in February 1792. They also arranged for a black community of twelve hundred men and women who were living in Nova Scotia to be relocated there. These three groups - the Falconbridges themselves, the company officials, and the sizable black convoy - were due to arrive at roughly the same time.

This wave of immigrants changed the composition of the colony for good. Resourceful and religious, the large black community was known familiarly as the Nova Scotians or the Black Loyalists because they had fought on the British side in the revolutionary war to emancipate themselves. As compensation, they had been expatriated to Canada and promised land which they never received.

Falconbridge tells the story of John Clarkson (brother of the famous abolitionist Thomas Clarkson) being dispatched to Nova Scotia to finesse the repatriation of the Black Loyalists to Sierra Leone. They contracted with Clarkson not only to accept land there in lieu of broken promises by the British government, but to 'form a colony' also.[10] One hundred died on route from Canada to West Africa. After he arrived, Clarkson was appointed governor of the colony, news that dismayed Alexander

Said

Falconbridge who had been half-promised the position.
Anna Maria Falconbridge was critical of the repatriation plan:

> A premature, hair-brained, and ill-digested scheme, to think
> of sending such a number of people all at once, to a rude,
> barbarous and unhealthy country, before they were certain of
> possessing an acre of land; and I very much fear will
> terminate in disappointment, if not disgrace to the authors;
> though at the same time, I am persuaded the motives sprung
> from minds unsullied with evil meaning (p125).

The present inexperienced administrators, she fears, will induce 'anarchy and chagrin' (p141).

She reports the disappointed reactions of the pious Black Loyalists to the discriminatory conditions they faced in the colony. This matched her own growing disapproval of the governing body (p201). The Nova Scotians quickly discerned exclusionary tactics: thrown in jail on trivial charges, castigated as 'black rascals', from the beginning their demands were delegitimated.[11]

But while John Clarkson remained governor - Anna Maria was one of his supporters - she downplayed the grievances of black settlers. She cannot easily confront the 'figure of the diaspora' returned. Thomas Peters, for example, the Nova Scotian leader who challenged Clarkson's administration, took literally the idea that 'civil, military, personal, and commercial rights and duties of Blacks and Whites shall be the same'. Apparently on reasonable terms with neighbouring tribal Africans, but coming to realise that the British had doublecrossed them once again, the Nova Scotians faced off against white bureaucrats; autonomy and economic survival were their goals. Falconbridge, however, only alludes in passing to letters and petitions about freedom that the Nova Scotians wrote from 1791 to 1792. While discussing life in the colony, she represents the ideological struggle there, almost, as one between diverse white communities. Thus she contributes to the 'epistemic violence that effaces the colonial subject'.[12]

Although recognising that their hard work benefitted the

British Directors, the Black Loyalists still cast their lot with the colony. Men cleared the brush while women washed and cooked. Eventually they built an encampment into which the original white settlers moved. Their industry notwithstanding, the Nova Scotians were forbidden to hold most administrative posts. The blandishments about equal treatment were palpably a mythology. Falconbridge's silent chronicle about the Black Loyalists and their demands marks her complex location - her desire for gendered authority on the one hand, her opposition to anti-slavery bureaucrats on the other. In some senses she writes 'not the history of the country which he [sic] plunders but the history of his own nation'.[13]

Alexander Falconbridge died in December 1793 after a tough struggle to initiate trade relations; three weeks later Anna Maria Falconbridge happily married Isaac Dubois. Her decision not to mention the name of her new spouse in *Two Voyages* or indicate beyond suggestive hints that she was remarrying signs her apprehension about claiming sexual freedom. The evangelical ruling class might have targeted her precipitous behaviour much as the sexual practices of slaves were targeted.

Not long after the marriage, the Company dismissed Clarkson, who had returned to London. Falconbridge and Dubois shared the settlers' disappointment with the news. Discord intensified. The newly married couple left Sierra Leone for good in August 1793, their differences with the colonial bureaucracy no longer reconcilable.

Meanwhile, Europe was at war. Hence, Anna Maria Falconbridge makes only a casual, passing remark about the fact that the Naimbana's son had died in July 1793, en route to becoming the Naimbana in Sierra Leone. West African internal affairs no longer rivet her attention. She had begun to reposition herself at a great distance from the colony, both physically and politically.

Back in London, Anna Maria demanded that the Director of the Company, Henry Thornton, fulfill financial promises that he made when the Falconbridges agreed to return to the colony for a second time. Thornton declined to comply. Perhaps her refusal to assume the role of widow for longer than three weeks had rendered her morally suspect. At any rate, fractures in the seemingly united white colonial front were evident to those in the know.

Parallel to Falconbridge's appeals to Thornton, Cato Perkins and Isaac Anderson had also arrived in London, on behalf of the Nova Scotian community, to present a petition signed by thirty-one black settlers. Representative agents of black settler destiny, Perkins and Anderson expressed their displeasure at broken promises and demanded fair and equal treatment. Where colonizers were concerned, they had learned, no a priori guarantees existed. As deeply religious men - Perkins was an ordained pastor - they could not be dismissed as hot-headed pagans.

As part of a contingent of former slaves rebelling for the third time, Perkins and Anderson circulated an oppositional discourse of emancipation; they pointed out why distrusting company officials made sense:

> *We have been so often deceived by white people, that we are jealous when they make any promises, and uneasily wait till we see what they will come to . . . The manner you have treated us [in], has been just the same as if we were* Slaves, *come to tell our masters, of the cruelties and severe behaviour of an* Overseer *(pp264-265).*

Where earlier she downplayed the existence of black settlers in Sierre Leone, now Falconbridge textually foregrounds Perkins and Anderson as ideological allies (weapons?) in her struggle against Thornton.

This opening up of liminal space, this foregrounding of black speech and self-determination, intensifies Falconbridge's textual ironies. Her location is persistently traversed by contradictions. By voicing former slaves who are the Directors' opponents, Falconbridge equates the anti-slavery ideology of colonisers with duplicity and injustice. Hence she makes good her prefatory warning to readers that her account will be 'uncompromising' and filled with 'unwelcome truth'.

Earlier quarrels with her abolitionist husband quietly resurface. And more has happened in the interim to complicate the scenario. In letter ten of *Two Voyages*, she mentions that the return voyage to London had changed her view of slavery; abolitionists, she claims, exaggerated the negative conditions aboard slaveships. Edging toward a pro-slavery stance, she aids the former slaves while arguing for private rights. Her fluctuating response constitutes a radical rupture in the text.

Though they return to Sierra Leone empty-handed, Perkins and Anderson accentuate the ambiguities of power through their sturdy actions. Their intrepidity signifies that the empire could not easily be solidified or codified. They exemplify the dynamic possibilities of even the colonising narrative. From Africa to North America and back again as representatives of their community, Perkins and Anderson inscribed and reinscribed themselves in the culture of resistance. Convention violators who were temporarily triumphalist, these involuntary yet subversive nomad-hybrids used Anna Maria's story, in Edward Said's words, 'to assert their own identity and the *existence* of their own history'.[14] They offered an alternate social experience and marked it as integral to the colonial quest. Falconbridge's text records this testimony and their feisty counterrefusal to be orientalised, to be placated. Yet willy nilly, the black petitioners served as Falconbridge's alibi for a not-so-veiled denunciation of the abolitionist-colonial administrators at home and in Sierra Leone itself.

AN AMBIVALENT TEXT

Anna Maria Falconbridge was the first English-speaking woman on the West Coast of Africa to articulate a response to the colonial settlement. Although her identity has not yet been fully exposed, the text was the 'first independent published report on the colony'.[15] She writes in a plethora of forms that include reminiscences, a pro- and anti-slavery critique, commentary on sexual politics, a manners-and-customs chronicle, a historical dedication and record, and a manifesto of burgeoning nationalism. Petitions, speeches, conversations, second-hand commentary, gossip, anecdote, omissions, and personal opinion are also included. With tribulations and highpoints juxtaposed, her polyphony of texts doubles as the literature of survival and the literature of conquest while she pointedly advances a political agenda of her own. An apparatus of power that affirms dominant ideology and advocates going slow on slavery, her text is transformative and heteroglossic. In Wilson Harris's words, it constitutes 'a trail of silent things'. [16]

The order in which Falconbridge wrote *Two Voyages* remains a textual ambivalence. We never know if she sent those letters and if she did, if the sender returned them to her. This indeterminacy about chronology and order destabilises the text. We also know from Falconbridge's preface that she was anxious to distinguish her account from another contemporary account of Sierra Leone, by Lieutenant John Matthews.[17] She will avoid the facts - she avows - that Matthews addresses. Falconbridge explicitly retains the gendered gaze that must eschew the 'objective' description of discovery favoured by male travellers. While underscoring her diffidence in emulating Matthews - she eschews being a mimic or a bore, she explains - she claims a different kind of discourse as her own. Falconbridge explicitly and unsentimentally personalises her account, asserts strong opinions, dramatises ideological oppositions, undertakes character assassinations and affirmations, and rarely shies from subjects (like prostitutes) scarcely deemed appropriate for a woman writer to discuss. She creates a gendered colonial discourse for female travellers that claims both class and race privilege. Inviting a dominant reading based on gender, she inscribes a critique of masculinist organisation and thinking. Her discourse complements the male coloniser's but she insistently separates and authorises herself on the basis of gender. The territorial imperative may still be primary but she sharply reconfigures it so as to manage a pre-slavery vantage point on colonial relationships. But despite her new angle of vision, uncertainty prevails; little comes to closure. Nothing is known of Thornton's ultimate decision but we suspect contrivance.

To add to the destabilising effect, Anna Maria opens *Two Voyages* with a complimentary address to the people of Bristol, a notorious slave-trading port; most of them would be repelled by an anti-slavery narrative. Bristol becomes a code word for pro-slavery supporters and plantocrats, with Anna Maria Falconbridge a prodigal daughter returning to the fold. She had eloped from Bristol with Alexander Falconbridge who is now dead. She had since married a man from the former American colonies whose parents may have owned plantations. Written at the end, or at least after the events of her husband's death and her own remarriage, the address to Bristolians functions as a reconciliation device: the apostrophe serves to placate members of the community who matter to her, but were repelled by her former behaviour. The attack on Henry Thornton consolidates this alliance with Bristolians. So does the appendix that she added between the first and second edition: it consists of a second letter to Thornton in which she refers to herself as an injured woman and to Thornton in calculatedly Christian terms, as an unrepentant malefactor.

In introducing the conciliatory opening and the self-justifying appendix, Anna Maria Falconbridge exemplifies the problems that a pioneer faces. As a female coloniser she has to create new conventions, construct an acceptable authenticity. Barring Lieutenant Matthews, no woman had travelled this proslavery path. Truth claims aside, unfeminine commentary is a problem because Falconbridge refuses to be constrained by the customary discourses of femininity. At the same time, since so many experiences and events are illegible to her, her text is always already decentered despite her hardy eurocentric efforts to represent a female gaze. Special conditions induce her to produce a different kind of text.

Thus Falconbridge's text seesaws among a panoply of meanings. By adding a panegyric to her hometown after she writes *Two Voyages* and has severed ties with the antislavery colonial administration, she absolves herself. Using a fractured chronology, she can present herself as someone sympathetic to a proslavery argument. Following the complicitous address, she can back up and contextualise her elopement with an ardently abolitionist husband. By implication, she excuses her behaviour on the grounds of youth and naivety; she asks her former community for forgiveness. She has already done penance - she hints - by combating abolitionist forces.

Embedded in the initial speech, these discontinuities persist. She socialises both with slave-traders and with John Clarkson who wrestles Thomas Peters. Falconbridge rarely mentions quarrels between Clarkson and Peters and certainly not Peters himself - a prominent figure in the settlement and a spokesman for the former slaves. But Clarkson's dismissal apparently changes her tune and empowers her to give the demands of the Nova Scotians more play. By then she had thrown in her lot with Clarkson's ally, Isaac Dubois, and opposed those who hired Alexander Falconbridge in the first place.

Yet when *Two Voyages* was published, she still used Alexander Falconbridge's last name, which was inextricably associated with abolition, a somewhat puzzling choice. Perhaps Dubois was 'too French' for a 1794 gallophobic English audience. Perhaps she thought that the familiarity of Falconbridge's name would attach more authority to her text and hence sell more books. More ironically, Anna Maria expropriates the last name of a famous abolitionist to undermine abolition. Her seemingly above-ground cultural work goes underground. She uses her dead husband against himself by using his name against what he believes in. He could hardly complain about the misappropriation, but in a sense she has him turning in his grave.

Falconbridge's insistence on female colonial power being taken seriously, down to the propriety of dress, would also have excited debate. Refusing to succumb to the fixed stance of widowhood, yet displaying herself as a proper English lady in the tropics, she asserts her position as an economic but not innocent player to whom the Directors were accountable. Highlighting gender as a mark of difference, she bestows a new legitimacy on female colonial narratives. Her epistolary chronicle challenges travel accounts by white male counterparts that exoticise women or erase them as subjects.

Hence her gendered travel narrative enhances the articulation of imperial meaning-making. Through female cultural inscription that privileges dress, hygiene, the sick, hasty marriage, and hastier remarriage, Falconbridge extends and complicates the colonial trajectory. Abolitionist Thornton declines serious negotiations, on the basis of her suspect views, most likely; but surely as an evangelical male he also takes umbrage at the permission Falconbridge grants other women to enunciate a controversial public discourse. The fact that she inflects the text with a clandestine seduction that speaks sexual desire less than a month after her husband's death clinches that separation between herself and Thornton: national decision-makers like Thornton cherished the spread of such landmark British values as morality and piety. Originally Anna Maria Falconbridge might have seemed a worthy import and model, a woman who could redeem a part of the world thought to be sunk in barbarism or vexed by rancour. Not to put too fine a point on it, Thornton might well have encoded her exceptional behaviour as part of the very ethos that the evangelicals sought to clean up in so-called 'uncivilised' Africa. Through aggressive action, she had declined the role of a 'fair and feminine' patriot in abolitionist terms.

Two Voyages, moreover, stages ambivalent relations to the Nova Scotians, to African peoples in Sierra Leone, and to the Company directors back home. Condemning the company's treatment of the Nova Scotians, and ultimately demurring about the enactment of a slave-free community, her evolving plantocratic stance only *seems* to clash with her concern for the settlers. She identifies with the denial of their rights because she felt similarly denied by the same company directors.

Hence at one level, Falconbridge's *Two Voyages* reads as an exposé of colonial mismanagement and ill-advised efforts to suppress black resistance, of administrators who promoted abolition but facilitated profit. The Nova Scotians themselves are caught in the twisting paths of the emancipatory trajectory, the much-touted civilising mission, and Falconbridge's own agenda.

But, motivation aside, Falconbridge's foregrounding of black settlers' petitions in both Sierra Leone and London ventures their demands into the void and exposes the veto of silence that the British government had unsuccessfully tried to impose. By centerstaging the Nova Scotian fight for autonomy, Falconbridge counters the contention that the relocating African community is fractious without reason. She explodes old equations about unvoiced otherness and ignorance, unmasking false representations of British colonialism in Africa. She constructs a platform from which Nova Scotians and Africans can make pronouncements - albeit mediated - 'newly empowered voices asking for their narratives to be heard'.[18] In the process,

Falconbridge denounces the double-voiced Sierra Leone
Company which opposes slavery yet denies black settlers'
demands: she returns a discourse about slaves to the original
geographical source of its institutional practice.

TWO VOYAGES AS IMPERIAL AFFIRMATION

Falconbridge's narrative is yet another filament of overseas
predation, the colonial mythology of origins early on in West
Africa.[19] Paradoxically, Falconbridge's publicising of black dissent
specifically advances the territorial enterprise: Nova Scotians
might be free people acting appropriately, but they also welcome
Falconbridge's assistance when the Sierra Leone Company wears
them down in London with a series of flat refusals and a waiting
game. Her aid to Perkins and Anderson is an affirmation of
something akin to plantocratic philanthropy. By underwriting
proslaveryites in this way, she links slave trading to a strong
national identity.

Falconbridge's controlling perspective configures an Africa that
only exists in the western gaze, as for example, in her dismissal of
the Naimbana's daughter as too unsophisticated to wear English
clothes. At the same time, Falconbridge verbally dispenses with
the fact that her narrative of colonial 'legitimation' in Western
Africa echoes that of Thornton and his allies in London.
Falconbridge and Thornton battle over ideological representations
of Africa, but they are still silently united in configuring the
continent and the people as the other of civilised Europe. Politically
they slide easily into each other, using the black Loyalists
differentially as a negative commodity. Consequently, Falconbridge
ends up representing herself as a mediator and saviour whose
avowal of a gradualist position on slavery - the eurocentric idea
that Africans must be slowly introduced to freedom - enables her
to justify pro-slavery proclivities. She acknowledges no crisis of
cultural identity; she had changed her mind, *tout court*.

Moreover, the charity she extends in London to Isaac
Anderson and Cato Perkins fudges this transformation from an
abolitionist who risked social ostracism to marry an anti-slavery
activist to someone who remarks on the acceptable conditions
of slavery that she observes on board a slaveship in the middle

passage. Since neither morality nor education can be found in unhappy Africa, she claims, the slave trade must be beneficial. Her standard of judgement is simple. She wants everyone to have freedom *who knows its value*, a catch clause that covers old ideas about allegedly ignorant Africans. In the end, she reverted unapologetically to a way of thinking shared by family and friends in Bristol. Her dedication to the inhabitants of Bristol, a major pro-slavery port and her hometown, couples the important of natal town and love - systematically denied to slaves - with her new attraction to a modified, pro-slavery perspective. She delineates novel boundaries within which she can exercise female authority.

Falconbridge's ideological shift (or reversion) is most transparent, however, in the changes to the title pages between 1794 and 1802. The original title page reads as follows: *Two Voyages to Sierra Leone During the Years 1791-2-3, in a Series of Letters, by Anna Maria Falconbridge To which is added, A Letter from the Author to Henry Thornton, Esq. M. P. and Chairman of the Court of Directors of the Sierra Leone Company.* The second title page recasts her politic, advocating the gradualist viewpoint on slavery favoured by plantocrats. It reads as follows: *Narrative of Two Voyages to the River Sierra Leone, During the Years 1791-2-3, performed by A. M. Falconbridge. With a Succinct account of the Distresses and proceedings of that Settlement: as description of the Manner, Diversions, Arts, Commerce, Cultivation, Custom, Punishments, &c. And Every interesting Particular relating to the Sierra Leone Company also The present State of the Slave Trade in the West Indies, and the improbability of its total Abolition.*

The expansion of the original title page without any alteration to the text itself suggests that Anna Maria Falconbridge wants readers to recast her discourse. Her second title page - she ventures - will provide an ideological gloss. Read it this way, she urges, and read it differently. The second title page also confirms that *Two Voyages* had become - even if it did not set out to be -a brief for European expansionist ideology.

Who speaks and writes for whom, then, is a crucial site of contestation. In voicing black settlers and silencing their narratives, Falconbridge highlights the fact that collective illiteracy, from an eurocentric point of view, constitutes self-erasure. Put another way, the question of signature characterises the civilising mission and the representation of indigenous people. The Naimbana, Cato Perkins, and Isaac Anderson all render their signatures as X. In the eyes of a European reading public, illiteracy signs inferiority; it revives the issue of Britons authorising themselves, throughout the history of the slave trade, to name Africans. Illiteracy justifies naming. Literacy permits (is) naming. Viewed ethnocentrically, collective ignorance unites Africans with Nova Scotians. Through self-representation moreover, Falconbridge offers new roles and new hope to planters: she softens the revulsion in which they are held, battling in London for different formulations of empire. Yet her very ambivalence marks a hegemonic stance; relative inequities matter because she perceives important differences between Nova Scotians and herself. Additionally, the emerging nation of combative communities has been founded - she claims - on unworkable principles. Besides, if Africans were not barbaric as most Europeans allege, then slavery would no longer be necessary; it would not be an issue. Ultimately, however, she bestows an imprimatur on the colony's existence. In cobbling together these contrary viewpoints, Falconbridge reinforces the pragmatic difficulty of the double-talking civilising mission, spotlighting the internal divisions among differently motivated colonisers. Yet the various traumas she hints at are not cut and dried. The narrative of colonialism cannot be neatly partitioned between coloniser and colonised.

Two Voyages, then, is integral to imperial implantation. Drilling the British public in a gradualist politic that represents England to itself, she articulates divers black self-representations. Her oscillations between an evolving pro-slavery vantage point and an economic self-interest is inextricably bound up with a suspect (and standard) philanthropic project. She proclaims the partiality and hence the inauthenticity of the overall picture, representing Sierra Leone only as she expected or wanted it to be. She constructs and confirms a certain national identity, a vocabulary of rights that supports both slavery and colonialism.[20] Proclaiming the reality of a coloniser, Falconbridge strains to construct a visible little England that upholds sartorial custom.

Furthermore, the popular epistolary form of her narrative authorises a certain handbook view of Sierra Leone; people back home can imagine the settlement through her eyes, they can identify with her goals, and hence learn acceptable parameters for a patriotic response to overseas rule.

Regardless of her altercation with the Company over political direction in Africa, the lives of the indigenous and repatriated Africans that Anna Maria Falconbridge chronicled in *Two Voyages* were built on the European imaginary. All she did was give the colonial project a new twist, a novel context for reconstituting the cultural geography of Sierra Leone and hence Englishness.

Notes

1. Anna Maria Falconbridge, *Two Voyages to Sierra Leone*. All references will be to the second edition, published by the Author, London.

2. For information on Sierra Leone, see Christopher Fyfe, *A History of Sierra Leone*; Oxford University Press, Oxford 1962; Joe A. D. Alie, *A New History of Sierra Leone*, Macmillan, London 1990; John Peterson, *Province of Freedom*, Northwestern University Press, Evanston IL 1969.

3. For the documents of Cato Perkins and Isaac Anderson, see Christopher Fyfe (ed), *'Our Children Free and Happy' Letters from Black Settlers in Africa in the 1790s*, Edinburgh University Press, Edinburgh 1991.

4. Alexander Falconbridge, *An Account of the Slave Trade*, J. Phillips, London 1788.

5. Here I am paraphrasing Martin Green, *Dream of Adventure-Deeds of Empire*, Routledge and Kegan Paul, London 1980, p37. The information about the French captain as a slave trader comes from Zachary Macaulay; see Viscountess Knutsford (Margaret Jean Trevelyan Holland), *Life and Letters of Zachary Macaulay*, Edward Arnold, London, p31.

6. Peter Hulme, *Colonial Encounters: Europe and the native Caribbean 1492-1792*, Routledge, New York 1986.

7. Mary Louise Pratt, *Imperial Eyes: Travel, Writing and Transculturation*, Routledge, London 1992, pp102-107.

8. For a compelling analysis of the construction of white femininity, see Vron Ware, *Beyond the Pale: White Women, Racism and History*, Verso, London 1992, ppxvii, 163, and passim.

9. For discussions of Englishness at this time, see Benedict Anderson, *Imagined Communities: Reflections on the Origin and Spread of Nationalism*, Verso, London 1986; Linda Colley, *Britons: Forging the Nation 1707-1837*, Yale University Press, Newhaven 1992. Gerald Newman, *The Rise of English Nationalism. A Cultural History 1740-1830*, St Martins, New York 1987. and Homi K. Bhabha, *Nation and Narration*, Routledge, London 1980.

10. See Peterson *Province of Freedom, op cit.*, p29.

11. Ellen Gibson Wilson, *John Clarkson and the African Adventure*, pp80-87. Information about Clarkson's administration comes from this text.

12. Laura E. Donaldson, *Decolonising Feminisms: Race, Gender and Empire-Building*, University of North Carolina Press, Chapel Hill 1992.

13. Frantz Fanon, *The Wretched of the Earth*, Penguin, Harmondsworth 1967, p40.

14. Edward W. Said, *Culture and Imperialism*, Alfred A Knopf, New York 1993, pxii.

15. Extensive archival research in Bristol and Somerset has yielded only scant information about Anna Maria Falconbridge. See Moira Ferguson *What They Wanted to See: British Women Writers and Sierra Leone*, forthcoming.

16. Wilson Harris, 'Books-A Long View', *Tradition, the Writer and Society, Critical Essays*, New Beacon, London 1967.

17. Falconbridge's fluid, explicitly political positions distinguish her narrative from the traditional format of univocal British traveller's tale, such as Lieutenant John Matthew's account; *A Voyage to The River Sierra Leone*, published in 1788.

18. Edward W. Said, *Culture and Imperialism, op cit.*, ppxx & xi.

19. For a brilliant account of the seemingly contrary colonial vantage points, see Pratt, *Imperial Eyes, op cit.*, especially pp58-85.

20. See Catherine Hall, *White, Male and Middle-Class: Explorations of Feminism and History*, Polity Press, Cambridge 1992, p207.

'AFRICA' AND CULTURAL TRANSLATION: READING DIFFERENCE

Kadiatu Kanneh

'Africa' has been a subject in its own right, with its own assigned codes and meanings, its own metaphors and myths, during a history which 'discovered', experimented with and interpreted Africa as a *whole*. In this essay, I am concerned with representations of Africa which, in diverse yet connected ways, locate and imagine the concept of Africa as a distinct and intelligible issue, one whose position in cultural analyses - either of the West or of Africa - is vital. Reading 'Africa' as a textual subject requires an awareness of how cultural interpretations inform one another: colonial anthropologies, travel narratives, ethnophilosophies and literary representations form a tissue of African narratives which often only make sense with reference to each other. The significance of colonial interpretations of Africa is evident, both in terms of resistance to and re-imagining of African cultural difference, and in terms of black or pan-Africanist responses to the already figurative meanings of Africa.

A BEND IN THE RIVER

V.S. Naipaul's *A Bend in the River* demonstrates, in its own self-conscious narrative, both the difficulties of representing or defining cultural others, and the inevitable historical and textual complicities underlying the location and legitimation of otherness. What the novel manages to enact, from the site of an implicated, yet detached authority, in anxious control of a subject which keeps slipping out of sight, is a sustained grappling with the *idea* of Africa. From an obsessive focus on the intense physicality of an African landscape, massively alive, massively secretive, to the repeated invocation of an African history without narrative structure, *A Bend In the River* deliberately writes itself against and alongside Joseph Conrad's *Heart of Darkness* [1]

The perplexity of the text lies in its constant engagement with cliché - the mystery, the violence, the impenetrability of African forest and African native - and, at the same time, its insistence on re-examining and dismantling the origins and meanings of cliché away from the dominating stance of 'foreign fantasy'.[2] What becomes clear is that the novel's subject and project is profoundly *textual*. Unable to represent an Africa which recedes behind the threat of bush and river, the novel lays contesting clichés, one against another, which compete bewilderingly against a backdrop of resolute mystery. Barred from the possibility even of *imagining* a direct engagement with the text's ostensible subject, the novel insistently foregrounds the monologue of its own displaced, postcolonial narrative, locked in the long history of European colonial encounter.

Exactly because the 'lost' and 'hidden' *meaning* of Africa is projected as lying behind the *presence* of African natural geography, African modernity becomes impossible to imagine. To make 'the land' (*Bend in the River*, p8) ... 'part of the present' (p9) ... 'this land of rain and heat and big-leaved trees - always visible...' (p42), its *visibility,* its offensive encroachment, must itself be annihilated. The precarious temporality of modernity in Africa relies on European order and is perpetually threatened by a violence and rage which is both historically necessitated (pp26, 81) and part of, 'some old law of the forest, something that came from Nature itself,' (p80).

The familiar colonial rhetoric of the timelessness of Africa, the emptiness of village life, locked in a fixed and lost dimension, the primitive savagery energizing the episodic destruction of order, lies against another familiar rhetoric of celebration which is positioned as another object, distanced from the narrative voice. The character, Father Huismans, a Belgian priest and self-made anthropologist, occupying the space of missionary and ethnographer, re-interprets the same Africa 'of bush and river' (pp62-3) as 'a wonderful place, full of new things'.

The crucial difference of his idea of Africa lies in his particular understanding of history as a dominating narrative destiny, intent on overriding and writing over what is, for him, *essentially* African. His veneration of Africa is actually a veneration of his own ability to seek out, to 'witness' (p65) African cultural objects, and, by placing them in his museum, located on the site of the European school, to *interpret* them. The force of European history, its power to exterminate Africa in the name of its own logic, becomes embodied by Father Huismans:

> *True Africa he saw as dying or about to die. That was why it was so necessary, while that Africa still lived, to understand and collect and preserve its things.* (p64)

The African masks in Father Huismans' museum become the locus of a war of interpretation, staged between the intense narcissism of the novel's own narrative and the clichéd philosophy of Father Huismans. Focusing on a carved African statue, the narrator, Salim, opposes Father Huismans' celebration of the artwork as 'imaginative and full of meaning' (p61), with an interpretation which insists on deeper ethnographical understanding. Salim's recognition of the statue as: 'an exaggerated and crude piece, a carver's joke' (p61), at once underlines the text's constantly *knowing* position as recogniser of clichés, and at the same time points to the subversive presence of other meanings beneath colonial discourse. These, in turn, disrupt and disturb any narrative certainty.

The previous reading of the African Ferdinand's face by Salim, which he confidently asserts was 'looking...with the eyes of an African' (p37), and which compares Ferdinand's face with: 'the starting point of certain kinds of African masks' (p37), must now be thrown under suspicion. This is a suspicion of which the narrative is very well aware and which it exploits in such a way that Africa's power, mystery and threat alternates with the mundane and the comic. Africa as a whole, represented by postcolonial Zaire - as a continuation of Conrad's Congo - both feared and mocked, is always superseded by the greater reality and textual order of Europe.

Independent, modern Africa, distanced from the hopeless, timeless secrecy of hidden forest villages, simply exists at the interchange of conflicting narratives, born of colonial discourse. Salim describes African modernity inconclusively as: 'Europe in Africa, post-colonial Africa. But it isn't Europe or Africa...'(p139.)

Out of the constant self-referencing self-consciousness of Salim's narration, caught in his own idea of postcolonial displacement, the novel identifies Africa as, inevitably, a site of its own narcissism: 'Those faces of Africa! ... They were people crazed with the idea of who they were.' (p269)

Sara Suleri's reading of Naipaul's novels and texts as indicative of a profound anxiety around the authority of *seeing* - of interpretation and judgement - is significant. She argues that: 'the text begins to acknowledge the narrator's bodily availability to interpretation, making it increasingly unclear whether the perceived or perceiving body is the greater redundancy on the narrative scene'. [3] The narrative of *A Bend in the River* returns obsessively to the narrator's position on the scene, constantly reiterating the priority of Salim's vision. What is perceived outside Salim's own body is repeatedly interpreted by and in connection with it, until the landscape itself achieves the drama of consciousness:

You heard yourself as though you were another person. The river and the forest were like presences, and much more powerful than you (p8).

This was how the place worked on you: you never knew what to think or feel. Fear or shame - there seemed to be nothing in between (p76).

This presentation of the narrator as interpreter and the victim of interpretation, where the text's object insidiously returns in control of the narrative, foregrounds the impossibility of 'knowing' otherness before its reduction to the Same. The recognition of anxiety as haunting the rhetoric of discourses which are invested in colonial values is a familiar one, and introduces a profound difficulty. *A Bend in the River* approaches the problem of representing otherness both by entrenching the notion of absolute difference, impenetrable to the possibility of dialogue, and by claiming its purely textual or romantic existence against the reality of the banal. This constant engagement with the self, emphasising the limits of ethnology, exposes the necessary gap between mysterious difference and the knowable familiar; the predication of mystery allows the obliteration of dialogue, placing interpretation *only* within the narcissism of authority. Suleri's insistence that: 'otherness as an intransigence ... further serves as an excuse for the failure of reading' points suggestively to those moments in the text where forest and river present a wall beyond which life without rationality or self-expression (the requisite of mystery) will be superseded by modernity.

This reading of *A Bend in the River* introduces a literary presentation of the issues which coalesce around discussions of African identity or African culture. The temptation to continually move from an examination of the particular, the local, to an obsession with the whole, the continent, is prevalent in texts about Africa. What makes 'Africa' different from the 'West'? How can we - if at all - discuss an African modernity? How have colonial discourses impinged on, or created, a modern understanding of African reality?

Naipaul's novel positions these issues as a problem of cultural interpretation, with a narrator who occupies the space of cultural interlocutor, or ethnographer. In this way, a deliberate disjunction is made between interpretation and what is seen, 'So from an early age I developed the habit of looking, detaching myself from a familiar scene and trying to consider it as from a distance' (p15). This distancing presents itself as a kind of privileged observation through Salim's own radical cultural displacement as an East Indian in exile in Zaire. Situated precariously on the edges of European colonial civilisation, trading European goods with the African interior, Salim is able to comment on the gaps between colonising and colonised cultures. What emerges, however, is not a transcendent narrative penetrating knowingly into pre-colonial African societies, but a mystified gaze remaining transfixed on the mystery of a doomed, deep forest. Repeatedly, the narrative revisits questions of time, the writing of history, and the problems of modernity, from a standpoint which recognises the permanence and ultimate authority of the written text, and the inevitable obliteration of local intransigence. Travel and displacement become the focus for a modernity which insists on a perpetual and unsentimental present, unstuck from the particularity of geographical place. Salim's entrenched self-reflexivity opposes itself to Father

Huismans' enterprise of entering and preserving a 'true' Africa by creating a museum of African masks. Rescued from the suffocating timelessness of the forest where, removed from the present, they can *mean* nothing, the masks become readable and contested cultural artifacts. This 'readability' can be premised only to the exclusion of a former context which, under the imposed temporality of colonial knowledge, becomes unreadable, without indigenous meaning. Sunday Anozie, however, attests to a differential semiotics of African masks outside the interpretive power of the museum:

> *In Africa, the mask certainly constitutes an iconographic or semiotic system: as a system of signs, it also embodies language; in sub-Saharan Africa, there is an authentic mask language, known sometimes as 'juju' language, just as there is an authentic drum language.* [4]

A Bend in the River is not an ethnographic text but a literary one. The novel's refusal to name its localities - whether countries, towns or villages - and to relate them only to the already metaphoric term 'Africa', emphasises its intertextual relationship with preceding literary and anthropological texts. The realities to which it primarily refers are textual. This does not, however, wholly remove its concerns from those of ethnography. The novel's continual foregrounding of the uncertainty of an authorial voice, the concentration on culture and time, link it very clearly with the theoretical problems of ethnography.

TRANSLATION PROBLEMS

Gaining knowledge of other cultures is not a simple, uncomplicated matter of neutral translation from one social order to the direct relativity of another. Cultural translation, which is central to the creation of ethnographic texts, paradoxically insists on the possibility of cultural relativism, and operates, at the same time, within a problematic which insists on radical non-relativity. Walter Benjamin's analysis of the task of the translator is useful here. His study of linguistic translation, which he describes as 'only a somewhat provisional way of coming to terms with the foreignness of languages', explores how meaning can be transmitted from one linguistic system to another. [5] Rather than forging a mutual space, or encounter, translation, on the contrary, forces a more rigid interface between languages which closes off the possibility of direct communication. The ideal translator insists that the secondary language - the translation's destination - itself undergo a rupture, a transformation of itself, under the onslaught of the original. In striving to approximate the essence of meaning in the original, the translation has to act upon the order and structure of the *second* language in order to produce a 're-creation' - not a copy - of the first (p80).

In cultural translation, the foreignness of languages also remains resolute. Vincent Crapanzano re-writes Benjamin's account of the desire for mimesis as a more complicated, dual project. For Crapanzano, the ethnographer aims, in his cultural translations, to 'communicate the very foreignness that his interpretations ... deny, at least in their claim to universality'. This idea, that the ethnographer must 'render the foreign familiar and preserve its foreignness at one and the same time', questions in practice the thesis of linguistic interrelatedness.[6] Insisting on the 'historical relationships which Benjamin temporarily suspends, the *equal difference* of languages becomes, in ethnography, *unequal disjunction*. The 'foreign' culture, which is made meaningful *and* strange, is historically in a position of disadvantage - a disadvantage which is produced from specific global relations of power. In this sense, cultural translation is also a form of cultural domination, or rather, translation depends on the existing dominating stance of one politically and economically powerful culture over another.[7]

Translation reads the signification (significance) of an other society within an economy of *nature* confronted with (and becoming) *culture;* or latent, *unconscious* experience confronted with a conscious will to knowledge. Michel de Certeau's reading of ethnology attests to this conditional inequality, emphasising the historical necessity to keep other ('non'-) cultures strange against the rational, unchanging Self:

> *The break between over here and over there is transformed into a rift between nature and culture. Finally, nature is what is other, while man stays the same.* [8]

Ethnology's profound resistance to the equal relativity of human societies, and its consequent relegation of less powerful cultures to a position of projected dormancy, opposes itself to Benjamin's study of relativity existing alongside the intractable nature of linguistic separation. A commitment to absolute relativity, claiming itself as a solution to this crisis of inequality, acts also as an encouragement to encounter only the self within discourses of the other. If ethnographical knowledge, conditioned by colonial histories of domination, repeatedly translates otherness into its own systems of imposed meaning, would not an insistence on interrelatedness perform a similar movement? The difficulty adheres to the problem of translation itself, where the act of re-writing, of making sense of another *differently*, performs an irreducible act of violence. Coevalness - perhaps the only immediate solution to the relegation of others to an inferior position within an imposed (foreign) system of meaning - risks the danger of enforcing an uncritical notion of universality, without guaranteeing an equal dialogue divorced from exterior and impacting relations of power. Christopher Miller's assertion that, to relinquish even the *desire* to coincide - the commitment to recognition - merely re-affirms the arrogance of unchallenged self-reflexivity; a serious corrective here.

This problem of relativism as an encouragement to the violent narcissism of impervious self-reflexivity can be re-thought through a re-configuration of cultural difference as the articulation, not of the *content* of opposing cultural units, but of the problematic of signifying difference itself, as the moment of enunciating cultural knowledge and meaning. Homi K. Bhabha's exploration of this issue usefully opposes the relativistic theory of 'cultural diversity' with a theory of cultural difference that emerges from the problem of interpretation:

> *Cultural diversity is an epistemological object - culture as*

an object of empirical knowledge - whereas cultural
difference is the process of the enunciation *of culture as*
*'knowledge*able*', authoritative, adequate to the construction*
of systems of cultural identification.[10]

Encounter *between* cultures is precisely the moment at which the
articulation of signs becomes apparent, caught between the
ambivalence, the 'in-between space', of contesting projections and
linguistic negotiation.[11] Cultural representation relies, inevitably,
on this conjunction, this clash of signification on the borders and
limits of cultures, which acknowledge and mediate cultural
meaning always as the articulation of difference and otherness:

> *'Cultures come to be represented by virtue of the processes of*
> *iteration and translation through which their meanings are*
> *very vicariously addressed to - through - an Other'.*[12]

This refusal of the depth of cultural content, which can be
'known' via the 'objective' lens of anthropology, enables a
further critique of Father Huismans' confusion, mistaking the
faltering of his own system of meaning in the encounter with
difference for the penetration into the (thus already known)
'Truth' of the Other.

Cultural translations of 'weak' by 'strong' languages take
place within an ideology which insists, not on a transference,
but on a *conferral* of meaning from one to another. In this way,
the object of translation offers up, not a text to be *read*, but
latent significance to be *written*. The object of ethnography
becomes a possible object of knowledge through the operation
of written inscription, which makes another culture *known*. This
ordering of 'unconscious' cultural signs into writing is one which
has long been practised with regard to Africa:

> *The discourse which witnesses to Africa's knowledge has*
> *been for a long time either a geographical or an*
> *anthropological one, at any rate a 'discourse of competence'*
> *about unknown societies without their own 'texts'*[13]

This system of unequal exchange has significant repercussions
for a project of knowledge which is founded upon literacy. If

written representation effectively erodes the chosen self-presentation of another, how can ethnographical writing allow another to speak for herself? Gayatri Spivak, writing about First World interpretrations of Third World women's lives, argues that the meaning of these lives, radically de-contextualised, displaced and retrospectively (at a distance) re-constructed through the process of writing, is not communicated via any active dialogism. Her conclusion that: 'The subaltern cannot speak' points to the structural inability of the written, Western text to give the Other her own voice.[14] Spivak makes her position clearer in an interview with Walter Adamson, where she retraces her interpretation of Bhuvaneswari Bhaduri's suicide in the previous essay:

What I was doing with the young woman who had killed herself was really trying to analyze and represent her text. She wasn't particularly trying to speak to me. I was representing her, I was reinscribing her. To an extent, I was writing her to be read, and I certainly was not claiming to give her a voice. [15]

Rather than claiming that her interpretations provide a *prior* or a *primary* text, Spivak claims instead that they form only a *second* text, which merely *re-writes* that which itself has its own context and meanings. The ethical consideration that remains is, then, a *contextual* one: 'What we do toward the texts of the oppressed is very much dependent upon where we are.' [16]

To bring literacy to another society is to impose a radically other way of being and of *seeing* the world, and the vital links between writing and the visual imagination have particular significance for ethnographic practice. Oral, or 'traditional' cultures offer themselves up for visual de-coding in the drama of landscape and environment; in the visibility of bodies and faces; in the contours of masks and art forms (all of which are 'scenes' recurring in *A Bend in the River*). Michel de Certeau outlines the collaboration of writing and visual interpretation in his reading of Jean de Léry's ethnological text, *Histoire d'un voyage faict en la terre du Brésil* (1578). Here, it is the physical bodies of native women, devoured by the ethnographic eye, offered up to revealed 'knowledge', which represent the aim of ethnology's uncoverings and discoveries:

> *From this labor, the women naked, seen and known*
> *designate the finished product metonymically. They indicate*
> *a new, scriptural relation with the world; they are the effect*
> *of a knowledge which 'tramples' and travels over the earth*
> *visually in order to fabricate its representation.'* [17]

This trampling, travelling knowledge, creating revelations through ocular penetration, effectively yokes together an ideology of space and distance with that of the violent incursion of visual representation. This mapping of the world through relentless movement has a direct relationship with the imagining of time, a significant aspect of the modernity which ethnology represents. Indar's comments, in *A Bend in the River,* provide a metaphorical reading of this link between travel and time, and the continual erosion of the specificity of other places and other times. The will to create an interchangeability of world spaces under a unitary, literate discourse of 'homogeneous, empty time'[18] has its figurative location in the image of the aeroplane:

> *But the airplane is a wonderful thing. You are still in one*
> *place when you arrive at the other...You can go back many*
> *times to the same place. And something strange happens if*
> *you go back often enough. You stop grieving for the*
> *past...You trample on the past, you crush it...In the end you*
> *are just walking on ground. That is the way we have to*
> *learn to live now.* (Bend in the River, *pp112-113)*

This 'learning to live' within the narrative of modernity is achieved through a learning to *read* the other through the language of history.

AMBIGUOUS ADVENTURE

Problems of translation impact heavily on Cheikh Hamidou Kane's novel, *Ambiguous Adventure*, which discusses 'Africa' as a space which is distinct and distant from the West, and yet profoundly implicated in Western cultural analyses. *Ambiguous*

Adventure interrogates the role of Africa in a modernity which negates and challenges African cultural systems, and grapples with the ethics of difference and dialogue. The novel seeks both to entrench an idea of African difference, and to demonstrate the ambivalence of this notion. Both the 'West' and 'Africa' are presented as radically encroaching on each other, in ways which disallow the simplicity of choice, the clarity of confrontation, and any unsullied connection to origins.

The discourse of the novel is balanced between an authorial voice and the developing consciousness of the main character, Samba Diallo. The narrative voice adds an illustrative dimension to the text, placing the psychological and spiritual aspects of Samba's consciousness within a larger historical framework. This context is a generalised overview of colonial conquest in Black Africa, referred to most directly in chapter five:

> *The entire black continent had had its moment of clamor...The morning of the Occident in black Africa was spangled over with smiles ...*[19]

This allegorical reference to colonial history in Africa serves as an ethical and interpretive background to the individual psyche of Samba Diallo.[20] In this way, Samba's specific experiences and private torments are given a symbolic status, as historically *typical* and collective African experiences of colonialism. The novel, set in colonial Senegal, providing an allegorical discussion of French colonialism within the specific 'Diallobé country' (p12), comes to represent the wider contextual and historical dimension of colonial Black Africa.

Ambiguous Adventure opens with a description of intense physical suffering, which is fused into a complex texture of love, spiritual exhilaration and ultimate subordination. The 'martyrdom' (p4) of Samba Diallo to the tenets of Islam is sustained, throughout the novel, as an inheritance fundamental to his identity as a member of the Diallobé and, more significantly, to his identity as an African. What are called, 'the values of death' (p27) within Islam, become the values of an African spirituality at odds with Western technological civilisation, and they create a further metaphorical link between notions of a dying civilisation, the superseded demands of dead ancestors, and the exigencies of sacrifice in the face of colonialist destruction.

What is both curious and deeply moving about this novel is precisely this tropic collusion of Islam as Truth with the crisis that challenges this. In other words, it becomes impossible to extricate a reading of the deepest philosophical or theological Truths of Islam from the tragedy of Africa's colonisation. Further to this, Islam itself represents a previous colonisation which forms a controlling layer over another, subdued 'Africa' beneath. What emerges within the text is a profound ambiguity around the stated fusion of African difference, or Diallobé culture, with Islam, and the status of 'absolute' human values, or Islamic Truth in a terrain irrevocably formed and complicated by French philosophy and colonial culture.

The equivocation between the inheritance of aristocratic Diallobé culture and the inheritance of Islam, both dramatised as utterly non-Western, is illustrated in the constant evocation of a pre-colonial past which is uneasily reconciled to Islam. For example, Samba Diallo's Night of the Koran is described in terms which insist on a historical and yet naturalised bond between Islam and the patriarchal descent of the Diallobé aristocracy, both united in the threat and celebration of death:

> This scintillation of the heavens above his head, was it not the star-studded bolt being drawn upon an epoch that had run its course?' (p72)

> ... For a long time, in the night, his voice was that of the voiceless phantoms of his ancestors, whom he had raised up.'(p 73)

What I have called the 'reconciliation' of the Diallobé to Islam, and yet the almost cosmic identification between the two, allows the novel to examine colonialism both as a fatal clash of two value systems, contingent upon history, and as a deeply disruptive collision between two fundamentally opposed metaphysics. The 'ambiguous adventure' which frames the novel is both physical and spiritual; individual and collective. Samba Diallo's initial exile from his father's house, to the Muslim teacher's hearth, is followed by his exile to the French colonial school and, later, to Paris. This journey is charted as a movement from the expansive, self-denying spirituality of Islam, described in terms of the immediacy and limitlessness of the voice, to a confrontation with objects, reflections, surfaces. During Samba's Night of the Koran, '.....in the humming sound of his voice there was being dissolved, bit by bit, a being who a few moments ago had still been Samba Diallo' (p72); Samba thus comes to recognise his new allegiance to textual signification and representation. Learning French at the colonial school, Samba begins a *written* communication with his father, which introduces a materialism fixed on the priority of sight and separated from the immediacy of thought:

> *This was to demonstrate my new knowledge and also, by keeping my gaze fixed on him while he was reading, to establish the fact that with my new tool I should be able to transmit my thought to him without opening my mouth (p159).*

This fixing of the gaze from the son to the father, in a kind of telepathic scenario, emphasises the use of a new power which resists the living tremor of the voice for the intransigence and timelessness of writing. This move from oral to scopic signification indicates a new relationship to representation and the word. Samba's communion with the Word of Allah in *pre*-literate years reveals the sufficiency of the moment of 'repeating the Word' (p4). The accurate repetition of God's Word through speech cancels any linear apprehension of time in favour of the totalisation of the moment: 'He contained within himself the totality of the world, the visible and the invisible, its past and its future' (p5).

Islam's insistence on recitation and the oral performance of Koranic Truth contrasts strikingly with the silence and visual orientation of literate communication. The interpretation of 'thought' here undergoes an important transformation from instant oral improvisation to the delay incurred in writing. 'Thought' moves from immediacy to history in a way which changes the interaction of father and son. Samba's insistence on controlling the written exchange with his father through the supervision of his gaze allows a temporal distantiation between the two which, similar to an ethnographic scene, is manipulated by the projection of watcher and writer. Writing operates as a 'tool' which separates the moment of writing from its destination. Here, before Samba's move to Paris, physical proximity and temporal dislocation are allowed to experimentally overlap. The intensity of Samba's gaze has an echo in the moment of confrontation between M. Lacroix (representing the incursion of 'the West') and the Knight of the Diallobé. Here, the Knight's sonorous voice, occupying the darkness of the space between himself and the Frenchman is perceived as an incorporeal being, which cannot be fixed and studied (evidenced) by sight:

> *He would have liked to scrutinize the shadowed face of this motionless man who sat opposite him. In his voice he perceived a tonality which intrigued him, and which he would have liked to relate to the expression of his face. (p79)*

Interestingly, Islam represents an intermediate stage between orality and literacy. The Word of Allah is memorised from written Arabic, understood as fixed and eternal. The Word lives in the endurance of memory, caught in the finitude of the body, a living manifestation which cannot endure beyond corporeal delivery, and yet claims its legitimacy beyond the temporality of life. Islam, in the novel, represents the temporary unity of body and spirit, conquered by the eternal spirituality of death.

The journey from spirituality to materialism, or from the infinity of death to the mechanisms of life, is also described in the Fool's discussion of his trip to Paris, where his confrontation with the terrible objectification of his own body brings on a powerfully physical revulsion:

> *My legs were soft and trembling under me. I had a great desire to sit down. Around me, the stone floor was spread out like a brilliant mirror of sound that echoed the clattering of men's shoes (p89).*

This assault of surfaces, mirrors and echoes becomes, for the purposes of the novel, the basis of Western civilisation, which exiles human experience from what Marc, in a later chapter, calls 'the intimate heart of a thing' (p151). 'Western civilisation' is consistently represented in the novel as French metropolitan culture. That Paris should become a metonym for the West in this text is historically contextualised by the French colonisation of Senegal, which itself stands as a metonymic signification of 'Africa'. The concentration on the materiality of Paris becomes aligned with the onslaught of literacy in 'the West' through the issue of visibility. M.Lacroix, for example, is criticised for his 'Western' ideas by the Knight: 'What you do not see does not exist' (p80).

Samba Diallo becomes a complex layering of identities which are ascribed to his position as an heir to the Diallobé, as a Muslim, and as an African acculturated into French values and ideas. The historical accumulation of these identities, from the familial, aristocratic order of the Diallobé to French acculturation, are no longer clearly distinguishable. Just as Islam has become a fundamental aspect of the organisation of Diallobé aristocracy and its values, so Samba's understanding of himself as 'African' is crucially informed by his absorption of French colonial education. In addition, the discussion of what Lucienne, a white Parisienne, calls 'Negroness' (p141), moves the ascription of difference from a historical, cultural or religious contingency to something more profound. Adèle, a Parisienne of black Caribbean descent, is immediately attuned to Samba's feeling of exile. Although born in France, her intuitive communion with Samba is allowed to be aligned to a form of racial memory or being - a Negritude:

> 'When she happened to discern in herself a feeling or a thought which seemed to her to cut in a certain fashion into the backdrop of the Occident, her reaction for a long time had been to run away from it in terror, as from a monstrosity (p157).

The 'ambiguity' in the novel's title can be attributed both to Samba's colonised identity, and to the impossibility of separating a critique of the West, signified through French culture, from its incorporation into and exploration of an Africa which is presented in opposition to Western influence. The existence of 'a non-Western universe' (p156) is, for Samba, in the country of the Diallobé. However, Samba Diallo's father tells Lacroix, an occupyng Frenchman that: 'The era of separate destinies has run its course' (p79). Not only is the world 'becoming westernized' (p69) and so, in an unequal way, somehow united; its separation was itself an arbitrary, not *natural* occurrence. As Samba Diallo puts it:

> *I don't think that the difference exists in nature...I believe that it is artificial, accidental. Only, the artifice has grown stronger with time, covering up what is of nature (pp152-153).*

This emphasis on 'artifice' points to the historical problem which haunts the novel. Unable to determine the meaning or constitution of 'African difference' outside the predicates of French colonial interest, the idea of antagonism and opposition can only operate within the predicates of French modernity.

Samba increasingly analyses himself and his position in the world with reference to the *different* philosophical underpinnings of French modernity. These underpinnings rely on the profanity of a literacy which is not an eternally fixed origin (unlike the Koran), and on the materiality of science: 'Your science is the triumph of evidence, a proliferation of the surface' (p78). Caught as it is in what becomes a despairing equivocation between French modernity and African self-understanding, unable, in the postcolonial world, to separate itself from the French culture on which it is so poignantly focused, the text posits a point of no return for the African world. Resistance, as well as existence, has become, to use Edward Said's term, a contrapuntal theme.[21] As Samba Diallo claims:

> *I am not a distinct country of the Diallobé facing a distinct Occident, and appreciating with a cool head what I must take from it and what I must leave with it by way of counterbalance. I have become the two. There is not a clear mind deciding between the two factors of a choice. There is a strange nature, in distress over not being two (pp150-151).*

The final chapter of *Ambiguous Adventure* presents what can be the only solution to Samba's exile in the form of an ultimate return to sources. In a passionate staging of the voice, which announces a continuous arrival to the 'moment which endures' (p177), the metaphors within the text are sustained: the move away from crushing objectivity, spiritual confinement, and the time-lag between written and oral expression involves a re-entry into the values and the reality of death. Death emerges as a celebrative instance, promising the only resolution to the pain of ambiguity, but, in its reconciliation of self with the heart of Being, it is an annihilation.

Samba Diallo is both ethnographer and native subject, the text performing its own self-conscious interlocution between Senegal and Paris, and remaining irrevocably caught between the two; able, finally, to resolve its differences through the performance of its own dissolution.

The narratives explore the confrontation of colonial domination with indigenous social order where a simple choice between two monoliths - 'the West' and 'Africa' are no longer possible. The conditions for *thinking* this choice are also the very conditions which create the ambiguity and nostalgia that profoundly complicate it.

POSSESSING THE SECRET OF JOY

I will conclude with a reading of Alice Walker's novel, *Possessing the Secret of Joy*, in order to explore a more recent approach to these issues in quite different terms. Walker's novel is significant for the particular constructions and appropriations of the term 'Africa' which are deployed in the text, which foreground how a kind of literary and cultural struggle around the meaning of Africa is being waged in Black literatures.

Alice Walker's novel, published in 1992, is separated from Kane's novel by thirty years, and deals more specifically with women's experience and cultural constructions of sexual difference. Taking as its main character an African woman, Tashi, from her previous novel *The Color Purple*, *Possessing the Secret of Joy* ostensibly presents a dialogue between the West and Africa through the interaction of American, African and

European characters. Tashi, from an imaginary African people, the Olinka, who are never given a location (although Alice Walker mentions that the actor who played Tashi in the film, *The Color Purple*, was Kenyan[23]), allows herself to be excised and infibulated as part of her expression of cultural independence from British colonialism. What follows is an intimate description of physical and emotional pain expressed through the corresponding frames of European and American culture. The text insists on a collective female experience, possible through empathy, and given coherence through the wider and supposedly universal lens of anthropology and psychoanalysis.

What results is an attempt to represent the practices of female circumcision not only as specific cultural practices, but as a metaphor for women's subordination and oppression on a global scale. In this way, the various operations of female circumcision can be culturally aligned with the Marquis de Sade (p132), or Western 'slash' movies - as when Lisette, a French woman, is reported as saying: 'It's in all the movies that terrorize women ... only masked, the man who breaks in, the man with the knife' (p131). The presence of Jung, the Old Wise Man of Europe, as Tashi's analyst, to heal her of the psychological scars of her excision, allows for a communion between European and African cultures in such a way that the novel can resist difference. Jung, named in the novel as simply 'the doctor' (p17), or 'uncle Carl' (p81), is described as being surrounded by what are called 'tribal' furnishings (p10). He is likened, by Tashi, to 'an old African grandmother', and he describes his relationship with Tashi and Adam (an African-American) in terms which form the basis of the narrative's insistence on absolute relativism and the possibility of a universal frame of cultural reference. 'Uncle Carl' says:

> *I am finding myself in them. A self I have often felt was only halfway at home on the European continent. In my European skin. An ancient self that thirsts for knowledge of the experiences of its ancient kin. needs this knowledge, and the feelings that come with it, to be whole ... A truly universal self (p81).*

The novel's celebration of the value of anthropolgy as the

understanding of African culture, taken as a whole, and a human collective consciousness, recoverable through sympathy, leads the narrative, in fact, to incorporate a version of Africa within rigidly North American terms. 'Africa' emerges as a dying culture; both *victim* - through the ravages of AIDS (pp233-236) and the suffering of circumcised girls - and as its own destroyer - due to the tyrannous collusion of female circumcisors with male sadism.

Tashi's agony makes her turn against both the Olinkan nation-state (p100) and the Olinkan woman, M'Lissa - both victim and sadist - who circumcised Tashi, at her own request. Tashi's pain and what is called her 'resistance' is seen to be contained within the logic of Olinkan culture (p196) whereas her affection, strength and salvation lie within Europe and the United States. Tashi's constant expression of her love for the United States (pp53, 158) leads to a vision of the United States as a microcosm of global empathy, representing and substituting itself for a damaged Africa. Tashi, as an African woman, is ultimately moved to see herself in an American reflection:

An American, I said, sighing, but understanding my love of my adopted country perhaps for the first time: an American looks like a wounded person whose wound is hidden from others, and sometimes from herself. An American looks like me (p200).

Tashi's voluntary circumcision, brought about by the fervour of nationalist decolonisation and the need to be: 'Completely woman. Completely African. Completely Olinkan.' (p61), allows the novel to reinscribe colonialism as the possibility of correspondence and unity between the West and Africa. Lisette's Paris becomes saturated with a paternalist or maternalist love of Algeria, symbolised by her son, Pierre, whose mixed race origins can be substituted for Algerian identity. The novel's moral frame - '"Black people are natural ... they possess the secret of joy"' - is attributed to the wisdom of 'a white colonialist author' (p255).

Tashi's names, oscillating between, or being hyphenated by, European alternatives - Evelyn and Mrs Johnson - are clearly intended to allow her to represent - and to be represented by - women of different cultures. She becomes the voice of Everywoman, articulated within the idealised terms of African-American womanhood, who, against the 'sliding gait' (p144) of broken African women, become icons of strength and power (p111). The repeated use of 'Evelyn' and 'Mrs Johnson' as substitute names for Tashi, and, in the final section, as progressive points on the road to salvation: 'Tashi Evelyn Johnson Soul' (p263) works to obliterate Tashi's allegiance to Africa and, indeed, the validity or value of her African identity.

Alice Walker's epilogue, 'To the Reader', is particularly significant for reading the structure and meaning of the novel. Discussing her use of fabricated 'African' words, the author claims: 'Perhaps it, and the other words I use, are from an African language I used to know, now tossed up by my unconscious. I do not know from what part of Africa my African ancestors came, and so I claim the continent' (p267-268). This claimimg, or appropriation, of a whole continent, for Alice Walker's literary anthropology, reveals the difficulties and dangers of a relativism which would seek to deny, not just the significance of cultural difference on a grand scale, but the validity of contextualising and locating where one is speaking from, about whom, and with what egotism. The novel is narrated by a range of characters who interpret Tashi's experiences and their relationship with her. They form part of a historical and psychological jigsaw of Tashi as a circumcised African woman - a kind of case history from the viewpoints of participant observers. In this way, Tashi's identity is owned, explained and transmitted by the people who *claim* her, and any discordancies or disagreements between the observers and Tashi about her own role and meaning are erased, to the extent that the observers *control* Tashi's self-understanding *for* her.

Both *Ambiguous Adventure* and *Possessing the Secret of Joy*, recognise the significance of colonial histories in perverting or creating cultural narratives and producing grand battles between a supposedly coherent West and a holistic Africa. The form that this recognition takes is different in each text, partly because Kane's novel, evidently caught in an irrevocable and unequal dialogue, insists both on the historical complications of African societies and on the massive propensities for loss and self-destruction in modern Africa's understanding of its related but local selves. In contrast Alice Walker's novel moves impatiently towards a modernity which can unproblematically include all peoples, all women, within a humanist framework which, via Jungian psychoanalysis, promises a terrain free of difference. Her claim on an Africa which is inherent to Black Americans manages to miss the dominating stance of the United States over Africa and the social and imaginative inclusion of African-Americans in Western narratives of Africa.

Notes

1. Joseph Conrad, *Heart of Darkness*, in Morton Dauwen Zabel (ed), *The Portable Conrad,* Penguin, Harmondsworth, 1987. See for example p536: 'Going up that river was like traveling back to the earliest beginnings of the world, when vegetation rioted on the earth and the big trees were kings. An empty stream, a great silence, an impenetrable forest.'

2. V.S.Naipaul, *A Bend in the River,* Vintage Books, New York 1980, p146.

3. Sara Suleri, *The Rhetoric of English India,* The University of Chicago Press, 1992, p161.

4. Sunday O. Anozie, *Structural Models and African Poetics: Toward a Pragmatic Theory of Literature,* Routledge and Kegan Paul, London 1981, p111.

5. Walter Benjamin, 'The Task of the Translator: An Introduction to the Translation of Baudelaire's Tableaux Parisiens', in Walter Benjamin, *Illuminations,* Hannah Arendt (ed), Jonathan Cape, London 1970, p 75.

6. Vincent Crapanzano, 'Hermes' Dilemma: The Making of Subversion in Ethnographic Description', in James Clifford and George Marcus, (eds) *Writing Culture: The Poetics and Politics of Ethnography,* University of California Press, Berkley 1986, pp51-76.

7. See, for instance, Talad Asad, 'The Concept of Cultural Translation in British Social Anthropology', *Writing Culture, op.cit.*

8. Michel de Certeau, 'Ethno-Graphy: Speech, or the Space of the Other: Jean de Léry', in *The Writing of History,* Columbia University Press, New York 1988, p220.

9. Christopher L. Miller, *Theories of Africans: Francophone Literature and Anthropology in Africa*, The University of Chicago Press, 1990, p27.

10. Homi K. Bhabha, 'The Commitment to Theory', in *The Location of Culture*, Routledge, London, 1994, p34.

11. *Ibid*, p38.

12. Homi Bhabha, 'Interrogating Identity', in *The Location of Culture, op. cit.*, p58.

13. V.Y.Mudimbe, *The Invention of Africa: Gnosis, Philosophy, and the Order of Knowledge*, Indiana University Press, Indianapolis 1988, pp175-176.

14. Gayatri Chakravorty Spivak, 'Can the Subaltern Speak?', in Patrick Williams and Laura Chrisman (eds). *Colonial Discourse and Post-Colonial Theory: A Reader*, Harvester Wheatsheaf, Hemel Hempstead 1993, p104.

15. Interview between Spivak and Walter Adamson, 'The Problem of Self-Representation', 1986, from G.C.Spivak, *The Post-Colonial Critic: Interviews, Strategies, Dialogues*, Sarah Harasym (ed) Routledge, London 1990.

16. *Ibid*.

17. Michel de Certeau, *op. cit.*, p234.

18. Walter Benjamin, 'Theses on the Philosophy of History', in *Illuminations, op. cit,* p263.

19. Cheikh Hamidou Kane, *Ambiguous Adventure*, Heinemann, Portsmouth 1963, p48.

20. Colonialism is ethically evaluated and indicted in phrases such as that of the Most Royal Lady, with reference to the French colonists: '"we must go to learn from them the art of conquering without being in the right."', (p37). See also, p152, 36 Miller, *Theories of Africans, op.cit.*, p296.

21. See Edward W. Said, *Culture and Imperialism*, Chatto and Windus, London 1993.

22. Alice Walker, *Possessing the Secret of Joy*, Jonathan Cape, London 1992, 'To the Reader', p267.

GENDERING IMPERIAL CULTURE: KING SOLOMON'S MINES AND FEMINIST CRITICISMS

Laura Chrisman

The publication of Said's *Culture and Imperialism* is arguably both symptom and cause of a new direction in 'colonial discourse analysis' - namely, the synthesis of colonial with imperial cultural studies. For too long, it seems to me, the dynamics of white colonial discourse and culture have been confusingly equated with those of metropolitan imperial culture, producing critical readings which, insensitive to the differences between the two, read the colonial material as simply the repetition and expression of primarily metropolitan problems and subjectivities, or else assume that the true psyche of the imperial West can only be mapped, and identified, in its colonial operations. These critical conflations have been particularly marked in analyses of H. Rider Haggard, a British imperial romance writer who spent several years of his youth as a colonial administrator in South Africa.

Since they are set in Southern Africa, Haggard's early and most famous works, *King Solomon's Mines* (1885), *She* (1886) and *Allan Quatermain* (1887) invite interpretations derived from Haggard's colonial administrative activities in Natal and Transvaal. Yet these books simultaneously demand to be read as emanations from a primarily metropolitan, not colonial, perspective, as responses to British domestic social, political and economic crises rather than as responses to Zulu and Afrikaner political contests and the developments of mining capitalism. There has been a set of critical readings which mostly tend to privilege either the colonial or the domestic British in Haggard's texts, or else implicitly equate the two spheres. A methodological contrast is offered in the way Said's book acknowledges the overdetermined, historically variable complexities of metropolitan imperial cultures in themselves and in their relations with the cultures of colonial resistance. In so doing, Said opens both a material and a theoretical space for the investigation of the constituent complexity of texts such as Haggard's, and more generally for the exploration of the non-identity as well as the commonalities of colonial and imperial discourses.

Said's work is also welcome for the way it relegitimises, in a sense, the critical study of fiction and literariness. By differentiating literature's aesthetic functions within imperialism from the functions of (for instance) social sciences, he points towards a revised methodology of 'colonial discourse' analysis - indeed, suggests that discourse analysis as we have known it may be nearing the end of its critical usefulness. These two issues - the relations between colonial and metropolitan-imperial ideologies, and the specific placements of literary productions within these ideologies - need to be more acknowledged, addressed and developed within feminist post-colonial criticisms and theories.

A partial exception here is the work of Gayatri Spirak; another is the work of Anne McClintock, whose study of *King Solomon's Mines* forms the starting-point of my discussion.[1] This novel has been a favourite candidate for a number of recent Anglo-American feminist analyses, including those of Sandra Gilbert and Susan Gubar, Elaine Showalter and Rebecca Stott. Their focus has been Haggard's construction of femininity, while Joseph Bristow (among others) has explored his versions of masculinity.[2] It is the work of Anne McClintock, however, which most stimulates my critical engagement because of its unusually materialist orientation.

Spivak's work directs critical analysis to the narrative dynamics both of human reproduction and production within imperial texts; one lesson I draw from her is that it is as crucial to differentiate between these two spheres as it is to link them. This dual focus is mapped in Spivak by her examination of the processes of human reproduction which inscribe women as bearers of eugenic, and finite, racial codes (the reproduction of racialised bodies), and the ways this subject-positioning meshes or conflicts with another nineteenth-century, missionary-inflected imperial ideology of the production of (universalised) human subjects/souls.

Spivak's interest in 'production' lies in the production of

human subjectivity itself; her emphasis is on a Kantian philosophical tradition and the ways in which a teleological view of humanity (man as end-in-himself) generates its own instrumental and violent narrative of colonial subjects (the coercion involved in *making* colonised people 'human'). Political economy underlies Spivak's discussion, insofar as she is arguing that the processes of capitalist production supply an analogy for, and share an epistemological/ontological matrix with, an objectified, instrumentalised notion of colonial subjectivity.

But critics can also explore the way in which the mechanics of imperial or colonial economic production can directly inform, and generate, cultural anxieties and literary themes. If the discussion of 'production' can be directed thus in the direction of questions of economy and labour, the discussion of 'reproduction' can be likewise extended from Spivak's discussion to include the ways in which imperial masculinity as well as femininity may be mediated through reproductive ideology.

This is precisely what McClintock's methodology at first promises to do. Her discussion of *King Solomon's Mines* derives from her conviction that 'a paramount concern of the book is the reordering and disciplining of two orders: female reproduction and sexuality within the black family, and labour in the production of mining' (p113). Regarding King Solomon's Mines as derivative of Haggard's 1870s South African sojourn, McClintock argues that the economic and political activities of the Natal administration against the self-determining Zulu kingdom. Crucial to this noncapitalist Zulu political economy - and to McClintock's analysis - was the productive labour of its women, organised through polygyny. Recognising this, colonialists targeted polygyny and imposed taxes which sought to force Zulu men into wage labour. Making it impossible for the men to 'depend' upon the homestead labour of women, the colonialists themselves appropriated the fruits of this labour and effectively supplanted Zulu males as patriarchs. Accordingly, McClintock suggests that *King Solomon's Mines* is an allegory of the ways in which colonial power wrested control of African women's reproductive and productive labour away from African men.

The authoritative condition of fatherhood was what both

animated and legitimated colonial activities, argues McClintock. By constructing white males as the 'father' of what came to be seen as a universal 'family of man', ideologues gave empire a biological/evolutionary - and hence, absolute - sanction. To back up her arguments that the thematics of fatherhood and family structures were fundamental to colonialism, McClintock cites contemporary discourses of European racial social science as well as South African colonial administrative discourses. She additionally draws upon aspects of Rider Haggard's biography to suggest that at the heart of Haggard's imperial/colonial psyche was the need to 'regenerate' himself through introducing 'the idea of the paternal origins of life'. *King Solomon's Mines* becomes an allegory of this regenerative idea as well as an expression of contemporary South African colonial practices.

Despite the initial plausibility of her reading, and its apparently demystificatory power, there is a tendency in McClintock's analysis to reinforce the very categories of power which she claims to be exposing. I want to focus on the way McClintock analyses the dynamics of labour and of racial/sexual degeneration, and to explore the implications of her methodology for feminist post-colonial criticism and theory. The second part of this paper will put forward alternative ways to conceptualise the operations of sexual difference in Haggard's imperial discourse.

Firstly, the question of labour. While I agree that African productive labour, and the processes of capitalist accumulation in South Africa, are crucial concerns within Haggardian ideology, I cannot share McClintock's view that the novel articulates Natal's colonial reorganisation of Zulu women's reproductive and productive 'labour' within the homestead. To support her argument, McClintock cites examples from contemporary colonial discourses on black idleness which justify the imposition of wage-labour and the challenge to polygyny by representing traditional forms of African production as emanations of a pathological male laziness, 'degeneracy' and excessive sensuality (hence the institution of polygyny). One would expect, accordingly, that *King Solomon's Mines* would be full of representations of idle males, using their many wives as slave labourers. But what is striking is in fact the total absence here of representations of productive labour or idleness within the African society of the (fictional Zulu-based) Kukuanas. There is a corollary absence of authorial negative judgementalism towards this community's production patterns.

Such absence of negatives can be explained, I would argue, by taking a quite different reading of Haggard: that far from being a fictional apologist for settler-colonialism in Natal, Haggard was actually highly ambivalent about the processes of capitalist modernisation both in the UK and in South Africa.[3] It is the presence of such ambivalence that led him to fantasise a precapitalist African society which is, at the close of the novel, guaranteed to remain free from entry into any colonial economy. I don't want to imply a critical fetish of ambivalence here: there were material reasons for Haggard's conflictual relationship to modernisation, which I will discuss later. Here, however, I want simply to point out that (as Said's recent work suggests), it is important to avoid identifying imaginative literature as an unmediated transcript of colonial administrative activities, especially when the literature concerned is the product of imperial-metropolitan as much as colonial experience and part of a fantasy genre, the imperial romance.

It is not the seizure of control over Zulu rural homestead labour, then, to which Haggard's representational agenda is devoted. On the contrary, his goal is the construction of an African political economy which stands outside the flows of capitalism, and the simultaneous construction of a model of imperial wealth acquisition (the mines' treasure) which also stands outside the processes of capitalist production through African labour. This reading differs from McClintock's argument that Haggard's text derives from the (colonial) apprehension of *women's* labour as the (sole) centre of the Zulu economy (itself a highly controversial argument advanced by the historian Jeff Guy). I am also sceptical about the way McClintock deploys the argument that Zulu women's reproductive labour is or was identical in economic terms to their productive labour: linked, certainly, but identical, no.

What McClintock is ultimately doing is presenting a mystical version of women's reproductive capability, in which women are held to be intrinsically 'powerful' regardless of whether they exercise any material control over the reproductive and productive activities of themselves or others. Thus Haggard's upper-class mother becomes, for McClintock, indistinguishable from his British domestic women workers and African women rural labourers: all signify 'generative authority' and therefore pose the same kind of threat to an imperial or colonial patriarchy. Class and race differences disappear from the analysis of femininity's functions, and so therefore does any possibility of analysing the *positive* role accorded to (white) maternity within imperial ideologies. This produces an odd reading of reproductive politics in *King Solomon's Mines*, one which I think has problematic implications for feminist criticism.

Something which is underrecognised in feminist criticism of imperial and colonial cultures is the difference between the representational politics of the land and those of human subjects. In *King Solomon's Mines*, for example, it is at the level of the landscape that any non-racialised generalisations about gender and symbols of reproductivity might safely be made; the representation of humans calls for gender analyses in which race needs to be taken into account. That said, evidence for the positive function of female wombs and bodies for imperial culture can clearly be found in the novel's feminisation of the landscape. The heroes' path to the mines takes them across a landscape which goes from a female 'head' (a waterspot) to her breasts (two massive mountains) and culminates in the vagina/anus (the treasure cave and exit). McClintock reads this as an allegory of male 'restoration of the paternal origin' (p118), in which the heroes travel across a hostile and temporarily castrating female body to the mineral wealth of the mines and the place of female reproduction [which] are fused: ' in a condensed, scatalogical image of particular neurotic intensity, which will be ritually conquered and reappropriated as white and male' (p115).[4]

What is absent from this account is an acknowledgment that the feminised landscape is constantly aestheticised (as beautiful and on occasion sublime), and that far from offering hostility it provides maternal sustenance - food and water - for the travellers. What I want to argue is that the 'body' of femininity, supplied in the African land, is indicative of the way in which the sexual sphere is instrumentalised throughout the novel, as a means of naturalising and hence legitimating economic imperial accumulation. Acquiring diamonds, Haggard tries to suggest, is as self-evidently 'natural' as male domination over women, with which it is he wants to render it analogous. Sexuality, in other words, functions as a means of resolving contradictions within the text's political economy, rather than constituting its economic 'essence'.

McClintock's discussion of racial/sexual degeneration contends that the novel is 'legitimised by two primary discourses of the time: the discourse on "degeneration" and the discourse on the reinvented "father" of the "family of man"'(p98). Drawing upon the social scientific writings of Galton, Broca and Lombroso, McClintock's use of 'degeneration' here refers less to the active process of decline from one condition to another inferior one than it does to a way of classifying a grouping as one which is seen to be essentially debased. *Should* an individual white male chance to actively 'decline', then his deterioration will take him down the evolutionary ladder; he will accordingly take on the characteristics of racial and sexual 'others'. This provides her with the hermeneutic key for *King Solomon's Mines*, which she argues to be an allegory of white colonial males finding regeneration by placing themselves as the evolutionary source and culmination of the human race/'family'. In the process they banish the necessarily 'degenerate' black mother figure (and by extension the black race) from their contesting tenancy.

The dynamics of evolution/degeneration here, as articulated by McClintock through these social theorists, derive from a number of central suppositions: firstly, that physical 'appearance' ('stigmata') is the primary key to, and sign of, all aspects of 'essence' (morality, intelligence, health, fitness, etc); secondly, and correspondingly, that there is only one, fixed, position that the classified group can hold within what is seen to be only one possible racial/evolutionary narrative (since humans are considered to be a single racial family). The 'meaning' of blackness, then, according to McClintock, is fixed, and singular: it denotes degeneracy of all kinds relative to whiteness. It also carries familial meaning: blacks are situated in the monolinear development of evolution as either 'child' from which whites/ parents have evolved, or 'mother' to which whites have (from ancient supremacy) degenerated. In this interpretation, white males are by definition the signifier of allround racial/human evolutionary value, with the aristocrat as the 'pinnacle' of white hierarchy (p102).

Yet, while degeneration is clearly a major concern of Rider Haggard's, it is not a concern which is notably or exclusively inspired by an epistemological desire to control or classify, racial and sexual 'others'. It does not assume that degeneracy is necessarily inherent in those others, or is measurable by physiognomy alone, or that white males represent its antithesis. On the contrary: degenerationist discourse, produced by Haggard himself and by a number of his late nineteenth-century contemporaries, is precisely where all those assumptions are *challenged*.[5] Degeneration is above all a fear of the debilitation of the imperial British race, occasioned by the development of modern industrial and financial capitalism itself. Modernisation, in other words, is held responsible, and in a number of ways: it enervates the proletariat, it destroys the labouring agrarian classes, it also threatens to debilitate ruling classes by either disenfranchising them or by making them indolent and hence making them susceptible to overthrow by more physically powerful races and/or classes. An obsession with the example of imperial Rome is a recurrent feature of such discourses.

Thus, whereas McClintock interprets degenerationist discourse as affirmative of Enlightenment developmental models of progress, in which whiteness as race and culture can only signify an evolutionary apex, I wish to claim that it is precisely because whiteness has, like other ethnicities, ceased to have a positive, transparent and unified evolutionary meaning, that degenerationist (and eugenic) discourses emerge and start to suggest that technological and economic evolution may produce ethical and biological decline.

Crucially, when he is seen to degenerate, the British male may not necessarily start to resemble racial and sexual others, lower down the scale. Those peoples considered less economically developed may on the contrary be idealised as repositories of the social, cultural and biological strengths which modernisation within the UK has lost. Regeneration is facilitated by a temporary exposure to, and participation in, such peoples' non-capitalist society, especially if it involves physical and military exertion. This, not a conviction of blackness as a totally degenerate condition, is what underlies Haggard's romanticised representation of the neo-Zulu Kukuana people (as opposed to their rulers) in *King Solomon's Mines*.

This reading is of significance for feminist post-colonial criticism in that it challenges that perspective on degeneration which produces a reading strategy which ignores differences of political and economic power within racial and gender categories. For an example of this reading strategy note the way in which McClintock interprets the king Twala and his adviser Gagool to be the sole representatives of (Zulu) blackness and femaleness within the text:

> *The Kukuana royal family is itself dangerously degenerate, offering spectacle of familial disorder run amok. In the features of King Twala's face* one reads the degeneration of the race. He is a black paragon of the putative stigmata of the race, excessively fat, repulsively ugly, flat-nosed, one-eyed...(p120, emphases added).[6]

Yet Twala is not the sole representative of the Kukuana family itself, since the heavily idealised and emphatically non-degenerate Umbopa/Ignosi is constructed to be just as much, in fact, more, representative. My claim then is that Twala's degeneracy is a function not of his 'race' but of his illegitimate and corrupt kingship - his *political*, rather than racial, identity.

Furthermore by equating Twala with the people whom he is shown to tyrannise over, McClintock overlooks the ways in which colonial and imperial commentators on the Zulu were prone to invest heavily in distinguishing between Zulu rulers and people when it suited them. She thereby inadvertently rules out the historical possibility and intellectual study of the ways in which colonial and imperial (ideological, political and economic) domination worked through as well as against colonised constituencies. This was achieved by, for instance, imperial alignment with the 'people' against 'oppressive' African rulers, or (rather crucially) with emancipatory and/or protective ideologies for African women.

Finally, I would argue that to base so much of her argument on the terminologies of father, mother and family is to court analytical difficulty. For McClintock's usage of these terms is highly indeterminate, and variable - and yet, if they are to be the intellectual linchpin for colonial, metropolitan political economy, culture and social science that she claims for them, it is essential that they carry a clear single meaning. Perhaps the indeterminacy is inevitable, because she constructs these words, 'father' in particular, as being words whose force is transcendent - whose 'meaning' is that they are to function as beyond particular meaning, the means of mystifying and facilitating an absolute power. But at the same time, their meaning needs to be self-evident, constantly and literally biological in order for her analysis to work. All of this seems to rest on the assumption that if 'family' is taken to be the explanatory mechanism for systems of power/ideology, 'family' cannot itself be subjected to careful definition and explanation.

We get figurative paternity described by McClintock in the ways it manifested itself through images and rituals of power - but then the status of such rituals becomes radically unclear. They appear to shift from *reflecting* that power to *constituting* it. What is at work, I think, is a kind of synecdochic logic: locate the image or the word of 'the father', 'the family', and you have already explained or identified the material power relations which go with it, since they are held to be summed up in the image. Thus, make of the reproductive woman the source and image of productive as well as reproductive capacity, and you no longer need to explain the processes of production within the literary text, and women's place within these processes. Or: identify fathers as the evolutionary and/or familial source and you don't need to detail the meanings of family and offspring in relation to the father, since these are implied in the 'founding' term.

What is ultimately missing from this analysis is any strong notion of relations, of practices rather than static conditions and images. The focus of the analysis rests primarily on what texts, like families, look like, not on how they *operate*. The synecdochic logic makes mystical talismans of the words mother and father, abstracting them from the context which endows them with meaning. Synecdochic logic, then, leads McClintock to equate (the representation of) African rulers with the whole society they rule over; it leads her to equate womb/labour 'power' with all forms of power (for women) and simultaneously to equate image 'power' with material power (for men).

Where, then, would I go in my search for a feminist critical methodology of imperial culture? As my criticisms of McClintock's synecdochic logic might suggest, I would want to recover a notion of the whole from which those parts are taken: to instate a working concept of a (not necessarily the) social-economic and textual totality into which patriarchy feeds and from which it is produced. In regard to Haggard's novel, this involves a macrological level of analysis and contextualisation which seeks to take account of political-economic developments in both Britain and South Africa. Haggard's ideological formation would then be seen not simply to be overdetermined by a cumulative series of metropolitan and colonial threats to patriarchy, but would instead become conceivable as a possibly diverse and even contradictory formation.

What I would want to argue is that Haggard's writing in general - and *King Solomon's Mines* in particular - reveals (even as it attempts to resolve) some of the discontinuities between imperial-metropolitan and settler-colonial interests and ideologies. There emerged in the British invasion of Zululand and the subsequent civil war a number of conflicting interests between politicians and populace based in Britain, and those based in Natal; Haggard's non-fiction discussions show him to be constantly torn between the two. Put overschematically, an imperial perspective would (in the mid-1880s) typically have a certain investment in the fantasy of an 'imperial', militarily powerful, sovereign Zulu kingdom, whereas a settler-Natal perspective would be interested in the material and ideological conversion of that Zulu into a wage-labouring indirectly-ruled colonial satellite.

Applied to *King Solomon's Mines* this contradiction is reflected in both form and content: the military actions of the imperial heroes in Kukuanaland correspond to, and reinforce, a colonial concern for establishing control over Zulu monarchy, but these are deliberately divorced from the political and economic relationships to which they would belong in a colonial ideology and material practice. What prevails instead is the *imperial* fantasy of an autonomous Zulu polity, restored with the temporary assistance of British men to its true, if slightly modernised form, after the aberrant blip of a tyrannous illegitimate ruler. The same applies with the text's approach to wealth accumulation: what is important, aside from the fact that the treasure is acquired without the structures of African labour, is the fact that the beneficiary of the wealth is England, not Natal.

In other words, there needs to be a methodology which can account for, and incorporate, differing imperial and colonial agendas. This is particularly important, I think, in the analysis of the fantastic genre of romance, which needs to include a notion of literary ideology as following something other than the norms of mimetic realism. The romance genre as pursued by Haggard here is more aligned with imperial-metropolitan than colonial ideology; Haggard uses African material to satisfy a primarily British readership's imaginary desires, and uses romance as a genre particularly well-suited to the symbolic resolution of material contradictions. The particular contradictions which seem most to concern Haggard at the time of *King Solomon's Mines*, I would argue, are those generated by the development of industrial capitalism in the UK, which were only just beginning to emerge in Southern Africa by 1885. What Haggard finds in the incipient mining industries of South Africa, and in the archaeology/mythology of the Great Zimbabwe, are potential analogues for the British process of modernisation and capital accumulation; what he turns them into is a corrective.

Any gender analysis of the novel really needs to take on this context of modernisation and Haggard's anxieties about it. Such anxieties have at least two sources or directions. One is the fear that urban modernisation is dangerous to national wellbeing because of its inhumane production of unfit humans, and therefore to be opposed. Another is the fear of the threat modernisation poses because of its association with democracy, and its potential destabilisation of the process of, precisely, 'real' political-economic growth and power. Haggard's elitist romanticism, then, generates a complex contradiction: 'the people', and equally the path of socio-economic development, emerge as both the victim and as the cause of contemporary decline. This gives rise to a fiction in which immense value is invested in the vision of non-reified, non-industrialised humans, whose production and reproduction belong to the workings of nature not culture. Simultaneous with this is Haggard's desire to find some way of vindicating material wealth acquisition as a natural and providential activity.

Within such a scheme, as I have already argued, the dynamics of sexual reproduction serve ideologically to naturalise economic production. It is taken as axiomatic that sexual difference, and reproduction, are natural processes, and it is here, through Haggard's twin concerns with capitalist reification and wealth accumulation, that I would begin an analysis of the ways in which the processes of reproductive and economic power are ideologically interrelated. There are sound material reasons why Haggard arrived at his contradictory position: some derive from his membership of a declining rural squirearchy class, which suffered from the agricultural depression and the development of urbanised industrial and international financial capitalism, although socio-economic class did not alone account for the entirety of Haggard's ideological orientations, nor for that of any other late nineteenth-century pro-imperialist. Unfortunately, I do not have the space here to develop this explanation, nor to enter into a discussion of class determinism in literary-ideological production.

I don't want to imply that all questions of gender are to be approached in an economically deterministic fashion. It is because the text so explicitly foregrounds the theme of economics, and equally insistently sexualises it, that I advocate this approach in this particular instance. But I also don't want to imply that all questions of sexuality, sexism and patriarchy in this text or any other can ultimately be explained by an exclusive attention to the issue of reproduction.

Along with the reintroduction of the notion of the totality in feminist criticism, I want to argue for the reintroduction of the notion of mediation. If a notion of the totality allows us to engage at a macrological and micrological level (social context and literary text, respectively) with the structures in which literary subjects are given ideological value, the notion of mediation allows us to engage with the ways in which those values are produced. This further involves us in developing more nuanced concepts of textual ideology, in which casual sexism, for example, can be distinguished from ideologically foregrounded sexism, and axiomatic sexism can be distinguished from sexism which is anxious and fraught. In the case of Gagool, for example, Haggard's representation depends on a basically non-fraught form of sexism which is manipulated to serve the exigencies of colonial and imperial political-economies. Through the mediation of the category of gender, Haggard's political ideology is furthered. But this is not the whole story: equally, a gender ideology is mediated through the category of political class. Trying to make either of these categories a 'cause' of the other is reductive: the notion of mediation is a way of avoiding reductiveness.

What I am suggesting then is that for feminist criticism of imperial and colonial culture to develop, it needs ironically to go 'backwards'. Back, in the sense that Said has gone back, to the study of the collective properties of imaginative literature as a distinct modality within imperial culture, and away from the analysis of such literature as functionally interchangeable with social science and administrative writings. Back to notions of totality, mediation and ideology as analytic tools and material operations. Back to formalism too, if what we mean by formalism is a careful consideration of the particular ideological configurations which individual literary texts reveal. The challenge for feminist criticism of empire is, in a sense, the challenge posed by 'difference'.

Notes

1. See Spivak's 'Three Women's Texts and a Critique of Imperialism', *Critical Inquiry*, 12, 1, 1985, pp262-280; Anne McClintock, 'Maidens, maps and mines: King Solomon's Mines and the reinvention of patriachy in colonial South Africa', in Cherryl Walker (ed), *Women and Gender in Southern Africa to 1945*, James Currey, London 1990, pp97-124.

2. See Sandra M. Gilbert and Susan Gubar, *No Man's Land. Volume 2: Sexchanges*, Yale University Press, New Haven 1989; Elaine Showalter, *Sexual Anarchy: Gender and Culture at the Fin de Siecle*, Bloomsbury, London 1991; Rebecca Stott, 'The Dark Continent: Africa as Female Body in Haggard's Adventure Fiction', *Feminist Review*, 32, Summer 1989, pp69-89; Joseph Bristow, *Empire Boys*, Harper Collins, London 1991.

3. See for example his *Cetywayo and his White Neighbours. Or, Remarks on Recent Events in Zululand, Natal and the Transvaal*, Trubner and Co., London 1882 (first edition) and 1888 (revised edition); his autobiography *The Days of My Life*, Longman, Green and Co, London 1926.

4. See for example the late nineteenth-century writings of Benjamin Kidd, Karl Pearson and James Cantlie on evolution and degeneration. See also Haggard's own non-fictional musings, found in a range of his writings on the decline of agrarian production, on garden cities, on Great Zimbabwe. These include his *Rural Rngland*, Longman, Green and Co, London 1905; Introductory Address to T. Adams, *Garden City and Agriculture*, Garden City Press, London 1905; Preface to A. Wilmot, *Monomotapa (Rhodesia). Its Monuments and its History from the most Ancient Times to the Present Century*, T. Fisher Unwin, London 1896.

5. Despite their oft-criticised problems, Fredric Jameson's arguments for a literary methodology grounded upon a conception of a social totality are potentially very useful here. See his *Political Unconscious*, Methuen, London 1981.

6. See my forthcoming *Empire and Opposition*, Oxford University Press, for an elaboration of my arguments here.